LISTENERS LIKE WHO?

Listeners Like Who?

Exclusion and Resistance in the Public Radio Industry

Laura Garbes

PRINCETON UNIVERSITY PRESS

PRINCETON AND OXFORD

Requests for permission to reproduce material from this work should be sent to permissions@press.princeton.edu

Published by Princeton University Press
41 William Street, Princeton, New Jersey 08540
99 Banbury Road, Oxford OX2 6JX

press.princeton.edu

GPSR Authorized Representative: Easy Access System Europe - Mustamäe tee 50, 10621 Tallinn, Estonia, gpsr.requests@easproject.com

ISBN 9780691257419
ISBN (pbk.) 9780691257426
ISBN (e-book) 9780691275093

Library of Congress Control Number: 2025935950

British Library Cataloging-in-Publication Data is available

Editorial: Rachael Levay, Erik Beranek, and Tara Dugan
Production Editorial: Nathan Carr
Jacket/Cover Design: Chris Ferrante
Production: Lauren Reese
Publicity: William Pagdatoon
Copyeditor: Norman Ware

This book has been composed in Adobe Text and Gotham

10 9 8 7 6 5 4 3 2

To the Squeaky Wheels of Public Radio

CONTENTS

Illustrations

Tables

Introduction

Arvand is a Middle Eastern American public radio employee in the United States.[1] I talked to him via Zoom in summer 2020 about his work as a public radio producer, editor, and broadcaster. He was working from home, as were most reporters at the time, given the COVID-19 pandemic. By the time we hopped on the video call, Arvand had had a long day—a long few years, in fact. He'd noticed in those years, his first in public radio, that he regularly heard nonwhite accents differently than his white colleagues did. When I asked him about the accents that made it onto the public radio program he worked for, he told me,

> People will still openly say, "We can't have that person on. Their accent is just too much." And then you go and listen, and you're like, "What are you *talking* about?" I understand everything they're saying. [. . .] It's almost like I'm looking through a different prism at the world than a white person. That's where it gets spooky and weird because we're hearing the same thing and hearing it completely differently.

Voice recordings from immigrants and communities of color sounded clear to him, while his white colleagues interpreted the same voices as unclear and, by consequence, unfit for airtime. Arvand mused that perhaps he was just better at understanding accents because his own parents had "heavy accents," then decided it couldn't be that alone:

> But no. I got Black colleagues who didn't grow up with that heavy accent. I don't consider any Black folks I know to have the accent my parents

do. My parents literally speak broken English. But even my Black colleagues heard it the way I did. There's something weird happening. That happens a lot.

Voice and narrative evaluations centered around a presumed white listener impact who (and what) makes it on air. During another interview, Sarah, a Latinx[2] reporter, told me she regularly faced pushback for how she reported on communities of color without a white referent. She told me,

> I know that I was hired to help us diversify our airwaves, help us diversify our audience. But I literally had a news director tell me—I made a pitch—and they literally asked me, "Why do white people care?"

This news director's reaction brings with it the suggestion to shift the sound of the piece immensely. If Sarah were to take their advice, first she would need to effectively justify her story, including a "hook" drawing an imagined white listener into caring about an issue largely internal to a racially minoritized community. Second, she might have to add in music or background sound design that fit that hook. Third, Sarah would need to include voices from outside the racially minoritized community she was reporting on, diluting the story for the benefit of a majority-white listenership.

Such an editorial orientation has ripple effects. The voices and stories available on air shape whether and how people feel they belong on public radio's airwaves and in the public debate. Take for instance Dr. Chenjerai Kumanyika, a journalism professor at New York University and a podcast creator. He had an unsettling experience when producing one of his first public radio–style pieces. Kumanyika, a Black[3] man, was not inexperienced at a microphone—he had been a DJ and rapper for over a decade at that point—but he found someone else's voice in his head: a mix of white public radio personalities like Roman Mars and Sarah Koenig.[4] In January 2015, in his "vocal color manifesto," Kumanyika described this sensation, which he attributed to the whiteness of public radio in the United States. He declared that the marginalization of nonwhite voices had, over time, shaped and curtailed the nonwhite stories available on the public airwaves.

Public radio in the United States espouses an egalitarian mission to serve all Americans through both news-based and cultural programming. What remains invisible, or inaudible, in this mission is the purveyor of the content. In the most traditional conception of radio journalism, the broadcaster is presumed to be an objective mouthpiece from which a diverse array of stories will flow.

And in some ways, public radio has broken this mold of an authoritative voice from nowhere. For example, in its over five decades of operation, it has been both critiqued and complimented for featuring prominent and influential white women broadcasters, for whom listeners have developed warm feelings and a sense of trusted connection. As an unprecedented number of nonwhite broadcasters have entered this space since the turn of the twenty-first century, however, their experiences have exposed the limits of the public radio industry's pathbreaking approach.

Public radio employees of color I spoke with for this project[5] routinely told me that the distinct public radio sound was unmistakably white. When I asked them to elaborate, I would sometimes get sonic descriptions, like a "nasally thin sound." For the most part, however, they would conjure up an image related to how a particular voice would make a white person feel: "a friendly, nonthreatening person"; "a white person"; or "somebody white people would like."

Descriptions like this are shifting, imprecise, and elusive. Yet the widespread association of the "public radio voice" with a narrow social group, even if the voice itself does not empirically index onto a neat set of linguistic conventions, tells us a great deal about power. We know from sociology and linguistic anthropology that utterances only receive their value—their symbolic capital and recognition by others as legitimate—when there is a structurally conditioned understanding of who can speak certain words in certain ways with authority.[6] And so white voice, or understandings of a voice as white, receives its power because of its synonymousness with authority and trustworthiness. The long-held association of public radio voice with whiteness consistently sets racialized standards that mark those heard as audibly nonwhite as not belonging on these official and respected airwaves.

When Kumanyika's vocal color manifesto took off on Twitter in early 2015, National Public Radio (NPR)'s *Code Switch* podcast dedicated its inaugural episode to the topic. Accompanied with #pubradiovoice as the conversation marker, prominent employees of color in public radio engaged with the piece and shared their experiences. It became clear that constructing an on-air identity in a historically white-dominant industry and company involved complex considerations for nonwhite broadcasters. Lourdes "Lulu" Garcia-Navarro, a Latinx host on public radio programming at the time, responded, "Sitting in host chair for first time I channeled white voice from [the] Midwest and lost my own. I had to fight my own brain!" Audie Cornish, a Black broadcaster and then host of *All Things Considered*, pointed out that her own voice often got confused as a "white one" and that "people

Lulu NYT
@LuluGNavarro

4) #pubradiovoice Sitting in host chair
for first time I channeled white voice
from Midwest and lost my own. I had
to fight my own brain!

FIGURE 1: #pubradiovoice tweet by Lourdes Garcia-
Navarro, January 2015. Source: Twitter.

usually don't react to my voice, they react to their google image search:).” In
writing about their relationships to their own voices, these women of color
highlighted the fact that there was—and is—a “voice of public radio,” and
that it was always presumed white.

Garcia-Navarro's and Cornish's tweets demonstrate how this idea of public radio's model voice stokes feelings of nonbelonging for workers of color. It
happens even if their voices fit the network: as Cornish described, listeners
experience a sort of dissonance when they look up her photo. Her identity
as a nonwhite reporter didn't seem to fit with the assumed whiteness of the
iconic public radio voice.

I learned a lot from public statements like these: public radio journalists
of color speaking out about their experiences both on Twitter and within
some of the NPR programming itself. But as I began my graduate studies in
fall 2016, well over a year after Kumanyika's vocal color manifesto found its
way into mainstream conversations, I found scant academic research that
reflected these employees' poignant articulations of their own relationships
to their voices vis-à-vis the voice of public radio.

This book sets out to fill that gap. I systematically delve into the factors
producing this discrepancy between Arvand's and his white colleagues' reactions to voice. I show that it is the arrival of employees from communities
of color into this white institutional space that produces this mismatch—it
is a breaching of an underlying and unspoken set of aesthetic norms and
storytelling practices embedded deep within US public radio's foundations.
The employees I spoke with do not just passively absorb industry norms
and practices. Instead, workers of color like Arvand often take on additional

people usually don't react to my voice
they react to their google image
search :) #pubradiovoice

FIGURE 2: #pubradiovoice tweet by Audie Cornish,
January 2015. Source: Twitter.

complex creative labor to expand who and what gets heard on public radio.
In other words, they resist in order to enrich the airwaves, often at great
personal cost.

Some might wonder why I've chosen to focus on public radio. There has
been a proliferation of news outlets and a fracturing of news consumption
in the past two decades, especially in the digital age. But NPR, unlike other
outlets, is what Rosina Lippi-Green calls a "dominant bloc institution"[7]:
its position in American radio broadcasting is enshrined in legislation, and
it has been in operation as a national network for over fifty years. Its network consists of more than two hundred affiliate stations on the local level,
which are funded by the Corporation for Public Broadcasting and air NPR
programming. In addition to its broad reach, the well-documented decline
of local print journalism[8] and the threat this poses to responsive journalism
that is connected to the communities it serves[9] has made the public radio
industry increasingly important as one of the last vestiges of local investigative journalism; if the public press is a bedrock of democracy, and if NPR
is a bedrock of the public press, it stands to reason that NPR's content, and
public radio's content more broadly, is crucially important to the polity.

Public radio's reputation as a voice seeking to "reflect America," coupled
with the narrower linguistic patterns of its output, maintains the notion
that there is an ideal, standardized language. The tension between the network's broad mission and narrow practice raises questions about who can
be heard in the public sphere. As Christopher Chávez puts it in his book *The
Sound of Exclusion*, "Despite its mandate to reach a broader public, NPR
has consistently delivered programming to a narrow audience of educated,

middle-class white listeners. By situating whiteness and privilege in its center, however, NPR has consistently moved minority audiences to the periphery."[10]

Understanding the Public Radio Industry as a White Institutional Space

Now let's dig into what public radio is. I conceptualize the public radio industry in the United States as a white institutional space.[11] This conceptualization includes NPR as an organization, the local public radio stations that have NPR memberships (its network), and the other nonprofit public radio distributors American Public Media and Public Radio Exchange. This set of organizations shares an egalitarian mission to serve the American public through a combination of news-based and cultural programming. Yet, as communications scholars Jack Mitchell and Jason Loviglio have noted, public radio content has taken on popularity with the American professional-managerial class, who are treated as identifiable listener-members who form a large part of the public radio listening community.[12] There has also been a societal recognition of public radio's aesthetic[13] and voice[14]; the iconic public radio voice has been indexed as mirroring the comforts and tastes of predominantly white, professional-class listener-members.[15] The mismatch defies recent efforts by the Corporation for Public Broadcasting, National Public Radio, and other public radio distributors to become more accountable to marginalized communities.[16]

But what do I mean by "white institutional space"? Space, rather than being a neutral concept, is politically and historically constructed, and spaces dominated by white cultural frameworks reproduce ideologies of white supremacy over nonwhite communities.[17] George Lipsitz and other scholars of white space extend this to consider how white ideologies are "inscribed in the physical contours or the places where we live, work and play."[18]

Organizational policy and practice can serve as the mechanisms that maintain white institutional space, even in organizations that embrace diversity and pluralism. Amanda Lewis and John Diamond, in their analysis of a well-funded suburban school in the American Midwest, show the endurance of Black-white achievement gaps despite the school's policies and values surrounding racial integration.[19] That is, the school is racially integrated, and its policies and rules are race neutral. However, organizational practices lean on existing schemas about potentiality and talent, and so the school, in practice, sorts gifted and talented students by race and entrenches the achievement gap.

White dominance pervades many other common meso-level practices: job market sorting,[20] normative structures and ways of thinking within organizations, and workplace labor distribution[21] among them. Joan Acker, a prominent scholar of gender and work, asserts that patriarchy, capitalism, and racism interlock in organizations to form "inequality regimes."[22]

I build upon and extend work that takes racism seriously as a structuring force in organizational and institutional life by illustrating how racism structured the historical development of the organizational form, policies, and practices of the National Public Radio network. Specifically, I consider how NPR is a racialized organization.[23] I then connect the historical formation of NPR's structure, policies, and practices to worker experiences today across the entire industry, not only NPR.

Public broadcasting in the United States has a robust archive that makes such a connection possible. The National Public Broadcasting Archive is a collection of documents established by the original authorizing legislation of the Corporation for Public Broadcasting (CPB). The archive, located at the University of Maryland, College Park, contains official documents, collections of informal intraorganizational and interorganizational correspondence, oral history interviews by institutional leaders in public broadcasting, and papers of interest from former employees at NPR and the CPB, dating back to the earliest days of the public broadcasting system.

These documents offer an account of organizational formation and practice over time. The archive, then, presents an opportunity to trace the formation of a racialized organization. How did the founders interpret the mandate to serve all Americans? What were the political and economic forces that shaped its foundation and persistence? What did the founders care about preserving when it came time for budget cuts?

This book goes beyond identifying the mechanisms that produce racial disparities in organizational life to emphasize points of contingency. By points of contingency, I mean the instances in which government bureaucrats, organizational founders, and managers made choices that entrenched or reinforced mechanisms of racial exclusion in the first place. Without identifying these actions, racial inequality seems to be generated "without racists,"[24] or at least without racial intent.[25] At each turn in the development of public radio that I document in the book, it is important to consider: Can we imagine government bureaucrats, founders, or managers making different decisions with different outcomes?

The policies and practices those government bureaucrats, founders, and managers chose had an enduring impact on public radio's story production process. Organizational policy decisions and their implementation accumulate to shape the contemporary experiences of people of color in public radio. How does the public radio industry's status as a white institutional space shape the evaluative processes within?

THE ROLE OF VOICE EVALUATION IN CULTURAL PRODUCTION

The human voice often serves as a marker of social distinction or social otherness. People infer class, race, and gender via a person's dialect,[26] and there is robust scholarship that points to how these inferences can lead to linguistic discrimination with material consequences. Sociological research on inequality has identified linguistic discrimination as one mechanism by which landlords and employers exclude nonwhite applicants when they seek resources from white institutional spaces. Urban sociologists Douglas Massey and Garvey Lundy demonstrate that racial discrimination in housing can begin at the moment of a phone call,[27] drawing on linguistic research demonstrating that Americans infer race via dialect.[28] Tracking linguistic discrimination is an effective way to identify racial discrimination in white space. But how and why does linguistic discrimination along racial lines form?

In contrast to the traditional sociological canon, linguistic anthropologists and interdisciplinary race scholars take seriously the co-constitution of racial ideologies and ideologies of language. Sara Trechter and Mary Bucholtz assert that studying whiteness through linguistic analysis goes beyond content to see how white norms are coded in language practices.[29] They find that linguistic analysis is a missing dimension of whiteness studies, and they call for a study of linguistic form as a way of looking at how whiteness and white racial dominance is constructed, in part, linguistically. Linguistic anthropologists Nelson Flores and Jonathan Rosa coined the term "raciolinguistic ideologies"[30] as an analytic concept to account for the ways in which linguistic norms are racialized by the socially conditioned, hegemonic white listening ear that shapes what can(not) pass as professional, trustworthy, or authoritative in public discourse.[31] From this perspective, it becomes clear that white institutional space, in making whiteness a credential, devalues markedly nonwhite linguistic performance. As anthropologist Jane Hill has shown, the process of racializing language makes public space into "white space" via voice evaluation.[32]

Ethnomusicologist Allie Martin demonstrates this process in her analysis of a 2018 municipal bill in Washington, DC, introduced to discourage street musicians from disturbing residents and workers in gentrifying Chinatown. Martin argues that the introduction and support of the bill singled out Black musical traditions, for instance brass bands and other Black sound traditions, when considering which music or performance was deemed disruptive. The bill, then, serves as a continuation of the ways "Black sonic creation has been consistently stigmatized and subsequently punished." Martin makes the stakes clear when she notes that "we are unable to understand how people build their worlds through music and sound if we are unable to listen to their multitudes, to the ways in which they impose and are imposed on in different forms."[33]

Turning this insight from public space to media representations, it is also evident that mainstream and popular shows are secured as "white space" through vocal stereotyping. For example, the well-known and long-running cartoon program *The Simpsons* faced critique after decades of using a stereotyped brown voice created by a white actor, Hank Azaria, as an Indian convenience store owner[34]; Azaria developed the voice in response to producers asking, "basically, how offensive can you make it?"[35] The critiques of Azaria's voicing of Apu received mainstream attention through a documentary, *The Problem with Apu*,[36] which connected comedian Hari Kondabolu's encounter with the cartoon character Apu to larger issues of how sonic brownface takes a psychic toll on those stereotyped by the process. While Azaria stepped away from the role in the months following the height of public critique, his ability to publicly use a mock "brown" voice in both *The Simpsons* and in public appearances[37] without pushback demonstrates the power of white institutional space to reinforce white supremacy through racial stereotyping of nonwhite voices.

Voice evaluation, then, is subject to the norms produced by the white institutional space in which the evaluation is taking place. In the cultural industries, similarly to the white public space that Jane Hill analyzes, nonwhite voices are stereotyped and commodified. Sociologist Nancy Wang Yuen documents, for example, how casting directors imagine and evaluate particular voices for different racial/ethnic groups, such as Asian actors of different nationalities.[38]

By analyzing the voice as an object of racialized evaluation, my analysis of public radio production processes in the second part of this book reveals the role of the Du Boisian sonic color line in the workplace. Adopting W.E.B. Du Bois's prognosis of the color line being the greatest problem of the twentieth century, sound studies scholar Jennifer Lynn Stoever has identified "the sonic color line" as an enduring, historically constructed mechanism that prevents white actors from hearing nonwhite voices in their full humanity.[39]

Stoever looks to Du Bois's *Dusk of Dawn* for this sonic metaphor for racialization. Du Bois describes the feeling of being a Black American in a vacuum, trying to be heard when asking for justice and equality, but separated from whites by a glass barrier. The whites do not even recognize the injustice to which those in the vacuum point:

> It gradually penetrates the minds of the prisoners that the people passing do not hear; that some thick sheet of invisible but horribly tangible plate glass is between them and the world. They get excited; they talk louder; they gesticulate. Some of the passing world stop in curiosity; these gesticulations seem so pointless; they laugh and pass on. They still either do not hear at all, or hear but dimly, and even what they hear, they do not understand.[40]

This barrier, a structured societal divide, shapes both how people can be heard in institutional contexts and the amount of communicative labor it takes for nonwhite voices to exist in white-dominant space. So in the workplace, you are already coded as having a deficit of authority; when you insist upon making the injustices audible to those around you, you are heard as unreasonable.

Attention to the sonic color line demonstrates that white supremacy in the United States is upheld in part through listening practices that mark racial difference through sound. Crucially, this set of listening practices has entrenched in dominant US discourses a "racialized auditory filter," setting sounds associated with white culture as normative.[41]

Recall Arvand from the opening paragraphs of this introduction. He noted of his white colleagues, "we're hearing the same thing and hearing it completely differently." These different evaluations came from a tape recording alone, without a photo pairing. A Middle Eastern American broadcaster raised in a nonwhite, low- to middle-class neighborhood, Arvand came to public radio later in life, only after he had established his own music career. His own subjectivity as an outsider within marks the whiteness of the space, and the white dominance of these evaluative processes around voices considered for public radio airtime.

Public radio's practices are shaped by the sonic color line in ways that challenge the industry's mission to provide a public service over commercial profits. In the public radio production process, the sonic color line manifests as a systematic racialized evaluation of voices. When voices evaluated for broadcast are coded as nonwhite, their clarity and expertise are more likely to be questioned. I analyze these patterns through the insights of outsiders within historically white spaces, like Arvand, who enter public radio with different practices of evaluative listening. The discrepancy between his hearing and that of his white colleagues is socially conditioned over time, and integral to understanding the reproduction of white supremacy via voice evaluation.

When sourcing stories, editors put extra scrutiny on guests without media training and with accents associated with nonwhite communities. Employees of color broaden the set of voices that make it on air by training guests and conducting bilingual reporting and interpretation work. In the case of producers sourcing live guests, some respondents feel a responsibility to protect the source from the whiteness of the space, acting as a cultural broker throughout the process. Further, as my respondents reflect on their own experiences trying to get sources on air, they propose alternative ways of listening to sources and evaluating whether voices are worthy of airtime.

THE INSIGHTS OF PEOPLE OF COLOR IN WHITE INSTITUTIONAL SPACE

Arvand's and Sarah's experiences show that even as people of color enter white institutional spaces, whiteness serves as a gatekeeping credential; the normative ways of performing in white institutional spaces prevent full belonging for nonwhite employees.[42]

So how does it feel to be a nonwhite worker in a white institutional space? Critical organizational research has found that the normative practices in white racialized organizations mark nonwhite and nonmale bodies as racialized and gendered and therefore deviant as they are measured against the default category of white and male. Tsedale Melaku theorizes the price for Black women professionals of existing in white institutional space as an "inclusion tax," due to the daily racism and misogyny they face in the workplace.[43] At the same time, their disruption opens analytical possibilities to denaturalize the unmarked, often taken-for-granted white dominance and patriarchy in racialized and gendered organizations.[44]

Beyond their very presence as disruption, workers of color gain experiences as they navigate the workplace that lead them to offer valuable insights into the inequalities that permeate the modern workplace. Perceptions of the world are shaped by one's social location in the racial order.[45] As Adia

Wingfield shows through an interview study with Black professionals, racialized emotions such as anger and frustration are coded as more acceptable and appropriate when white in the workplace. The professionals that Wingfield interviews know these feeling rules very well, even if their non-Black colleagues do not.[46] The ways workers of color perform emotional labor in organizations are rendered invisible by colorblind ideologies.[47]

I center how employees of color articulate their own experiences in and responses to their workplaces as what Patricia Hill Collins calls "outsiders within": people in elite spaces who are from marginalized communities or who hold historically marginalized identities.[48] The outsiders within white racialized organizations challenge the organization's moral legitimacy by laying bare who is *not* included in the existing organization, its output, and its audience. Further, they bring a unique standpoint to the social structure in which they are marginalized. Thus, I have found that the racialized self-formation of outsiders within the public radio industry often produces a unique standpoint on understanding the sonic color line in the workplace.

This book offers a study of public radio in the United States that considers those who are marginalized within the industry as vital voices to help us better understand it. I have often been asked why I am asking nonwhite employees to talk to me, when I am considering whiteness as the structuring mechanism that shapes their exclusion. There are two reasons.

The first is that while hostility against nonwhite bodies in white spaces is pervasive, this hostility can remain relatively invisible to the white people moving through the space. Elijah Anderson shows how tenuous white space is for Black individuals, noting:

> A particular organization—for instance, a corporation, a nonprofit, or a public sector bureaucracy—may pride itself on being egalitarian and universalistic and not recognize its own shortcomings with respect to racial inequality. The generalized effect of the iconic ghetto is often subtle; the issue of race can remain unspoken, but in the white space it can count for everything.[49]

Anderson here is addressing the anti-Blackness of white space, but as Wendy Leo Moore points out, nonwhite racial groups face distinct yet interrelated subjugation in institutions structured by whiteness.[50] While outcomes and experiences may differ, they share in subjection to conceptions of what is good, appropriate, and right being set by historically white (and historically racially exclusionary) structures. David Embrick and Wendy Leo Moore note:

The mechanisms of White institutional space are so deeply constitutive of the infrastructure of U.S. organizations and institutions that they become tacit, implicitly understood without conscious thought, normalizing White superiority and successful attainment of institutional resources and characterizing non-White inferiority as normal in these social spaces.[51]

In other words, white bodies and white authority are naturalized and conceptualized as the universal norm in white space. The pervasive and deeply embedded character of white supremacy allows it to operate without much notice to white employees.

Second, while white employees might have difficulty seeing or hearing these mechanisms of exclusion due to the seamlessness with which they operate in the space, cultural workers of color in white organizations tend to develop what I call a "sonic double consciousness": an awareness of the racialized evaluation of voice in white institutional space.[52] Cultural workers of color form or further develop this awareness when producing and voicing stories, due in part to the interactions with the white world that this labor entails. So while white people remain largely unaware of these dynamics of language and racism, interviewees of color recognize the racial exclusion that occurs in their workplaces daily, whether it happens to them or to their colleagues.

By undertaking qualitative interviews with cultural workers of color in the industry, I *start* with those who were not included at the decision-making table at the organization's inception. That way, the discussion is less about how we get more people to the table than about reconsidering the insights once excluded and the ways these exclusions enshrine racial inequalities. In this way, I offer up this book as a modest corrective to existing public radio historiography—a corrective that is not all-encompassing, but one that offers one starting point for a more inclusive history of the industry, decentering the dominant voices in the archive.

Literal and Metaphorical Voice in the Contemporary Public Radio Industry

To recap, we know from existing research that (1) white institutional space shapes who has authority and resources in a racially exclusionary way; (2) racism shapes voice evaluation in white institutional space; and (3) people of color in white institutional space offer a unique vantage point on these uneven power dynamics.

From these insights, I argue two points. First, white institutional space is a site of reproduction of the sonic color line, or the racialized evaluation of nonwhite voices as nonnormative in mainstream (white) American listening practices. Second, nonnormative bodies in white racialized organizations, due to their increased awareness of the space's whiteness as outsiders within, may develop a linguistic responsibility to other nonnormative speech communities. This sense of responsibility guides their work to get a wider diversity of sources on air.

When I analyze how voices of color are perceived in public radio, I am considering them in both the literal and the metaphorical sense. By "literal voices," I refer to the exclusion of voices that fall outside of legibility for a presumed white, professional-class audience.[53] In other words, analyzing "literal voices" is the analysis of how the industry evaluates accents, cadence, and tone. This exclusion of literal voices is what Arvand refers to at the beginning of this introduction when he notes a mismatch between how he perceives an accent's intelligibility and how his colleagues do.

By "metaphorical voices," I refer to the perspectives and content of voices, including how such voices are framed, narrated, and curated. In other words, what the voices say politically. The cultural studies scholar Nick Couldry speaks to how crucial voice and listening are to human agency:

> All human beings have the capacity for voice, to give an account of their lives. [. . .] This irreducible feature of human agency requires recognition, as a feature of every human agent, and therefore as a feature mutually shared by any two or more humans who interact with each other.[54]

Mutual recognition, then, requires not only the ability of individuals to voice their own opinions in social space. The person voicing their perspective within an organization must be heard and seriously considered on their own terms; otherwise, the power imbalance in the interaction is exacerbated.

When Sarah, introduced in the opening of this introduction, is faced with the question of why white people would care about the stories she pitched, she is being implicitly instructed that she must pitch the story on the terms of the dominant racial group. When this consideration is embedded in the cultural production process, one risks disseminating distorted narratives about minoritized groups already misrecognized in society.

While the question of why white people would care is distinct from the question of whether an accent is intelligible, the two issues are intimately linked. B, a Black woman reporter in the southern United States, noted these efforts at her local station:

I have also really been trying to push where I can [on] accents. I think often our rural [white-dominated] location is used as a reason to not put on somebody with an accent. [. . .] I did a story about this coffee shop. It's a hub for resettled refugees outside of the city. And I was like, "We need to have someone on [the air] who is a refugee!"

B went on to note why the inclusion of these voices is important for public service:

People need to get comfortable with accents and understanding accents on the air, 'cause that's just the direction this country's coming in. I think it's a public service, even—if you wanna go that far—to put different accents on the air that people will have to really kind of think about and get used to.

When B insisted on covering an important gathering spot for refugees in her station's coverage area, she considered voice on both the literal and the metaphorical level. On the literal level, she platformed refugee voices despite conventional concerns that their accents as new arrivals would not be easily understood by listeners born in the region. On the metaphorical level, she platformed their perspectives by producing a story that centers those points of view, rather than speaking for them. B's insistence is rooted in a developed practice of listening across difference.

Listening across Difference

Fatima, a Latinx reporter I spoke with, was tired of the limited perspective that emerged when trying to make different voices and accents fit within the typical public radio form. She insisted that reporters must defy this expectation:

I think I should push back on that, because it's not always to entertain. The goal is to actually empathize or learn or push and ask more questions. Hear from someone that you typically wouldn't hear from. Not just be like, "Oh, yes, wow. They sound really smart. They're a good talker."

Fatima articulates an alternative way of thinking about public media: What if the goal was not to capture the attention of the white professional class, but to expand the soundscape of public media beyond that audience's racialized auditory filter? She and her colleagues feel an obligation to listen that resonates with media theorist Tanja Dreher's concept of "listening across difference."[55]

The concept of "listening across difference" is a powerful one as it shifts the focus from ensuring that everyone has a voice in media, to considering how and whether "diverse voices" get listened to. As noted above, the sonic color line has inhibited recognition across axes of racialized difference because of the way that race has structured our society. Thus, it requires active work to create an institutionalized practice of listening across difference.

Dreher's focus on listening shifts responsibility away from marginalized speakers being made to contort themselves into legibility for the white American listening ear. When applied to this research, it is clear that my respondents actively work to listen across difference. Nicola, a Latinx reporter, described a *learned* ability to hear a wider variety of accents as intelligible as having a "sympathetic ear":

> I have a sympathetic ear because I've also taught English to non-English speakers and I've taught ESL in this country. I love that. The reason I'm bringing up the phrasing of that word is I love that word of having a "sympathetic ear." There's the linguistic part of that. Let's actually listen to people and what they're saying and what they're trying to say and come back to them—"Is this what you mean? Did I understand you correctly?"

Nicola proudly explains that she has developed this sympathetic ear over time, through concerted efforts and training to do so:

> And that's something that I learned from teaching a language, and I had some really good teachers in journalism school, of really talking to people and listening to comprehend so that you're having the best possible interviews at the end of when you write something out. That's to say, I wanted to speak to people with different accents.

She insists that this type of learning can be embedded into institutional training:

> We've got to train all of our reporters to listen to our sources and be less worried about accents. If your problem is the accent, if your problem is the language, then just give the translation. Give the summation. I feel very strong feelings about that.

The ethics of listening across difference that these public radio employees of color bring to their interactions with sources gives us a glimpse of what a more capacious, and antiracist, auditory filter might sound like.

By offering an account of both obstacles to and strategies of resistance, this book shows the challenges that lie ahead while keeping in mind the potential embedded in the day-to-day strategies of employees of color to dismantle the sonic color line. Once we apprehend the mechanisms that reproduce a racialized set of listening practices, might we be able to build a more ethical framework for listening across difference in the American public sphere?

A NOTE ON ANONYMIZATION

While the eighty-three employees of color I spoke to for this project range from temporary contract workers to prominent, well-established employees, I have anonymized every interviewee for the purposes of telling the story of public radio through their perspectives. Any journalist or public figure named in the text has spoken on these issues in other outlets or on social media, and I cite them accordingly.

As Sara Ahmed offers in her book *Complaint!*, complaints are often (mis)heard as obstacles to progress, as stickiness that leaves people in negativity. I join her reframing of complaint as a practice that enables people in institutions to "show what you know."[56] Indeed, Garcia-Navarro's and Cornish's tweets about their need to contend with the presumption of whiteness in their organization revealed to me a deep well of knowledge, one that only further deepened as I began to speak with interviewees lower in the workplace hierarchy. Yet many of the workers of color I interviewed are facing conditions of workplace precarity. Some live on permatemp status; others worry about their status as the "only one," putting them in the position of constantly speaking out and taking professional risks. Thus, their anonymity is key as they continue in such workplace struggles.

I heartily believe that this collection of voices can be a tool for organizing for people of color in public radio and in the audio industry more broadly. I feel that this can be better achieved when considering these experiences as part of an industry-wide phenomenon—something that might be obscured by naming individuals.

When I presented preliminary findings to a group of radio and podcast producers at one of their professional conferences, I opened space during the discussion for audio workers of color to voice their own concerns. While they discussed being "the only one" at their respective stations and organizations, they also indicated that these findings offered a point of legitimation—hearing others' similar accounts showed that they weren't alone in the ways they experienced storytelling in their organization.

I give an overview here of the experiences of a wide range of public radio employees of color; their commonality is their self-identification as people of color. Beyond that, they do experience other distinct systems of oppression differently: women, nonbinary people, and femmes are subject to patriarchal constraints; working-class people of color must contend with structural elitism; Black people experience not only white supremacy but also the structural anti-Blackness that both white people and non-Black people of color can benefit from.[57] I draw these distinctions out through examples, but the throughline of the book centers the role of whiteness in shaping the experiences of all my participants. This move is meant to center points of possible solidarity across racialized workers.

While I do my best to reflect a wide range of experiences, I know that the accounts featured in the book are only partial; not all employees of color in public radio will see themselves reflected in this patchwork. But I do hope there are points of resonance with readers who have experience in the industry; or, if not, then generative points of dissonance!

This book is meant to serve as another reminder for workers of color in the industry, particularly those in "the only one" position, that they are not, in fact, alone. Their complaints are manifestations of the deep institutional knowledge they possess from their position as racialized subjects. May my research serve as a point of solidarity and a driver for change.

The Story Arc

The book consists of six empirical chapters.

In chapters 1 through 3, I examine the roots of the public radio industry. National Public Radio formed under the Corporation for Public Broadcasting as a white racialized organization because it drew on practices from the existing, white-dominant nonprofit radio field. It became a network that championed voices of white women and challenged the authorial masculine voice. And it became a network that sought out donations from the white professional class, given its perpetual struggles with underfunding. Each of these practices has contributed to the formation of the "voice of public radio" as it stands today, in its progressive elements, in its positive impacts, and in its imperfection.

In chapters 4 through 6, I analyze the contemporary industry practices that maintain public radio's signature sonic aesthetic, with a focus on the constraints that employees of color face in trying to break away from the network's traditional narrative framing and sound. These constraints faced by producers, editors, and journalists of color can lead to distortions in the stories available in the public sphere; at the same time, they give rise to robust forms of resistance among people of color and other storytellers with a racial consciousness.

I conclude by turning to the broader relationships between racism, voice, and the public sphere—and what all this means for the future of public media. I highlight three main ways we might challenge the trenchant sonic color line within this industry: namely, reassessing public media's sense of moral certitude, changing public radio's funding structure, and shifting production practices according to the insights of employees of color. I end by discussing how the implications of this research can move beyond the cultural industries, showing that linguistic discrimination maintained through institutional logics can be embedded in seemingly nonracial processes in consequential social organizations, from health-care settings to schools to realty offices.

Whether it be in a newsroom, a school, or any other institution, the same ethical responsibility to listen across difference remains. Because until we dismantle the sonic color line everywhere, we're never going to hear the whole story.

PART I

Public Radio's White Racial Structure

If you have some familiarity with public radio in the United States, you already know the public radio tote bag. It is made of canvas fabric. By some accounts, it costs about six dollars to produce. Barbara Sopato, the director of consumer products for NPR, explains in a piece in the *Atlantic* that tote bag giveaways began in the 1970s for practical reasons: its matter-of-fact utilitarian simplicity "fits in with public radio. It's very affordable, very useful. We're grassroots people."[1]

This account of the object's simplicity is technically true. Yet it understates the complex social markers that are associated with carrying the tote. An outward show of public radio listenership, the tote has become emblematic of a *type* of person in the United States. A person who carries a public radio tote, either from NPR or from a local affiliate, expresses that they have donated to and support public media. Others can see that the carrier has the time to listen to the news, the civic-mindedness to care about nonprofit media, and enough discretionary spending to make a sizeable donation to the network.

Even if you don't have familiarity with public radio itself, this type of cultural capital via canvas tote bag manifests globally across white-dominant countries. As noted by Alexandra Dane in her analysis of the role of tote bags in American, Australian, and British contemporary literary festivals:

FIGURE 3: *This American Life* public radio tote bag. Source: WBEZ Chicago online store.

The canvas tote bag, often branded with the name and logo of a popular cultural institution or bookstore, has become a shorthand for an individual's accumulated cultural capital; this seemingly innocuous accessory has the power to signal to one's peers the level of their engagement with the cultural and creative industries in a seemingly casual but deeply coded manner.[2]

Like those found at literary festivals touting the *New Yorker* brand, a simple public radio canvas tote bag is an iconic object that signals what Elizabeth Currid-Halkett refers to inconspicuous consumption. This form of consumption involves the purchase and display of items that themselves do not cost much, but despite their low cost, they serve as discrete boundary symbols because of their connotation with deep cultural knowledge. Currid-Halkett finds that inconspicuous consumption has become more prevalent in the twenty-first century as luxury goods have become more widely available to a larger mass of consumers. While the twentieth century's leisure class spent ostentatiously to set themselves apart, today's elite are more likely to do so by signaling that they are virtuous consumers, focusing on experiences and informed choices rather than luxury goods.[3]

There's an added layer to the tote displayed in figure 3, sold by WBEZ Chicago's *This American Life*. The slogan "This is the tote bag they keep talking about on public radio" serves as a sort of wink to its potential buyers—and those who will see it on the street. This layer of self-awareness of the reputation of public radio has become commonplace.

Public radio's location in the media ecosystem no longer surprises people. We already know very well public radio's tendencies to serve well-educated, professional-managerial-class baby boomers, as noted in existing histories of NPR.[4] Although public radio's reputation is well cemented, we cannot take NPR's social status within the media ecosystem for granted if we wish to dismantle the inequalities it produces. Part I of the book unpacks how we got here.

The Work of Part I

In the following three chapters, the first empirical section of the book, we go back to a time before public radio and public radio listening became associated with white liberal culture. I ask, what is the *structure* of public radio, and how does whiteness shape it?

Chapter 1 examines how a legacy of racial exclusion marks National Public Radio as a white racialized organization. First, I outline nonprofit radio programming in the Golden Age of radio (1920s–1950s) to demonstrate the racially unequal conditions that NPR inherited. I then turn to NPR's founding and its first ten years of operation. Using organizational meeting minutes, external reports, oral histories, and founder memoirs, I show that the early implementation of station membership criteria, hiring practices, and programming priorities, while considered race-neutral decisions by the founders, inhibited the inclusion of nonwhite voices into NPR's workforce, station membership, and programming.

Chapter 2 analyzes public radio's signature sound. The network has often been credited with legitimating feminized voices of authority on the airwaves.[5] This understanding of the network's voice became further entrenched in 2021 with the fiftieth-anniversary canonization of NPR's "Founding Mothers": Cokie Roberts, Susan Stamberg, Linda Wertheimer, and Nina Totenberg.[6] The chapter considers the role of whiteness and patriarchy in this canonization, asking: In cementing these voices as iconic in public radio, what other pathbreaking voices were precluded? The chapter analyzes a combination of founder memoirs, oral histories of the Founding Mothers, and interviews with employees of color. The data show that the sonic aesthetics of white womanhood included in NPR's sonic formation are now associated with public radio storytelling. This shift, while progressive, has unintentionally upheld race and class hierarchies.

In the words of one of my participants, Samiya, "It's always been white public radio. [. . .] The weird thing is, it was wonderful and experimental at first and still very white. And then it became more corporate and still very white." Chapter 3 takes us through this shift from white experimental to white corporate, focusing on public radio's relationships with both donors and corporate underwriters in the 1980s. NPR member stations, understood at their outset to be local organizations meant to reflect the entire public of their respective regions, became dependent on a narrow set of donors, and by consequence, those donors' tastes. This chapter reviews existing public radio historiographies alongside a unique analysis of contemporary public radio marketing materials to show the rise of a white, professional-class donor base and corporate sponsorship from 1980 to present. The marketization of public radio has turned listeners into consumers rather than publics. This reconceptualization impacts the demographics that public radio is accountable to, disproportionately centering an affluent, well-educated, predominantly white consumer base.

Taken together, these three elements—the founding conditions, the sonic aesthetic, and the network's relationship with white donors—constitute the white racial structure of public radio and the terrain people of color navigate in the contemporary context.

1

To Serve All Americans

Following June 2020, when George Floyd was murdered by police in Minneapolis, activists and community members on local and national levels fought for accountability. The movement critiqued not only anti-Black police violence but racism embedded in American institutions more broadly. Journalism as a profession had reached a visible breaking point; Black journalists in particular pushed for long overdue paradigm shifts in the ways the media covered Black and brown communities.[1]

The American public radio system was no exception. NPR's national headquarters and its local affiliates were forced to confront the inadequacy of their reporting on racism and their internal newsroom practices. Public media newsrooms were called to task for the mismatch between their espoused values—with a mission to "reflect America"—and the white dominance of their newsrooms. As laid out in local NPR station WNYC's show *The Takeaway*:

> Across the country, journalists and staff are speaking out at public radio stations about failed attempts at diversifying newsrooms and troubling stories of racism in the workplace going back decades and stretching into the present day.[2]

Having been studying racial equity in public media for four years before this historic juncture, I received quite a few queries as to whether I was surprised by this development. But this discourse felt familiar; it resonated with the more than fifty-year arc of public radio, and it took me back to the archive. Because if you opened the *New York Times* on November 26, 1978, you would see a very public account of public radio's shortcomings on race. Journalist Richard Shepard writes:

> Public broadcasting has been delinquent in meeting the needs of minorities in every aspect of management, employment, training, programming and decision-making, according to a detailed and voluminous report issued by a task force that spent 18 months examining the problem.[3]

Shepard was describing "A Formula for Change," a 1978 report of the Task Force on Minorities in Public Broadcasting. For the report, Dr. Gloria Anderson and twenty-eight other researchers conducted an extensive study filled with critiques on public broadcasting's lack of racial diversity. They included seventy key recommendations for addressing the problem. The introduction summarized the findings and declared,

> After 18 months of study and 11 years after the taxpayer subsidy began, the Task Force must conclude that the public broadcast system is asleep at the transmitter.[4]

The report was a disappointment for NPR, an organization that had consistently voiced commitment to reflecting the racial diversity of the American public. Programming manager Bill Siemering's vision for public radio, written in 1970, stressed the need for specialized audience programming, insisting that "[a]s man pulls himself out of the mass society to develop his unique humanness, his minority identification (ethnic, cultural, value) becomes increasingly important."[5] But seven years after he published these programming purposes, the emphasis on minority publics in this foundational vision had failed to manifest.

By 1977, per "A Formula for Change," NPR was dedicating only 3 percent of its budget to creating programming focusing on minority groups within the US population. Out of the 1,543 hours of radio programming that NPR produced that year, only 71.5 hours were designed for minority audiences. Furthermore, NPR's board of directors was all-white and all-male. Less than a decade into its operation, there was already a yawning gap between the organization's intention and its production.

To more deeply understand the contemporary experiences of people of color who work in public radio, we first must take time to understand the roots of the public radio industry. In this chapter, I review the racial inequities that public radio inherited from its predecessor, educational radio; introduce the original decision makers who sought to create a new type of organization in response to the legislation that formed a public broadcasting mandate; and explain how these decision makers, all white men from the professional class, shaped the character of the organization in their image for years to come. When the founders translated existing social norms into a new workplace, they created a white racialized organization.

White Racialized Organizations

At first mention, it may sound counterintuitive to deem a nonhuman entity such as an organization as "having a race." But sociologists who study racism in organizations have demonstrated that, in organizations, race is not just an individual demographic variable. Racial ideologies often structure organizations and inform their cultural practices;[6] therefore, "organizations are not race neutral."[7]

This insight is often understood as common sense when we talk about nonwhite organizations; we don't bat an eye when someone refers to "ethnic" restaurants, Black barber shops, and Latinx grocers. To talk about a white organization in popular discourse, on the other hand, often only conjures up images of white *power* organizations like the Ku Klux Klan. But in reality, many more commonplace mainstream organizations in the United States have white normative ways of thinking and structuring resources. The dominant white racial character of these organizations persists even as the organization includes nonwhite individuals through hiring and admission.[8]

Take law schools, for example. Wendy Leo Moore demonstrates that the institution of the legal system—and, subsequently, legal education— were developed under conditions including the racial exclusion of nonwhite social actors. Thus, the logics of both the legal system and the curriculum surrounding it reflected the dispositions of white people in a segregated social system and naturalized such logics as race neutral.[9] When nonwhite students, faculty, and staff enter a law school today, the history of the place haunts their present experiences. They enter halls filled with portraits of white men that tell their perspectival narratives as founders and creators of legal doctrine.[10] Their curriculum, despite being steeped in racist and segregationist origins, is presented often without the racist social context in which laws were formulated and enacted.[11]

Moore was clear that law schools were merely one sort of racialized space. Indeed, well beyond law schools, historically constructed processes of segregation and exclusion often become institutionalized and perpetuated through organizational practices. The founders forming public radio, while

looking ambitiously toward an attempt at pluralism in their journalistic practice, had not properly reckoned with the history of the radio broadcasting
field as they built their network, and so they, too, formed a white racialized
organization.

When public television and public radio developed in the United States,
both legislators and founders stressed the novelty of these systems. In a
speech, President Lyndon B. Johnson noted that in passing the National
Public Broadcasting Act of 1967, Congress had "created a new institution."
As Jack Mitchell, NPR's first employee, recalls the formation of NPR: "No
stations or individuals, as in television, stood ready to lead. No constituency
demanded action. No expectations existed. The slate was blank."[12] It was
technically true that NPR and the Public Broadcasting Service (PBS) were
new organizations, as was the Corporation for Public Broadcasting over-
seeing them. However, the slate, far from blank, was historically white and
racially exclusionary.

Where Did American Public Radio Come From?

When I began this project interested in contemporary experiences of public
radio's workers of color, I knew I would have to trace organizational decisions across the network. But it soon became clear that I had to go back even
further, before NPR hit the airwaves. While there was no "public" broadcaster in the United States before the 1967 act, there was a robust educational broadcasting system that produced and disseminated noncommercial
radio content.[13] Educational radio was regarded as a tool for progressives to
advance democracy throughout the twentieth century,[14] particularly during radio's Golden Age. To the extent that educational radio that predated
NPR included minoritized communities, however, it was through a white-
dominant framing aligned with US interests at the time.

For instance, while there was US-sponsored programming heralding Latin
America as a modern and desirable place for the United States to engage in
diplomacy and commerce, there were few accounts of Mexican Americans
in the United States experiencing racism and xenophobia in educational radio
stations. Instead, Mexicans in the United States who detailed issues of interest
to Latinxs operated on the margins, on low-funded community stations and
US-Mexico border stations, as detailed by historian Dolores Inés Casillas in
her account of twentieth-century US Spanish-language radio.[15]

Another prime example of educational radio's white American perspective can be found in the broadcast series *Americans All, Immigrants All*. In

1938, the United States, recovering from the Great Depression and gearing up for the Second World War, used radio as a tool to promote national unity. The US Department of Education partnered with CBS to create this twenty-six-part radio broadcast series, which simultaneously attempted to celebrate diversity and flatten both difference and inequality.[16] *Americans All, Immigrants All*, noncommercial and government funded, was meant to incorporate American immigrant groups and African American descendants of slaves into a patriotic narrative of a united US populace.

The *Americans All, Immigrants All* series was put forth to celebrate the accomplishments of non-Anglo settlers, the extent of their success measured by how helpful they had been to the "typical" Anglo settler. The measure of accomplishment by this definition is clearly highlighted in the nation-building poster shown in figure 4, a promotional tool for the series.

In the map, marginalized groups are situated as laborers, laudable because of what they contributed to "America," or perhaps, more appropriately, to the white racial project of the United States.[17] Notably, Englishmen are positioned offshore in the Atlantic Ocean, providing law and order as well as settlement. In this poster, labor exploitation and forced removal by Anglo settlers are reformulated as "contributions" by the exploited. Through narrative racecraft, Indigenous peoples' role in America is relegated to their existence on reservations, without the consideration of white American settlers forcing their removal from the land into designated areas, while Black people grow cotton, sugarcane, and rice in fields, somehow without white Americans dehumanizing, enslaving, buying, owning, and containing them to force such work.

By the end of the twenty-six-part series, the narrators declare that their story "has been your story. The story of your friends and your neighbors." Both the aesthetics and narrative of the series specified the "you" as an ideal white citizen, as the program normalized white ways of thinking and speaking as *the* American story, one to which all "others" are welcome to listen in on, contribute to, and emulate. This programming, of course, far preceded public radio as an industry. Racial categorizations have changed dramatically between its airing and the birth of public radio. But this example is indicative of the white perspective inherent to the programming of the educational radio that public radio's infrastructure ultimately drew from.

Not only was noncommercial radio framed for a white audience; it was also majority-white controlled. The main institutional precursor to NPR was the National Association of Educational Broadcasters, founded in 1925.[18]

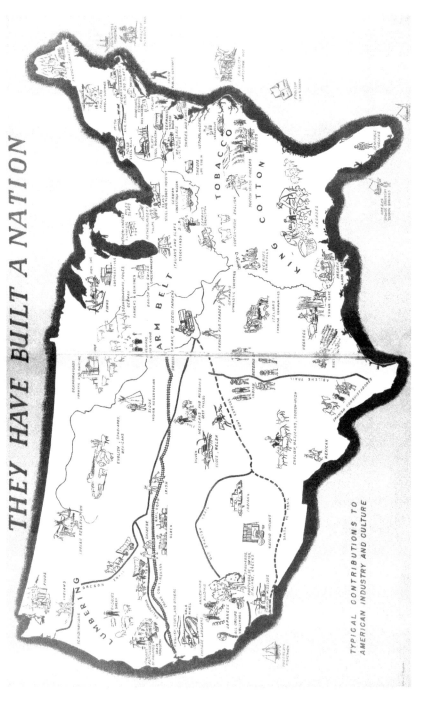

FIGURE 4: "Typical Contributions to American Industry and Culture." A promotional poster for *Americans All, Immigrants All.*
Source: Project Gutenberg.

Its aims were to "promote, by mutual cooperation and united effort, the dissemination of knowledge to the end that both the technical and educational feature of broadcasting may be extended to all."[19] They also used their collective power to fight back against the overly commercialized airwaves as radio grew and became commodified.

Educational broadcasters fought against airwave commercialization by lobbying the Federal Communications Commission (FCC) to reserve more channels for noncommercial radio in a landscape increasingly dominated by commercial interests. By 1938, they had successfully reserved five channels of the airwaves for noncommercial radio purposes, a number that grew to forty by 1945. These noncommercial stations were dominated by white licensees.[20] From the 1940s through the 1960s, much of noncommercial radio was educational: this designation meant that station ownership was largely in the hands of white-dominant universities. In this context, station producers and managers were white men who drew from their predominantly white student body to recruit radio trainees.

Still, the National Public Broadcasting Act of 1967 passed during a time of progressive change in conditions for women and people of color. During this civil rights era, grassroots social movements led by radical activists fought for and achieved legislative victories for racial and gender justice. The federal government institutionalized the legislative victories of the civil rights era in the years following under the Richard Nixon administration.[21] Public broadcasting was part of this ambitious set of changes, legislated in the hopes of making quality broadcasting that reflected the diversity of the American public. Many of the founding members shared this mission.

To make good on the mission, though, and break through into a new, more inclusive type of noncommercial radio, the founders would have had to contend with the legacy of the prior decades of segregated airwaves. Despite the civil rights era's political shifts, by the time NPR was founded in 1970, white men had already dominated the noncommercial radio field for over four decades. Thus, the educational broadcasting system inherited by NPR was normed to a white American audience.

Creating Public Radio from a White Perspective

Despite ambitions of pluralism, NPR's founders, like most white people of their generation, were socialized into a "white habitus"[22] that oriented their worldview and actions. A habitus is a set of practices and beliefs that people acquire over time in their social environments.[23] When sociologists Eduardo Bonilla-Silva, Carla Goar, and David Embrick explored the concept's racial dimension, they found that white people socialized in segregated spaces tended to develop a white habitus: a shared value system of racialized attitudes with racially exclusionary implications. In the sociologists' study, this white habitus was reinforced when subjects' viewpoints weren't challenged or marked as particular to their own segregated context.

White habitus is a useful concept for understanding how racially unequal outcomes occur through both historically developed social structures *and* the behaviors of the individual social actors who are dominant within such social structures. The white habitus simultaneously is conditioned by and upholds white-dominant norms of larger institutions in American society.

NPR's founding members had been socialized on the white-dominant side of a legally segregated system throughout their entire lives. They trained within historically white universities, apprenticed within the historically white organizational field of educational broadcasting, and received their most salient feedback from white audiences. As communications scholar Michael McCauley notes, "NPR, in the most basic terms, is a network founded by well-educated baby boomers and targeted toward listeners with similar demographic and psychographic profiles."[24] The founders did not see their "similarities" to their target listeners as racialized, but as entirely natural.

Figure 5, a group photograph of NPR's incorporation meeting, highlights visually the homogeneity of decision makers in terms of race and professional aesthetic. The collective inattention of NPR's founders, and the employees they hired, to their own whiteness and to the whiteness of their models inhibited them from seeing their own perspectives as particular, not general, in this endeavor—and perhaps from seeing the possibility of other perspectives altogether.

Central to the founders' shared white habitus was a recognition of a civic duty to "the public interest," coupled with misrecognition of the "public" and its "interest" in largely white (and professional-class) terms. NPR's founders were conditioned to have a civic-minded understanding of their work by defining a stated commitment to create a radio network for all Americans. Yet, they were hampered by their racialized habitus. They acted in ways that contradicted their commitment to serve all Americans because they failed to see the existing stations and programming, let alone their own fledgling network, as white dominant.

FIGURE 5: National Public Radio incorporation meeting at the Corporation for Public Broadcasting, Washington, DC, 1970. Seated, left to right: Dick Estell (WKAR East Lansing), John Macy Jr. (Corporation for Public Broadcasting), John Witherspoon (KPBS San Diego), and Bernard Mayes (KQED San Francisco). Standing, left to right: Joe Gwathmey (KUT Austin), Karl Schmidt (WHA Madison), David Platts (WFSU Tallahassee), Marvin Segalman (KPFK Los Angeles), and Bill Kling (KSJR Collegeville, Minnesota). Not pictured: Bill Siemering (WBFO Buffalo). Source: National Public Broadcasting Archives.

Creating a White Racialized Organization

So, how did these two elements—fieldwide histories of racial othering and the founders' shared white habitus—come together to make NPR into a white racialized organization? Organizations within a given field[25] tend to resemble one another for social reasons. Like humans, organizations are not purely rational economic actors subject only to competitive pressures of the marketplace. Instead, they are subject to institutional pressures of the organizational field they belong to. Organizational theorists Paul DiMaggio and Walter Powell have outlined three pressures that potentially lead organizations to resemble one another.

First, organizations face *coercive pressures* to conform to fieldwide technical standards. This pressure is, most often, a set of legal standards. This is the mechanism that leads car manufacturers to adopt new federal environmental regulations. Manufacturers do not do this because it affects their products' market value; rather, they are forced to by their position within an organizational field subject to governing bodies. **Second**, organizations face *normative pressures* to gain legitimacy through the field's professionalization. This pressure is the mechanism that causes employers to require certain credentialing for entry-level positions, even if there is no objective market value to doing so. **Third**, organizations experiencing uncertainty face *mimetic pressures* to model their organizations after legitimate and successful organizations in the field. This pressure is the mechanism that caused the tech industry to adopt open-concept floor plans for their offices en masse; while the setup was not empirically proven to improve workplace morale or the company's position, this office layout began to signify legitimacy because it had been adopted by the more powerful entities in the tech industry.

These three fieldwide pressures give rise to what DiMaggio and Powell have called "institutional isomorphism": "a constraining process that forces one unit in a population to resemble other units that face the same set of environmental conditions."[26] Managers and employees play an integral role in institutional isomorphism, as they shape the organization through their daily actions.[27] Fields, rather than passive sites of norm diffusion, are "relational spaces" in which managers and employees of one organization may feel pressure to conform to the practices of other organizations in the field.[28] Conceptualizing organizational fields as relational spaces and organizational members as actors rather than diffusors of macro-level norms leads us to examine how inequalities are generated through relational processes.[29] Lauren Rivera, for instance, demonstrates that, in the hiring process, interviewers consider cultural fit in their assessment of candidates, often considering a candidate's match with current staff along race, class, and gender lines, a process that exacerbates inequalities in white-dominant fields.[30]

I focus on how organizational founders actively translate old norms into new organizations. What were the *decisions* that led NPR's founders to adapt features of the educational radio field into the new organization's practice? I identify three white institutional isomorphic pressures from the noncommercial radio field. These pressures are racialized norms that shape the practices and standards adopted across organizations within a given field.

a. *Coercive isomorphism* in how founders implemented membership criteria that precluded many nonwhite community stations from membership while privileging university stations;

b. *Normative isomorphism* in how founders sought out hires through informal connections; and

   c. *Mimetic isomorphism* in how the founders set NPR's programming priorities by privileging national news programming that reflected the perspective of what the board and hired employees deemed general and appropriate, based on the larger educational radio field.

These combined pressures led founders to adopt criteria and institute practices that ran counter to their theoretical commitment to pluralism. White institutional isomorphism provides an analytical lens through which to view organizational fields as relational spaces within which deeply embedded racialized norms are spread.

Coercive Isomorphism: Determining Membership Criteria

I spoke with José, a Latinx freelancer, in 2021. He had spent his early career in the late aughts working for public radio stations in the southern United States. He noticed a pattern across stations.

> The South at the time had overwhelmingly white news directors in areas where there was a large Black, and in some cases Latino, population. And they really did not like stories about race, and they really did not like stories about economic inequality.

But why was there such a mismatch between upper management and the communities being served? To fully understand this mismatch, we must consider the lack of station ownership by nonwhite individuals and organizations. Despite interest and advocacy by prominent Black scholars, including W.E.B. Du Bois,[31] there were no Black-owned noncommercial stations on the air until 1949. The stations that served Black audiences were owned by white licensees; of those, there was only *one* recorded Black manager for a Black-centered station owned by white licensees.[32] Further, Black voices were relegated to the realms of entertainment, excluded from general news broadcasts.

Notably, a 1966 peer-reviewed report in the *National Association of Educational Broadcasters Journal*, which asked "Is Educational Broadcasting Segregated?," concluded in the affirmative.[33] By 1970, then, there was an established pattern of excluding Black individuals from controlling the means of radio production: only sixteen radio outlets of eight thousand nationally, commercial *and* noncommercial, were owned by Black individuals, a dismal .002 percent![34]

By the time April 1971 rolled around and NPR's board of directors stated their standards for station membership, they had not fully reckoned with the extent of this structural exclusion. So when they committed to "utilize the most advanced techniques of the medium, introduce new concepts and have the highest technical standards in the field,"[35] they were creating an uphill battle for historically marginalized communities.

In radio transmission, stations with higher wattage have higher technical quality. The founders of NPR had to consider airwave standards for national station membership when creating its membership network. The board deferred to the expertise of the experienced educational broadcasters in the room, like board member Al Hulsen, who'd spent a decade as a reporter and educational radio manager.[36] Hulsen embraced the technological standards of the field as a given. For a station to become an NPR member station, it would have to have a higher wattage. This is an example of a coercive pressure—a *technical* regulation imposed on all local stations seeking membership.

According to founding members, Hulsen's imposition ensured excellence; by limiting the range of stations that could receive national funding, NPR functionally raised the barrier to entry for hopeful member stations. On its surface, the selection of high technological standards does not appear to be racialized, unless you consider the already long-standing racialized inequities in station resources. President Herbert Hoover passed the Radio Act of 1927 in an attempt to regulate the airwaves. The act created the Federal Radio Commission (FRC), which controlled station licenses and reduced the number of stations on the air. Stations applied for frequencies, and the decision about which broadcasts deserved airtime on a given frequency at a particular time was left to the commission's discretion. Unsurprisingly, the commission often deferred to stations with the most capital—that is, for-profit stations.[37] As the cost of a license for a noncommercial station was prohibitively expensive for the community centers and nonprofits in which nonwhite communities most often participated, those educational stations that banded together to form a larger network were largely the province of white-owned universities.

Fledgling community stations had to find the funds to match membership standards, or they would not receive national funding or national programming. Adding a layer of difficulty, the operating budget of each station had to be at least $75,000 per year prior to receiving any community service grants.[38] Taken together, these criteria eliminated a disproportionate number of minority-owned community stations from eligibility as NPR member stations; in raising barriers to entry and providing only limited grants for station development, these standards discouraged would-be members without existing formal institutional backing. Note that, in 1977, only 10 of 195 public radio stations in the continental United States were controlled by nonwhite managers.[39] In contrast, established stations were rewarded for existing infrastructure backed by university funding, despite their disproportionately white and elite racialized and classed composition. By 1977, "[t]he lowest level of minority participation on public radio boards was found among stations licensed to universities—6.4 per cent (56 of 869)."[40]

To NPR board members, race had nothing to do with the decision. Relying on the expertise among them, they rarely consulted local stations about such challenges. Had they realized that they were operating against their stated goal, they could have acted to ensure greater racialized equity; however, their shared white habitus made the racialized impact of the technical standards invisible to them. Elizabeth Young, the first station relations associate, reflected in 1977, reasoning that NPR's technological standards in fact encouraged minority group stations to rise to higher standards:

> I mean we now have stations that are owned and operated by minority groups, like American Indians, Eskimos, what have you. Sometimes those communities are finding it difficult to meet the criteria. [. . .] [H]aving them has thrust forward the thinking: well, if this is what we have to do to get the money and get the programs, we'll do it. Which is probably not all bad.[41]

Hulsen himself, looking back on this decision in 1978, described the process of implementing the technological standard as painless—neither he nor the board had much contact with the affected stations: "I never felt too terribly uncomfortable with any of that because, first of all, you have to remember the structure. There weren't a lot of national meetings. There weren't a lot of get-togethers. Most of the business then was done by small meetings of boards of directors."[42] Hulsen advocated the exclusion of any station below ten watts; he justified his decision in this same interview, quipping: "Democracy has its place; but if you believe that educational radio is important, you might just say that the boards ought to do it. [. . .] [T]he boards did a pretty good job. [. . .] [T]hey were conscientious and careful in their dealings."[43] His attitude revealed the prioritization of the growth and coherence of national station membership over consideration of lower-resourced stations and reaching the racially diverse publics who listened to those stations. NPR's founders had the option to garner input from local stations but recognized that opting to do so would open lines of dissent and slow the process. Moving forward with the ten-watt standard exacerbated inequality among community radio stations, rewarding well-endowed stations and punishing those historically disadvantaged.

Hulsen, in translating fieldwide standards into NPR membership standards, remained insulated from the racially biased implications. Because of his shared socialization process among his peers within a white-dominant field—his white habitus—he considered his decision solely one about technological limitations. Isolation from smaller, ten-watt stations allowed him to overlook the racialized resource allocation that the standards promoted. This insulation relied on his confidence that his own view—along with the view of his white colleagues from similar backgrounds—was *sufficient* to make decisions on behalf of the public interest. Hulsen admitted that he felt "life might be a lot better today if they had less national meetings and more actions by boards of directors."[44] This sentiment reveals that his structurally conditioned ignorance, contributing to racialized inequality, was in fact welcomed and beneficial, as it facilitated the all-white board's ability to set standards in line with the larger fieldwide standards with few objections or roadblocks. Had the board been more reflective or responsive, it might have recognized how its actions resulted in a legacy of exclusion from the early days of radio, when resources were concentrated under the umbrella of (white-dominant) university stations.

Normative Isomorphism: Hiring Networks

In July 2020, I spoke with Sasha, a Black broadcaster who had worked in public radio for decades. She outlined how intractable the issue of racial diversity in station workforce is, particularly in smaller towns and cities:

> If you're in the middle of the country, you've got a middle-aged white guy who's been your general manager for twenty-five years or longer. And your staff is all white and you need to diversify, but they've all been on staff for ten years; who are you going to fire? What are you going to do? How's that going to be accomplished?

Her reflections speak to the deep entrenchment of majority-white hiring networks in public radio, referring to white employees who end up staying at the station and inhibiting demographic changes across the network. The recruitment process of NPR's original executive board and employees reveals to us how we got here. The fields of government service and educational radio both shaped the racially exclusionary formation of NPR's workforce.

The decision to rely on colleagues and familiar figures in the educational radio and public service fields demonstrates NPR's reliance on field-based legitimizing professional markers in constructing its initial workforce. Processes of recruitment for positions on the board and executive staff reveal the salience of governmental and educational radio professional networks during the founding years of 1968–1972. Again, despite the new network's commitment to serving a diverse plurality of Americans, its processes undermined the goal. Hiring became a prime example of normative pressures, because of the need to legitimate the network through professional credentialing via the informal "vouching" provided by personal and professional networks.

I present in figure 6 a simplified organizational chart that illuminates each organization's relationship to the other. The National Public Broadcasting Act of 1967, passed by Congress and signed into law by President Lyndon B. Johnson, established the Corporation for Public Broadcasting (CPB) as a nonprofit organization in the United States dedicated to providing funding for public radio and television. Johnson appointed his colleague Frank Pace, third US secretary of the army, as the first chairman of the CPB. He was concurrently the cofounder and president of the International Executive Service Corps,[45] established to consult developing nations with neoliberal policies on private enterprise. The CPB was charged with establishing exactly *how* it would promote public broadcasting, which it did through the establishment of NPR and PBS.

The corporation's executives sought expertise from existing educational radio networks, relying on preexisting professional norms to garner legitimacy and a swift formulation of a path forward. Don Quayle from the CPB consulted Robert (Bob) Mott, executive director of the National Educational Radio Network (NERN), to brainstorm candidates to head the Radio Division. The short list consisted of educational radio producers affiliated with the NERN. By Quayle's account: "Working with Ward Chamberlin [chief operating officer of the CPB] and Frank Pace [chairman of the CPB], we went through a number of possible candidates for the CPB radio job. We came up with young Al Hulsen. [. . .] Al had worked with me at Ohio State, and at WGBH, and with the Educational Radio Network."[46]

Jack Mitchell, NPR's first employee, was hired by Bill Siemering under Don Quayle's presidency three weeks after Quayle's election. Mitchell's account of *his* good fortune to be hired reflects a shared orientation toward action, a habitus, illuminated in the decisions analyzed throughout this chapter: "By happenstance of birthplace [Michigan] and year [1941], I landed in

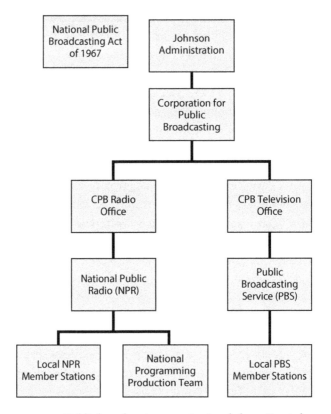

FIGURE 6: Public broadcasting organizational chart. Created by the author.

the right place at the right time to play a part in launching public radio."[47] In addition to these bits of serendipity, his birth on the right side of the color line structured his life chances in this place and time.

Meanwhile, Frank Pace had recruited his friend and squash partner Ward Chamberlin as chief operating officer of the CPB. Chamberlin was a corporate lawyer with no public broadcasting experience, let alone educational radio experience. Still, Pace and Chamberlin were entrusted with stewardship of the new public broadcasting system based on their positions as well-connected leaders in government. When they made decisions on the workforce of the CPB's executive Radio Office, they, in conversation with Quayle, conformed to normative pressures of the white-dominant field of educational radio by favoring personnel with professional training in the same industry. Their department, like others, ultimately reflected existing, majority-white educational radio stations.[48]

The use of such closed networks in hiring CPB executives cascaded through to NPR's executives, because the CPB's architects were then charged with constructing a board of directors for the public radio network. Quayle, who transitioned from his role at the CPB to becoming the first president of NPR, delineated the search process in a retrospective interview: "NPR was set up by consensus of regional meetings. Hulsen and Mott, and sometimes [John] Witherspoon, went out to talk to all of the [local station] managers, and to have them elect six [members]. These six elected three more [public members], and that constituted the Board of Directors of National Public Radio. Working with legal counsel, they wrote the by-laws, the charter, etc." In other words, recruitment relied on tapping into professionals' existing networks, over and over again. Of the original thirteen board members of NPR, none identified as women or as members of racialized minority groups. These thirteen white men were tasked with selecting NPR's president and working with this selected president to recruit its executive staff.

When NPR's founding President Quayle and the newly elected NPR Board of Directors worked on hiring initial executive staff, it started with Quayle cold-calling close friends and professional acquaintances he believed were good fits and placing them in management positions.[49] His trust was contingent on previous contact through professional networks within the existing organizational field—networks that were inaccessible to people of color at the time. Like the hiring process within the CPB, Quayle hired largely through informal networking to create an NPR workforce that reflected the white field of educational radio of the time.

Accounts from early NPR employees' oral histories demonstrate a similar pattern in hiring throughout the fledgling network. For the position of director of station relations, Quayle hired Elizabeth Young, who had been working with Quayle on the CPB radio staff at the time and who had already asked Quayle for any job within NPR. By her own account, when Quayle was elected, Young "went to him and said, 'I don't know what I want to do, but I'd like to work for you.' [She] went on board with NPR in September of '70."[50] By contrast, Lee Frischknecht had never heard of National Public Radio before he was recruited for one of its lead positions, director of network affairs, recalling: "Don Quayle calls from Washington. He says, 'Hey, what do you know about National Public Radio?' I said, 'I never heard of it.'"[51]

The contextual details of these hires differ—in particular, Young was already embedded in the CPB while Frischknecht was not privy to the project—but they are united through their informality. Rather than conducting an open job search, NPR's president used his existing national networks in noncommercial radio to find good fits for these executive positions. Recall that DiMaggio and Powell highlight how normative isomorphic pressures lead organizations to seek homogeneity in training their professional workforce. Drawing on previous professional experience as a marker of legitimacy for job candidates, despite the known racialized exclusion within the professional field, resulted in further racialized exclusion; however, Quayle's white habitus, or social conditioning within a predominantly white field, blinded him to the connection between network recruitment and the resulting whiteness of his executive staff.

The normative isomorphic pressure to legitimize the public radio profession lessened the potential for a diverse racial and socioeconomic base of radio professionals within NPR, as professional credentials were structured by whiteness in the fields of noncommercial radio and universities from 1967 to 1977, the era immediately following Jim Crow. As sociologist Victor Ray notes in his explanation of whiteness as a credentialing mechanism, "access to mainstream organizations facilitates cumulative advantage processes stretching across the life course, as much of what counts as 'merit' in hiring or access to education is produced through prior access to credentialing organizations."[52] The shared white habitus of NPR's board conditioned the board to understand its own credentialing process as a race-neutral way to screen people for experience and potential in the noncommercial radio field.

Launching back to the present, Sasha declares that this hiring network is still strong, despite her and her colleagues offering suggestions of another path forward. When she and other coworkers invested in diversity insist upon more managers of color when open positions *do* emerge, the outcome remains the same:

> And even when you have an open conversation [about hiring], and we say, "you must do 'x' to support your workforce." It would be best if you hired a person within these parameters. We tell you what we want. And then you hire a white woman with no audio experience.

Although the woman that Sasha spoke of had no audio experience, whiteness remains a credentialing mechanism; her own lived experience, different from Sasha's, becomes the cultural capital required to be considered a good fit in a white racialized organization.

Mimetic Isomorphism: Programming Priorities

The reason behind wanting a more diverse set of managers is to shift what many of my respondents consider to be misguided programming priorities. When I spoke to Juan, a Latinx reporter, he spelled out this logic:

> The hope is that if we have a manager of color, then the manager of color can be the one to tell everyone, yes, this is a story. Instead, we are put in an adversarial position in our way with our editors who don't get it. But [the editor] is my boss. I think it's important that those managing the newsroom understand our stories, because that helps us have a better idea of what we can aspire to be.

As outlined in the previous section, the founding board members were tasked with deciding on station standards, selecting NPR's president, and working with the president to recruit its executive staff. They also met to set priorities for what programs NPR would offer on the national level, an ambiguous task for the first national programming network of its kind.

Mimetic isomorphic pressures arise around those areas of uncertainty in organizational decision making—moments when there may not be a clear way to ascertain the *best* decision for organizational practice. In lieu of a clear best practice, organizations tend to mimic, or model themselves off existing legitimated paradigms. NPR aimed to produce national content, in part because there was an insufficient number of high-quality local noncommercial programs to air nationally.[53] The founders, despite believing they were working with a blank slate, were influenced by characteristics of other noncommercial radio programming, and sought to model themselves after it.

Recall that, in the abstract, there was a commitment to diverse publics: board member Dick Estell, in a discussion about his aims for the programming, stated that "aside from the human compassion which should dictate a service to these groups, it must be remembered that minorities comprise part of the 'Public' in National Public Radio."[54] However, in conversations about what national programming would cover and sound like during NPR's first board meeting in January 1970, there was no clear mandate to cover particular topics over others, nor was there a format required from the new broadcaster. Given this ambiguity, board members faced a mimetic pressure to conform to existing (and already legitimated) paradigms.

Much as the educational radio field was well established as a medium dominated by the perspective of white Americans,[55] board members decided that minority groups would be served by their local communities. NPR's national team, instead, would only focus on "general programming of interest to the whole nation." The whole nation, of course, became conflated with a narrow part of it—the part to which the board members belonged. Board members "agreed that NPR should not be duplicating local stations' efforts, nor should it initially be providing a special service to minority groups, except in so far as 'minority' programs were of national interest."[56] It soon became clear that general programming of interest, defined by the board and national programming staff, would not be about communities of color.[57]

The board's discourse differentiated between general and specialized audience programming; as noted, they believed that NPR would handle the general daily programming, whereas local stations would provide more specialized community programs, such as shows for racialized and ethnic minorities. Implicitly in this vision, a general audience was understood as a white audience. NPR allocated just 3 percent of its programming budget to specialized audiences over its first seven years of operation. When Gloria Anderson and the Task Force on Minorities surveyed 1,543 station hours, they showed that only 71.5 hours were designed for a nonwhite audience; the majority of those 71.5 hours consisted of music programming rather than news or culture.[58]

The national programming that NPR did invest in was a unique shift from either commercial radio or more traditional molds of educational radio. Programming manager Bill Siemering insisted that they develop a show akin to a newsmagazine, covering a variety of topics within three hours. By May 1971, *All Things Considered*, staked as the network's flagship program, went on the air.[59] As I discuss in the next chapter, NPR was notable in breaking with gender norms; white women dominated and led the programming's voice rather than white men.[60] Ralph Engelman, in his political history of NPR, notes that while this form deviated from archetypal news broadcasts, its form and content mirrored those programs that station employees worked on before they came to NPR.

> Various precedents are said to have influenced its format—among them, Al Hulsen's former show *Kaleidoscope* on the Eastern Educational Network, a program called *This Is Radio* broadcast by WBFO/Buffalo during Siemering's tenure as station manager, the CBC's early-morning offering *America as It Happens*, and the public and cultural affairs programming of the BBC, which influenced Jack Mitchell, another veteran of WHA/Madison who helped create *ATC* [*All Things Considered*].[61]

Aesthetically innovative and experimental in format, the program's models came from existing nonprofit radio in the United States, Canada, and Great Britain,[62] whose workforce and audiences were predominantly white. Given the shared habitus of NPR's board, this whiteness was unremarkable to the group.

Again, the assumption that local public radio stations would automatically reflect the demographic diversity of their locales ignored the history of racialized exclusion in noncommercial radio stations. Yet NPR was drawing from these local stations as partial inspiration for national programming. Passing the responsibility of creating "specialized" programming down to local-level stations implied that the national interest was the interest of the white majority. The embrace of racial pluralism without a corresponding investment in nonwhite stations was illogical—unless you understand how a white racialized habitus facilitates a normalization of white dominance. Furthermore, the model of local stations providing minority group programming proved insufficient, given the anti-Blackness endemic to noncommercial radio. For instance, Detroit's local station served a majority-Black district, and the white staff wanted to create specialized Black programming. The white station manager lamented to his fellow public radio professionals at a 1971 public radio conference:

> As a white person you're not exactly in the most advantageous position to determine the needs of the Black community, or to judge the standards of programming by and for Blacks—that is, the Black aesthetic. That's why you need to find a committed Black to do this for you. But where do you look?[63]

The sentiment was shared across this 1971 conference, as the write-up from the meeting of public radio managers and board members declared that "many managers who stated they were interested in minority programming said they didn't know where to start."[64] The statement that they would need to "find a committed Black to do this for [them]" is reminiscent of practices spanning back decades, of Black Americans being called on to consult and comment on their own communities but not to become station owners, or even members of the station, as was the case in Du Bois's engagement with radio.[65] This attitude has been shaped by the reliance on segregated white networks of friends and coworkers, and the historical exclusion of minority-owned stations, which might have been training grounds for more nonwhite staff.

In considering the recruitment of Black voices, the white manager does not consider the possibility of nonwhite management. As Mitchell noted candidly, "[p]ublic radio and the broader academic world are liberal or progressive in their thinking but are not radical. They are not about to jeopardize their own comfortable situations by fostering fundamental change."[66] NPR's founders and employees sought to promote pluralism, but from a position within the white-dominant organizational field of noncommercial radio. In their uncertainty about which programming to air, they faced mimetic isomorphic pressure to imitate the stylistic choices of existing fieldwide norms. The resultant politically liberal programming demonstrated an appreciation of pluralism and of different perspectives, curated through the ears of the white liberal producers, managers, and reporters.

The Reproduction of White Racialized Organizations

In viewing NPR's founding process as the development of a white racialized organization, it becomes clear how NPR failed to serve nonwhite publics in its first ten years. Their membership criteria, hiring practices, and programming priorities were shaped by existing norms of the historically segregated noncommercial radio field.

NPR's founders would have needed to actively resist the field-level legacy of racially exclusionary decision making to achieve their organization's stated goals of pluralism and service to all Americans. Yet, NPR founders were hesitant to consult outside their board meetings, staff meetings, and immediate social circles for the sake of efficiency. Had they been attuned to the historical inequities of their field of noncommercial radio, the discrepancy between their own insular decision-making processes and their desire for racialized inclusivity would have been apparent. Instead, NPR's founders and original workforce puzzled over outreach to racialized minorities without questioning, for instance, the lack of nonwhite station managers.

This, of course, bears out across the journalism industry. Communications scholar Gwyneth Mellinger shows this in her exploration of the American Society of Newspaper Editors demographic parity plan, and how it ultimately failed to reach its goals.[67] Mellinger finds that, through attempting to achieve a more racially diverse membership, editors made policy and public statements that commodified racialized subjects, concentrated on new entry-level hires rather than retention and promotion, and allowed the inclusion of racialized subjects without avenues for those employees to exert influence on the existing workplace culture.

This failure, while not unique, is particularly troubling in nonprofit media, given its mission to serve beyond commercial interests. In the executive summary of the 1978 Task Force on Minorities report, Gloria Anderson states, "The scenario would not be so dismal for minorities however, if the public broadcast industry were alone in negating the minority presence and the positive aspects of the lives and cultures of the diverse racial and ethnic minorities in America. However, finding no place set for them at the commercial broadcasting table, minorities have discovered that they must look further than public broadcasting to find a place at all."[68] In other words, National Public Radio's formation was not an aberrant case—and that was known as early as 1978. As an adopter of existing organizational norms, NPR was reflective of racial inequities across broadcasting organizations. Founders, when embedded in institutional spaces they set out to shift, can become agents of fieldwide norms.

In 1980, NPR published a thorough response to the report that included updates on its progress. It documented substantial progress on employment and training programs. Within the two years following the report, for example, NPR hired more minority employees as primary decision makers, corporate officers, and managers, using training programs to provide a chance for minority employees to work their way up to these managerial positions.

However, the organization was unable to take direct action on broadcast policies, which they argued required a larger governmental intervention. Additionally, NPR pushed back against the task force's finding that only 71.5 hours of programming were designed for nonwhite or nonmale audiences. It argued that its news programming was not directed at any *one* public, so the finding was misleading. This pushback reveals a long-standing assumption that the generalized program served all publics and was wrapped up with the notion of objectivity in journalism and communication.

The perspective that fueled NPR's response was that its generalized programming was designed for all, despite its use of mostly white journalists and experts to choose and report on local and national stories. Ultimately, NPR's refusal to acknowledge its own white subjectivity in 1980, despite an urging by the Task Force on Minorities, was a decision that perpetuated its white perspective and alienated a growing market of listeners from underserved minority communities.

Gloria Anderson and her task force in "A Formula for Change" highlight the importance of outside actors to promote accountability. The task force critiques pushed those at NPR in the late 1970s and early 1980s to increase minority employment and training programs. Further, the Corporation for Public Broadcasting made new grants available to minority producers in noncommercial radio stations outside of the national public radio network, creating opportunities for Spanish-English bilingual community radio to grow and gain popularity.[69] The Task Force on Minorities report also highlights why racial diversity in decision-making bodies matters. By providing a bird's-eye view of the policy reasons behind limited diversity, the report threw into relief the larger constraints of the US funding structure for public media, ever reliant on funding from the majority-white government supplemented by majority-white private philanthropy. Indeed, Lewis Raven Wallace interviewed Cecilia Garcia, a Latinx TV producer and one of the members of the task force. She reflected on the funding structure specifically, noting: "There are winners and losers when we fund things the way we do here [in public broadcasting], and, inevitably, people of color have been on the losing end of that equation."[70]

While condemned by the Task Force on Minorities for its racial exclusion, NPR fared far better than its mainstream counterparts from the beginning with respect to one progressive measure. White women were prominent creators and voices of authority on the network at a time when white men ruled the airwaves. In the next chapter, I will consider how this divergence from fieldwide organizational norms occurred, how it impacted the American soundscape, and how the "voice of NPR" is heard and interpreted.

2

A Trusted Voice

She seemed like some Upper West Side, New York lady leaning into the microphone, mensch-ily talking into the radio.
—IRA GLASS, IN AN INTERVIEW FOR THE *NEW YORK TIMES*,
DESCRIBING THE VOICE OF BROADCASTER SUSAN STAMBERG

I hear middle-aged white dudes who sound like they just drank some really warm coffee.
—DR. A. D. CARSON ON PUBLIC RADIO PROGRAMMING

There are two main narratives floating around about today's voice of public radio. Some listeners draw upon the warmth and inclusiveness of its more feminized sensibilities, emphasizing its difference from traditional masculine authority in broadcasts. Others pick up most centrally on the whiteness of "the voice" as an alienating force. This chapter delves into people's different responses to the public radio voice, where those responses come from, and what they mean for the US public sphere.

As we learned in the previous chapter, National Public Radio and its affiliate stations were largely managed by white men during the network's formation and first ten years of operation. Yet in a time of masculine baritones dominating mainstream TV and radio, the network developed a voice of authority associated with femininity. Indeed, as radio historian Jason Loviglio notes, public radio's voice is a marked shift away from "the stentorian diaphragmatic speech typical of US male broadcasters, from

Edward R. Murrow to Walter Cronkite and Dan Rather."[1] Compared to the deeper voices that these famous broadcasters are known for, public radio's soundscape is associated with higher pitches and softer forms of authoritative sound.

How and why did the US public radio network develop a feminized voice of authority in a male-dominated broadcasting space? And how does the "public radio voice" today evoke different reactions shaped in part by one's racial identity and class upbringing? As seen in the quotations above, while white radio personality Ira Glass hears in the network's history the feminization of authority and the allowance of "menschiness"—a welcome inclusion of female and Jewish voices—Black communications professor Dr. A. D. Carson hears whiteness as the primary feature. In talking to his friend Dr. Chenjerai Kumanyika, Carson summed the voice of the network up as "middle-aged white dudes who sound like they just drank some really warm coffee." That's fine, he insists; it's just not for him:

> And I'm not against it. It's just that, I know that there is just a lot going on there, and a lot of it is captured in that voice. In that—you know— warm coffee sippin', whispering almost. It sounds like the whole joint is recorded in the back of Barnes & Noble.[2]

I provide in this chapter an account of public radio's development of a distinctive voice. At a time when the male baritone ruled the airwaves, four women reporters on NPR's staff, later characterized as "the Founding Mothers," developed NPR's iconic voice in the 1970s. The shift brought legitimacy to more feminized voices of authority on the airwaves,[3] and thanks in particular to on-air personality Susan Stamberg, acceptability to the combination of white womanhood and Jewishness. It was a dramatic shift in the American soundscape in a time when white men were the only mainstream broadcast authorities. For upcoming reporters like Ira Glass, the voice of NPR provided permission to fight against the "deep voice" and "gravitas" of a typical broadcaster voice. In later describing Glass's radio voice, *New York Times* columnist Alexis Soloski quipped, "he sounded urban, Jewish, a little fretful. Most of all, he sounded like himself."[4] Glass built on Stamberg's voice, along with a mélange of inspirations from outside of public radio, to further redefine what authority sounded like, defining it in some ways against the hypermasculine aesthetic of commercial broadcast news.[5]

At the same time, the unique broadcasting soundscape that NPR created in the 1970s was indelibly marked by its omission of nonwhite voices, a tradeoff that continues to haunt NPR's voice today, even as women of color hold four flagship host positions at the network as of this writing.[6] In its first ten years, the network crafted a distinct sonic aesthetic based on the characteristics and sensibilities of NPR's four "Founding Mothers." Their names are Susan Stamberg, Nina Totenberg, Linda Wertheimer, and Cokie Roberts, though they are often referred to by their first name only among the NPR set as Susan, Nina, Linda, and Cokie. All four are well-credentialed white women who came of age in mid-twentieth-century America. In platforming their voices, the network opened opportunities for women and Jewish people and gave NPR a distinctive voice. At the same time, the formation of a distinctive voice associated with white womanhood foreclosed possibilities for voices of color to find their footing in the tapestry of NPR's early soundscape.

Listening habits among the general public have expanded over NPR's fifty years of operation, yet the shared set of understandings about acceptable voices on air is still governed by the "sonic color line," a set of racialized expectations about sound and voice based in the racism undergirding America's social system and dominant culture.[7] As noted by historian Tom McEnaney, the "new nasality" and "nonaggressiveness" used to describe Ira Glass's voice are features that linguistic anthropologists often link to whiteness.[8]

It's not hard to see, then, why public radio has struggled to find as fervent a listenership among people like Dr. A. D. Carson. Today, as I explore at the end of this chapter, the network is in the midst of a "vocal reckoning"[9] in which the public radio voice's whiteness has come to the fore as an alienating sonic aesthetic. I draw from a combination of popular parodies of "public radio voice" and interviews with people of color in public radio to analyze how outsiders hear the network's contemporary sound and how this differs by socialization in white spaces. I consider the extent to which we are in a new moment of opportunity as voices of color have entered the industry at unprecedented rates, and I outline the challenges for the network as it tries to once again shift the mainstream broadcasting soundscape.

Sonic Conventions and Inequality in the Public Sphere

To understand the iconic voices of NPR and how they have collectively formed the "voice of public radio," it helps to take a step back and ask: What makes a set of sounds socially distinct? In the arena of performance, sounds become convention through shared social associations with an aesthetic, or artistic style. Sociologist Howard Becker, in his foundational work *Art*

Worlds, uses the example of music composition. When a composer creates a musical piece, they draw upon shared social conventions to evoke particular emotions. Those socialized in a dominant American soundscape will recognize a minor key as "sad," so a composer can use this convention as shorthand to communicate sadness to the audience. The same goes with laugh tracks for TV producers: laugh tracks are a sonic stimulus to connote humor in a show, making viewers more likely to see a scene as comedic.[10] Shared socialization primes audiences to respond to certain sounds in certain ways, and these sonic conventions become useful shorthand in artistic practice and performance.

Similarly, a person's aesthetic judgments begin with seemingly spontaneous initial affective reactions; such judgments are conditioned in a significant way by existing understandings of social difference and an implicit understanding of a status quo.[11] Aesthetic conventions, whether in the performance arena or in daily life, are *never* neutral or unbiased. Dominant aesthetic conventions can include the use of gongs for shorthand in communicating a stereotyped Asian scene, and bird and nature sounds alongside Indigenous sonic practices to conjure up a static view of Indigeneity as operating outside of modernity.[12] We can learn a lot about our society through interrogating our shared understandings of sounds, where they belong, and what they elicit in us.

Further, the human voice as a type of sound carries with it social baggage more clearly linked to identity, difference, and bodily capital. Sociologist Tressie McMillan Cottom expresses how white supremacy pervades American aesthetic convention in an essay on beauty wherein she notes that, through her upbringing at an integrated school, she learned that "beauty is the preferences that reproduce the existing social order."[13] Indeed, we know that lookism, or the bias toward or against a person based on their attractiveness, is racialized and gendered.[14] But these biases are not limited to the visual; such preferences extend to the human voice, as seen in instances of linguistic profiling. There are studies, for example, that show that housing applicants are rejected based on racialized accents and tones.[15] Sonic biases also come to the fore in the resistance to putting women's voices on air or on stage, unless directly called for, due to their perceived shrillness.[16]

If existing societal biases shape which voices gain prominence, how do shifts in sonic conventions become possible? We like to believe that artists and performers are in control of their own innovation. However, a sociological approach to art and culture emphasizes that innovation and changes in taste are facilitated or inhibited by exogenous or external factors—such as changes in who gets to participate in art and the distribution of resources to create art.[17] According to sociologist Jenn Lena, such factors create a unique "opportunity structure" upon which individuals produce or sacralize cultural forms. From the start, NPR's voice shifted away from the existing sonic convention of an authoritative male broadcaster voice. This shift was facilitated by a unique opportunity structure, which facilitated the entrance of well-credentialed white women into broadcasting roles in turn.

New Voices of Authority: NPR's Founding Mothers

In the previous chapter, I showed how hiring managers during NPR's first years used their existing networks to recruit leadership, making hires based on prospects' credentials in the segregated field of educational radio, their ties to government bureaucracy, or both. These hiring practices yielded a majority-white leadership structure. Yet there was, even early on, a marked contrast between the male-dominated board of NPR and the makeup of the programming teams: over half of the reporting and producing staff were women. These women, even though relegated to assistant roles, were central to setting the agenda for flagship programming, to setting the stage for the kinds of questions that future reporters at the network would ask during interviews, and to setting the standard for the tone and cadence public radio reporters would use. In the words of Jason Loviglio, from its founding, "the voice of NPR has very often been a woman's voice."[18]

NPR's voice made waves in the 1970s. It was outside of the realm of normal broadcast speech. "Normal" broadcast speech at the time was a masculine baritone that represented men's concerns.[19] It did not laugh; it did not pause to ask about childcare or "domestic" concerns when interviewing government officials. Laughs had no place within reporting, and such questions were thought by conventional journalists to fall outside the realm of public concern. But when NPR came on the airwaves, the abnormal became everyday. As Lisa Napoli describes it:

> Male reporters would query lawmakers about defense spending. Women, once they were allowed, posed questions that had previously gone unasked about different essential matters, such as health care and schools and equality. What was a policy's impact, they demanded to know, on the family, on the elders, on the children?[20]

A unique combination of factors created an opportunity structure for public radio: public radio's underfunding, alongside internal advocacy for women's voices, enabled the Founding Mothers to gain prominence on NPR's airwaves. The formation of NPR occurred during the late 1960s and early 1970s, at the tail end of the civil rights movement, just as there was a precipitous increase in married, college-educated women's labor force participation.[21] White women's professionalism in this era was often seen as in response to Betty Friedan's "problem with no name"[22]—the ennui, boredom, and deep existential frustration that arises from being well educated but unable to pursue a career due to one's oppressed position in the patriarchy. Economist Claudia Goldin finds that this era's cohort of women no longer needed to choose between their profession and family, as had been the case for earlier generations. They had the option of doing both, despite the continued structural difficulties in doing so.[23] Of course, given the consistent underrecognition of reproductive labor as skilled work in the United States,[24] the cohort Goldin speaks of is a very particular one—those privileged enough to have a profession and to be able to pay for largely women of color to help in childcare work, making their careers possible. In many cases, they were credentialed women who didn't *need* to work in a financial sense; they *wanted* to for fulfillment and purpose.

So, NPR came on the scene just as a new, expanded cohort of professional women did. It was also short on money. Public radio was an underfunded afterthought adapted from the educational radio network system, and its operations were even more poorly funded than PBS's. With well-credentialed men accustomed to earning "family wages" (that is, enough to support a family with a "breadwinner" salary), and more seasoned journalists wary of jumping ship to join a brand new, untested network, NPR's hiring committees would need to look for newer, cheaper options.

On the hiring of these four (white) women for NPR's early programming, Lisa Napoli wrote, "[i]t helped that some were subsidized by parents or husbands, which made them able to agree to the low pay he [Bill Siemering] could offer. A man expecting to support a family on what NPR could pay couldn't make do."[25] These women had the right education, few other opportunities, and lower pay requirements than men in the field. That they would become household names was a boon yet to be realized.

Among the Founding Mothers who would shape the sonic aesthetic in the 1970s, Susan Stamberg was the first hired. She embodied characteristics that departed from the "normal" broadcast voice in key ways. Again, in Napoli's words:

> Susan didn't sound like an announcer. She sounded like a person. She spoke the way she wrote, in all caps and exclamation points and ellipses,

with energy and enthusiasm, like she was gathered around the piano in her parents' living room on West Ninety-Sixth Street, inhaling that glorious nicotine, chatting up a gathering of friends as if at a salon.[26]

NPR had not yet amassed a large audience, but its emerging voice was meaningful to those listening. This meaning was often transmitted in written form; Stamberg has kept her fan mail, housed at the National Public Broadcasting Archives in College Park, Maryland. The letters she has received are telling of how her fans heard her.

Both men and women remarked upon two things: her joy and her preparedness. Listener Marion Vanderveen told Stamberg that she and her entire family admired the way she was able to "zero in" on a good question while remaining cheerful. Beyond being a deliverer of the news, fans heard Stamberg as a "companion" who helped them become personally invested in the news.

The audience tuned in to hear both Susan Stamberg the reporter and the personality. Since 1971, Stamberg has shared her mother-in-law's cranberry relish recipe annually,[27] while also interviewing artists and world leaders. The mixture is indicative of a tone that the network was setting; the programming was to encompass both deep news features and slice-of-life audio portraits, and the women on the air facilitated this breadth.

Each of the Founding Mothers brought her own voice to the reportage and to the host seat. While Stamberg had no interest in the world of politicians, Nina Totenberg, Linda Wertheimer, and Cokie Roberts transformed the DC reporting landscape. Totenberg doggedly chased down leads and cultivated sources that led her to consistently break Supreme Court news. Wertheimer was a White House reporter who was able to cover Senate debates live and communicate the jargon plainly in real time. Roberts gained fame in her prominent political reporting, but her celebrity also extended to the fact that "she seemed like a woman in your book club, someone you ran into at the local farmers' market who remembered your husband's recent surgery, or your daughter's recital—a PTA mom consumed with her own family, canning tomatoes from her garden, rushing to church on Sunday morning."[28]

Despite their different approaches, a key feature united them: they diverged from the assumption that they had to be neutral and dispassionate. Instead, they treated their interviews conversationally, revealing surprise, consternation, or other spontaneous reactions throughout. To have all of them appearing prominently, and concurrently, on a national broadcaster

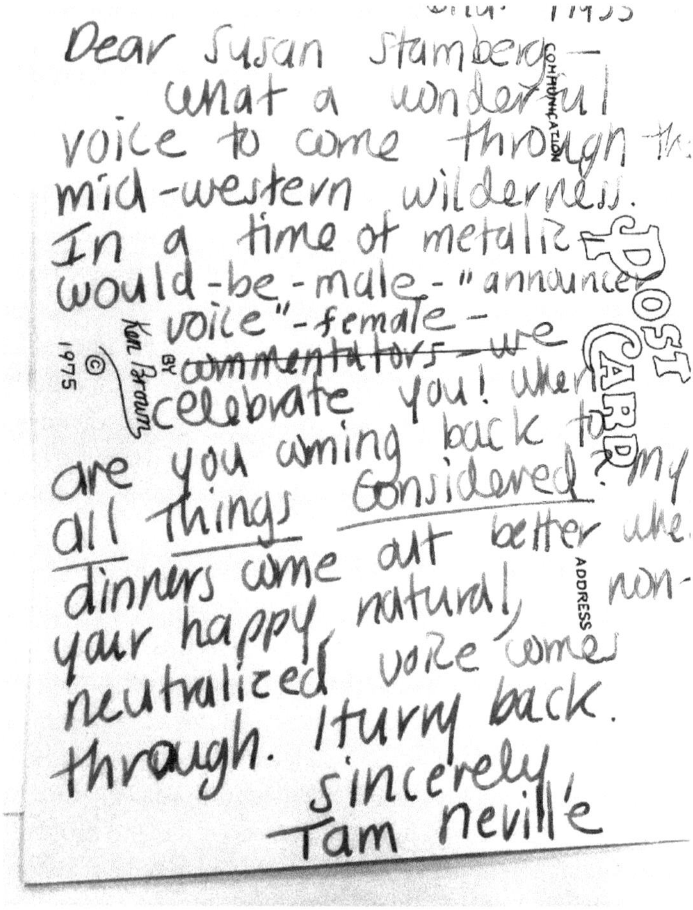

City: 1955

Dear Susan Stamberg —
what a wonderful
voice to come through th:
mid-western wilderness.
In a time of metaliz
would-be-male- "announce
voice"-female-
commentators—we
celebrate you! when
are you coming back to
all things Considered? my
dinners come out better when
your happy natural, non-
neutralized voice come
through. Iturry back.
sincerely
Tam neville

FIGURE 7: Susan Stamberg fan mail from listener Tam Neville.
Source: National Public Broadcasting Archives.

throughout the 1970s and 1980s indicated an influential shift in the American soundscape.

The voices that are allowed on the radio both reflect and shape our under-standing of social norms. Thus, radio historians have found that the set of human voices allowed on air has the potential to shift society's understanding of whose voices belong not just on air, but in public. Women's voices have been shown to destabilize patriarchal authority in a way that is transgres-sive. Christine Ehrick, for example, finds in her study of Argentinian and Uruguayan radio from 1930 to 1950 "that radio itself provided women with a new venue from which to speak and be heard at a time of significant rene-gotiation of gender roles."[29]

At the same time, these voices and their ability to transgress are complicated by the constraints of the society in which the airwaves get broadcasted. Anne Karpf, in her appraisal of white women's challenges to break through as reporters in early twentieth-century Western broadcasting, noted their double bind: they were deemed too sexy when articulating in a low voice, and not serious enough when articulating in a high voice.[30] Thus, the path to making women the model broadcasters on NPR was not a simple or straightforward one. While they amassed a loyal following, the reporters and hosts were demonstrably still subject to the sexism of listeners, even fans. Men wrote in with backhanded commentary. Some noted their surprise at liking a woman voicing the news. One listener, Ray Dougherty, remarked, "I have to admit I've always had a bias against female media personalities. You are, however, something special." Other men made advances, sending flirtations, requests for photos, and confessions of ardor (such as from Dave Martin, of San Francisco, who wrote to Stamberg, "I'm afraid I'm falling in love with you"). One fan sent a Tabasco label with a lipstick mark on it, telling Stamberg it was a "hot kiss," while Jeff Knorek of Michigan wrote in a poem that he wished to sleep not with Brigitte Bardot, but with Susan Stamberg's voice.

There was backlash. NPR's workspace gained the nickname "fallopian jungle," a misogynistic, snarky nickname given to the group of four women in the office indicative of the power these women held within the office itself. The women knew of this nickname, but they focused more on consolidating their power: sharing resources where they could and ensuring that women like them got more on-air opportunities at NPR than at other networks.

INTERNAL ADVOCACY FOR WOMEN'S VOICES

NPR's position as a new entity in the broadcasting space provided a unique opportunity for such voices to make waves. The organization's lack of funding to hire established broadcasters made the voice of white women a prudent one to invest in.[31]

Yet, these factors alone did not ensure white women's space on the NPR airwaves. Indeed, the voice of white women met much resistance in mid-twentieth-century broadcasting. It would require ongoing, internal advocacy to establish the Founding Mothers as on-air personalities during the first decade of NPR's operation.

Bill Siemering, as the network's first programming manager, proved instrumental. Siemering, a white man, had articulated his vision for the network in his now famous programming purposes. He believed that NPR would "regard the individual differences among men with respect and joy rather than derision and hate [. . .] celebrate the human experience as infinitely varied rather than vacuous and banal [. . .] [and] encourage a sense of active constructive participation, rather than apathetic helplessness." He also insisted that the sound and tone would be "quieter, more constructive, and more illuminating" than the voices of commercial broadcasting.[32]

Siemering hired Jack Mitchell, a veteran of educational broadcasting, to be a program producer. As producer of *All Things Considered*, Mitchell then hired Susan Stamberg.

> What Mitchell was drawn to was Susan's resemblance to the perfect diplomat's wife—not in the white glove, pinkie-finger-in-the-air-while-sipping-tea way, but because of her authentic and inherent interest in everyone she met.[33]

When local stations or management complained about her voice, Mitchell held firm on his decision and did not filter this feedback to Stamberg, as she was creating the content. Don Quayle, president of NPR at the time, had previously hired Stamberg to work at another educational radio station, but he disagreed about her prominent host position on *All Things Considered*. But "Mitchell pushed back on the pushback, all the while shielding Susan from it, not wishing to dash her confidence."[34]

Throughout the 1970s, the women on air advocated for and hired more (mostly white and college-educated) women for positions in all areas of programming. Then, as public radio gained its foothold in the public consciousness in the 1980s, it turned out that another broadcasting voice was doing its gender work: conservative talk radio.

> While NPR built on and elaborated the more socially conscious, antiviolent, aesthetically appreciative versions of manhood as articulated on free form, talk radio provided a platform for what can best be called male hysteria, a deft and sometimes desperate fusion of the desire to thwart feminism and the need to live with and accommodate to it.[35]

In its contradistinction to the chauvinist brand of talk radio, public radio's feminized aesthetic was heralded as a calm and well-reasoned alternative. This understanding of the network's voice became further entrenched in 2021 with the fiftieth-anniversary canonization of NPR's Founding Mothers, celebrated for their mentorship of other women and their willingness to nurture a sense of warmth, belonging, and collegiality among public radio personalities.

As noted at the beginning of this chapter, Ira Glass looked up to Susan Stamberg as an iconic voice model. His own journey to prominence within NPR was far from smooth. He was originally heard as "too quirky" and thus off-putting, and he struggled to get airtime at the national organization. Instead, his voice gained prominence over time through his local station, WBEZ Chicago, which produced his program *This American Life*—and it came to represent another step away from traditional forms of masculinity dominating the airwaves. Loviglio remarks upon the common misconception that Glass is gay due to his "high-pitched, softly inflected" voice.[36]

The public radio voice marked an important shift in our notions of gender in broadcasting. The iconic voice also made space for Ira Glass's pathbreaking voice in the twenty-first century, a voice that is now known as the dominant voice in podcasting. Although gendered voice conventions were challenged in the public radio industry, racial ones persisted.

How Outsiders Within Hear the Founding Mothers

When one describes the Founding Mothers' pathbreaking voices, the modifier "white" often remains unspoken and unnoticed. But the voice of public radio has been unmistakably associated with the norms of white, professional-class liberals over time, in terms of both tone and style.

As I noted in the introduction to part I above, the public radio genre has reached the point of parody. Take, for example, a popular *Saturday Night Live* (*SNL*) skit in which Ana Gasteyer and Molly Shannon play two NPR hosts on a show called *Delicious Dish*.[37] The skit's characters, Teri and Margaret Jo, are two meek white women whose idea of glut and opulence is asking for a wooden bowl and oversized index cards for Christmas. Alec Baldwin appears on their holiday special, playing a bakery owner named Pete Schweddy. Baldwin uses an uncharacteristically soft, gentle voice as he talks about his holiday treats, which he terms "Schweddy balls." The skit juxtaposes the milquetoast demeanors of the three interlocutors with an array of vulgar second meanings. The hosts ask Schweddy to "whip out his balls" in reference to his pastries, and they remark on how big they are, apparently without intention of a double entendre. The two hosts and guest, in their blissful unawareness, elicit howls of laughter from the *SNL* audience. The joke relies on an understanding of NPR as gentle, innocent, and civil, as well as a bit nerdy, recognizable not only in vocal tone but in style.[38]

A more recent *SNL* skit parodies the first season of the 2014 hit public radio podcast *Serial*.[39] In the original series, Sarah Koenig revisits the murder of eighteen-year-old Korean American Hae Min Lee, including interviews with Lee's ex-boyfriend, Adnan Syed, who was charged with the murder. Spoofing the original series, the skit transforms the case into an investigation of how Kris Kringle the elf could have left toys at so many children's homes.

In this parody, Cecily Strong plays Koenig, duplicating the reporter's measured, calm tone and confessional vulnerability, a combination noted by writer Teddy Wayne as iconic to the twenty-first-century "NPR voice."[40] In this voice, Strong provides context to the Kringle case by noting how elves "are seen as shifty and secretive" in American society. Kyle Mooney plays white elf Kris Kringle while retaining a vocal impression of Adnan, who is Pakistani American. Kringle, like Syed, is reactive to Koenig's questioning, heavily rehearsed to seem light and curious. The skit works because it mimics the way the audience is meant to feel intimacy with Koenig as the narrator. As Laura Sim describes in her analysis of the podcast, we are made to feel empathy through embodying her journey as the reporter.[41]

Each of the skits works because of contrast: in the first, the contrast between the actors' tone and demeanor and their vulgarity, and in the second, the contrast between "Sarah" and "Adnan." Public radio as a genre is ripe for parody precisely because it is recognizable as a distinct sound—a speaking style associated with calm white people. Hearkening back to how NPR formulated its voice originally, it makes sense that this juxtaposition works so well. To push back against the commercialism of for-profit media, Siemering decided to avoid the masculine loudness of commercial broadcast reporters when possible. We see this throughline in today's instructions to contemporary broadcasters at the network. A Black broadcaster named Kevin told me, "Generally I was told not to sound like a TV reporter. That was the definite no-no. Whatever you do, don't sound like a TV reporter."

Jackie, an Asian American editor I spoke with about the sonic aesthetic in public radio, remarked on the way that the quiet minimalism she heard when editing stories chafed against her immigrant sensibilities:

> I've thought about this a lot in terms of art and design, where the attention to its—like, "hiding the work" is a very white aesthetic. You go into a house that is like a high-class white house and, you know, like to me, like the epitome of this is minimalism. Like a certain type of minimalism where you want to pretend that there aren't wires that bring electricity into your house.

So public radio is often defined as distinct from commercialism, and this distinction is accomplished through directives to be quieter, more measured, more restrained. As media scholar Christopher Chávez puts it, NPR's conversational style is not necessarily a reflection of spontaneous delivery but rather "a highly disciplined practice that is meant to mimic spontaneity"; it is also one, he argues, that is used to secure NPR as a "white space."[42] The voice then, while deviating in terms of masculinity from broadcaster performance, hews tightly to the well-established understanding that some voices are "excessive," a characteristic that is often associated with nonwhite cultures.[43] Chávez spoke with communication studies scholar and audio producer Chenjerai Kumanyika, mentioned earlier in this chapter, about Chávez's book on public radio and the Latinx public:

> [Kumanyika] stated that, in his opinion, NPR's controlled way of speaking does not reflect some of the more emotive ways of speaking sometimes associated with ethnic speech, what he referred to as "bigness." [. . .] [H]e loves hearing the range of voices on commercial radio, particularly those who work in hip hop and sports, stating, "you just hear folks be animated and you see all kinds of linguistic aesthetics come out."[44]

Whereas Stamberg's warmth, use of ellipses, and exclamations came to define the network, as did Glass's rehearsed voice of neurosis, other forms of deviation still fall outside public radio's core aesthetic. In the words of Stacey, an Asian American reporter, her program makes excellent stories, but they are "emotional stories told in an unemotional way. Not too earnest. Humorous in a very dry, intellectual way, often."

Understandably, reporters of color have admitted to feeling alienated by public radio's model voice. Marta, a Middle Eastern American reporter, admits that she struggles to listen to her own station sometimes: "I don't know how to describe it, but it's like, when I listen to it, I force myself to do it, and it feels like they're talking to, like, either young woke white people or old retired people."

Often, when I asked employees of color to describe the sound, they would conjure up the vision of a person who either possessed whiteness or had proximity to it. In their words, the model voice was "a white person," "somebody white people would like," and "a friendly, nonthreatening person." Cultural critic Doreen St. Félix has considered how, although voices associated with whiteness evoke particular associations, "white voice is an ideal that not even the white man can attain."[45] Yet, as we will see in the second half of this book, the iconicity of "public radio voice" consistently sets racialized standards, marking those heard as audibly nonwhite as not belonging. Nonwhite employees who "successfully" adopt the voice sometimes find that it is so tightly coupled with whiteness in the public imagination that, well, their race comes as a surprise to listeners.

PUBLIC RADIO AND CLASS DISTINCTION

The public radio voice exemplifies both whiteness and cosmopolitanism. As former public radio employee Lewis Raven Wallace notes in his book *The View from Somewhere*, despite diversity programs that bring people from marginalized communities into the industry, "when people talk about 'public radio voice,' they still mean a white East Coast or midwestern person with a smooth tone."[46] Some of my participants identified with the voice through their own socialization in white space. Indeed, their listening practices were often embedded in commutes within predominantly white spaces to white-dominant institutions. Lisa, a Black producer with parents in the professional class, was very clear about this, noting, "My dad used to play it all the time in the car. I grew up in a very white, wealthy suburb and both my parents listened to a lot of public radio, so I heard it filtered through them." She, along with other respondents, remarked that this commute was often to a predominantly white school, which mirrored the sensibilities of the on-air public radio sound.

Overall, my sample of nonwhite broadcasters commonly had the cultural competence to speak in a way that was legible to a majority white, professional-class audience. This is partially because educational attainment shapes which nonwhite broadcasters are filtered into the public radio infrastructure, as does the financial capacity for unpaid internships and precarious contract work. My respondents noted that a large portion of their colleagues of color had attended elite, private schools—one Latinx reporter at a local station told me that her vision of a typical NPR broadcaster was "someone with a really straight back posture—white male, or white liberal woman, super-educated Harvard grad type person." An Asian American reporter said of her station: "It's culturally homogeneous. Everybody is white. Most of us have master's degrees." Many respondents who noted that their voices could be coded as conforming to the public radio voice were people of color raised in predominantly white suburbs, or with some access to elite education, or both.

Several broadcasters noted that they had once been "backseat listeners": children listening to NPR because their parents controlled the radio dial. A Latinx reporter, Helen, noted that she was a "classic NPR backseat baby. We'd listen on long car trips. I didn't really listen independent of my parents, but it was always on and around." Janice, a Black reporter, remembered that it was part of her regular routine growing up: "I listened to NPR every morning from when I was in sixth grade till when I was a freshman. My dad drove us in the morning, and he liked to listen to NPR." A key part of this backseat listener existence is how the network was regarded as a taste acquired over time. "My parents are NPR listeners, my dad in particular. I'm like everyone else, where I remember being a kid and my dad put the news on and I thought it was really boring. And then somehow I ended up in it."

Other participants stressed the depth of their connection with the sound of public radio. "Growing up with my dad, he was a big public media guy. He would drive me to school, in elementary school, he would usually have NPR on. It's been ingrained in my head since I was a kid. It's so deep in me." Further, Faith, a Black public radio producer, reflected on how strong a connection she feels to one of NPR's theme songs: "I think that cadence is ingrained in me."

Lisa, Janice, Helen, and Faith all had class origins that shaped their intimate knowledge of public radio prior to entering the industry. This ingrained knowledge of public radio voice was cultural capital that facilitated their entry into the industry and relative ease within that industry, in comparison to their peers from working-class backgrounds.[47]

In later chapters I will elaborate on these different pathways for employees of color based on their voice's association with public radio voice. For the purposes of the present chapter, it is important to note that across class origins, the bulk of my interviewees were attuned to public radio's voice as being *both* raced as white and classed as professional or cosmopolitan. And through its purposeful distinction from commercialism as its aesthetic developed, public radio voice had also come to be defined in terms of what it was *not*: it was not brash, it was not colorful, it was not bombastically male, and it was not big.

The particularities of public radio voice are made clear when confronted by a voice that does not adhere to these norms. I asked Carmel, a Black reporter at a local public radio station on the West Coast, whether there were times when guests clearly did not fit the mold. She recalled a live show where she thought that the guest was excellent:

> One of our shows will occasionally go to guests live. One show, when the host welcomed the guest, he responded [in a loud and excited tone], "Hey, whattup [city]?" The interview went fine. Coming out of this show, I was like, "That was a really great interview. Good job."

The host, however, had a different reaction. Carmel remembers the host responding to her compliment: "Yeah, to be perfectly honest with you I was really worried when he first came on air, that 'what up' thing . . . what was that? Am I right?"

This sounds like a minor detail: a discrepancy in how Carmel and the older, white male host heard this guest. Carmel, who was not new to media but was new to public radio at the time, found the guest to be engaging and open. But the host considered the "whattup" response to his welcome to be strange and out of place. It was louder than the host's voice, per Carmel's retelling. And notably, the "whattup" is informal in a way that matches slang from minoritized communities, not the "how's it going" that would pass muster as an appropriate colloquialism in white space. This reaction makes sense only when you consider that public radio's sound is often intimately linked to the lifeworld of the white professional class. Tom McEnaney draws this point out in his reading of an interview with Ira Glass in which Glass reflects on how he and his producers pick programming. He declares, "We simply put on what we like. We're all suburban kids. We feel we have the most normal tastes in the world. We think: If we like it, other people will like it."[48]

McEnaney rightly notes that this statement and others like it work to "normalize and universalize a class experience and perspective," one borne from growing up in the suburbs, presumably in a professional, middle- to upper middle-class family. In a 2005 radio piece about backseat listeners, a preteen whose parents listened to NPR said confidently that although she did not currently listen independently, "I know I'll be an NPR listener. I've grown up with these people that brought me the news every night."

As evidenced by my respondents who reflected on their upbringing in majority-white, professional-class suburban settings with a liberal- or centrist-leaning demographic, the sound of public radio marks and defines the family commute, inculcating a particular sonic sensibility in backseat listeners. And this sonic sensibility can mark guests saying "whattup" as outside the realm of normal broadcast speech, even for a network known for breaking convention.

A Vocal Reckoning

The Founding Mothers broke convention against entrenched sexism and decades-long norms of masculine baritones as the voice of authority. The time of the network's foundation at the tail end of the civil rights movement, combined with key advocates inside the organization and various organizational hurdles, facilitated this impressive break with tradition.

We now find ourselves at another inflection point. Public radio's whiteness has become a well-acknowledged problem. Could we imagine a new break with convention, puncturing the sonic color line to further expand the voices associated with the network? Certainly, it would be in line with NPR's mission of pluralism, and thus it is more thinkable than in commercial spaces.

Further, the sounds that appear on the network have the potential to impact how we hear each other in daily life. A Black reporter at a local station, Jillian, pointed out its significance for the public sphere:

> When you hear different voices and accents, and people [. . .] that you would never speak to, it really opens up your mind to be a little bit more accepting of those kinds of people. I think that's one great benefit of that if we were to do that.

Macro-level shifts suggest the potential for a new break, yet there is always the risk of institutional inertia preventing change. NPR is in a much different financial and reputational position now than it was forty or fifty years ago. Compared with 1971, people now have a deep, long-standing connection with the network and the voice it has become known for. A Black host, Grant, noted that the audience now expects a certain sound from NPR, and that means he gets policed when he and his colleagues don't live up to it.

> The policing wasn't coming from people in the building. People were telling us they hated the way we sounded, literally telling us that they hated the sound of our voices. It's the way you get letters from NPR's very, very dedicated listeners who are like, "Why did you use this word? Why use slang?" That kind of thing.

The network's established listeners have also become quite lucrative for the network. To alienate them risks financial consequences. In the next chapter, I will review how a particular set of listeners turned into "NPR's best customers," and how they have gained a grip on NPR that prevents the full realization of the network's pluralistic impulses.

3

Listeners Like You

A group of mostly white, mostly affluent individuals have become a core group of "listener-members" of public radio. This moniker was intentionally coined when financial constraints on the public radio system provoked a dependence on private contributions; audience research firms encouraged NPR to use the term "listener-members" because their research indicated it would foster loyalty among white, professional-class listeners. The donor group's importance to NPR affiliate stations and their sustainability, in turn, shapes the experiences of employees of color, particularly those from low-income backgrounds, in the public radio workplace.

———

Fatima, a Latinx reporter, had never heard of NPR growing up, and her engagement with it as an adult went no further than watching viral Tiny Desk Concert videos. Still, a public radio editor sought to recruit her at a regional networking event for journalists. The editor noted how valuable Fatima's bilingualism would be for a position at the local NPR member station. The recruiter was kind and welcoming, but Fatima was hesitant. When Fatima mentioned that she did not know public radio, people from the journalism field were flabbergasted:

> People were like, "*All Things Considered*!!!" So, I was like, "Okay, I'll consider it." And then they were like, "That's the show! *All Things Considered*!!" And I said "Okay." And then they kept saying other things, like,

"Do you know Ari Shapiro [host of *All Things Considered*]? What about this person? This show?" And it's like, I know this is all very important to you, but I don't know what any of this is.

We both began to laugh. Public radio participants—both public radio's loyal listeners and its employees—have a distinct attachment to public radio's iconic figures and flagship programming. This bears out in NPR's own audience research: according to a nationwide "personal effects" survey, 84 percent of NPR listeners say that public radio is "very personally important to them." This factor, personal connection to NPR, makes listeners more likely to give regular financial contributions to the network.[1] Indeed, when asked why they give, some common refrains from donors are that their local public radio station is akin to "part of the family," expressing love, gratitude, and dependence on the programming for the rhythm of their day.[2]

But Fatima hadn't listened growing up, so she had no such personal connection. It was instructive to puzzle through the moments when she was confronted by these different cues and signifiers, and how she made sense of them. Perspectives like Fatima's are particularly useful in evaluating who public radio is for, beyond the institutional-level insistence that public radio is for everyone.

———

I asked Fatima, "Who is public radio for?" She started out by recounting what other people have asserted. "I'm told, 'NPR: it's public radio. It's for everyone, the whole public.'" Again, while smiling at the mismatch, she quickly produced a rebuttal:

> If it was [for everyone], you would have different kinds of broadcasting. I think there are just times that I'm like, "You're lying to me!" And you clearly know you're lying to me, too, because this is only for somebody that has a bachelor's degree or higher, that probably lives in a city, or probably lives on the coast, that speaks English, that both spouses have a job. Their income is probably roughly $80,000 per individual or above. Right? I'm smart enough to know that [this claim] is not accurate.

The first employee of National Public Radio, Jack Mitchell, sums up the relationship between the public radio network and its core listenership in his memoir: "Public radio has a symbiotic relationship with its listeners, who are well educated and societally conscious and who feel so connected to their medium that they are willing to support it financially." He is candid about the fact that public radio is molded by highly educated, well-off "baby boomers," a group that is predominantly white, and has been consumed most consistently by that same demographic.[3]

What strikes me is the consistency between Mitchell's and Fatima's accounts of NPR's listenership. In fact, across the public radio industry, there is a remarkably steady view of who constitutes the typical listener. This group of loyal listeners, sometimes referred to as the "listener-member class," emerged as public radio's core audience in part out of financial necessity. While public radio's stated mission within the 1967 Public Broadcasting Act was to serve all Americans, it was never provided with nearly enough funding to do so. When we look at public funding models like the BBC in Great Britain or the CBC in Canada, we see far less reliance on individual and corporate contributions. By contrast, like many other American institutions lacking adequate government funding, NPR has been forced to consider market-based solutions for survival.

Economic constraints on the institution of public radio have narrowed its intended audience, especially following NPR's near-bankruptcy in the early 1980s. It was the rise of audience research that offered public radio executives a solution to their ongoing financial woes: in attracting and serving an audience able to financially support it, public radio could not only survive, it could grow substantially. The privatization of public radio, however, inevitably turned listeners from *publics* into *consumers*. This redefinition impacted the demographics to which public radio is accountable, disproportionately centering an affluent, well-educated, predominantly white consumer base. The relationship allowed NPR to grow despite, and perhaps because of, consistent threats by various administrations to cut funding, yet negatively impacted the experiences of employees of color, particularly those like Fatima, who have not been targeted within audience researchers' formulation of the modal "listener-member."

In these workplaces, the dynamics unveiled in research on donor relations and on people of color in white-dominant workplaces come together. We see how privilege-dependence in a major nonprofit organization creates a tension between the industry's ambitious aims of pluralism and its chronic underfunding. What was once a saving grace for the network—and remains a consistent source of growth—NPR's narrow focus on an implicitly raced and classed category of listener-members has proved alienating for workers and, potentially, listeners of color.

Donor Relations and Privilege-Dependent Organizations

Nonprofit organizations, when seeking funds, make a combination of emotional and practical appeals to potential donors. These appeals are bolstered by the potential donor's own social networks, bringing pressure to give a combination of their time and money.[4] The pressure is higher for people with high socioeconomic status and high formal educational attainment, as they are more likely to be surrounded by people who also donate and volunteer.[5]

A sociological understanding of philanthropy and donor relations explains the use of social networks and appeals to audiences to foster loyal donors. Still, this literature does not offer a picture of the inner workings of organizations such as NPR member stations. To understand how donor relations impact organizational priorities, and as a result the experiences of employees, I turn to the notion of privilege-dependence, a feature of the public radio industry that alters intraorganizational practice.

The term "privilege-dependent" applies to an institution that derives social and economic status from the high-income constituents it serves. Sociologist Jess Calarco finds that public schools are heavily dependent on families with high socioeconomic status, which leads to an unequal enforcement of rules within the school. For those without "helicopter parents," Calarco found that the rules on homework were enforced as stated in the handbook. However, those kids whose parents had the time and resources to be heavily involved in the school received leniency. Given that public schools are privilege-dependent, relying on the satisfaction of upper middle-class parents for their prestige and rankings, teachers cater exclusively to these parents for financial survival.[6]

This is a useful conceptualization in that it explains how donors and other influential outside members of an organization shape its internal dynamics. However, research on the school Calarco highlights and on other privilege-dependent institutions, like museums and retail stores, focuses on the impact of prestige dependence on the visitor or consumer. What about the employees themselves—the service providers—who must adjust their job responsibilities to cater to the more prestigious consumers, or, in the case of public radio, audiences?

As we have seen, NPR was founded as a white racialized organization, and its emergent privilege-dependence sustains its ongoing resistance to genuine racial change. My empirical focus on the workplace experiences of people of color brings a theoretically different vantage point, allowing me to examine NPR as a case study in the effects of donors on nonwhite employees' experiences within racialized organizations.

THE CONSTRAINED BUDGET
OF AMERICA'S PUBLIC RADIO SYSTEM

Before we delve into how employees of color experience public radio's white, privilege-dependent workplace, we should recap just a bit. NPR is a nonprofit organization meant to serve as an alternative to commercial influence over the public airwaves (a trend enshrined by the Communications Act of 1934).[7] In the words of Raymond Williams, public media was meant to offer a "palliative" to the already immense and dominant commercial system of broadcasting constructed in the 1930s and entrenched throughout the ensuing decades.[8]

Given its aims to serve as a counterbalance to this commercialization, how has public radio become so tied to a particular subset of the American public? Ten years after the National Public Broadcasting Act created a national public radio system, NPR and its television counterpart, PBS, had demonstrably failed to serve minority publics. Several different minority groups in the late 1970s and early 1980s articulated a strong critique of public broadcasting, characterizing it as too inbred, "too reflective of a white, male, upper middle-class outlook that was much more closely associated with established unprogressive forces in the social and economic order than it realized and hence [. . .] substantial alterations in policy for funding and oversight were necessary."[9]

At the same time, executives had to fight for the system's survival, which was far from guaranteed. The public radio system struggled financially from the start. Radio was an afterthought amid public broadcasting's institutionalization in the 1960s and 1970s—a last-minute addition to the National Public Broadcasting Act, originally intended for television broadcasting only. Accordingly, it received only 20 percent of the funds allocated to the fledgling Corporation for Public Broadcasting.

NPR's budget was paltry in relative terms, too. Other industrial nations with public broadcasting systems are far more generous in their per-citizen allocations. Historian Willard D. Rowland Jr. argues that this financial situation put NPR on the defensive from the very start. It is always seeking more funding and always on the brink of financial insolvency. Throughout the medium's existence, public radio executives have expended significant time and resources arguing for the continued provision of federal funding for broadcasting.

The system's financial situation started off in a bad place and worsened over time. From 1977 to 1983, under Frank Mankiewicz's leadership, NPR underwent a financial transformation. Mankiewicz was committed to simultaneously putting NPR on the map and releasing its dependence on government funding. During 1982–1983, the FCC produced a report compiled by its Temporary Commission on Alternative Financing for Public Media that normalized the notion of private contributions as fundamental to public broadcasting.

Mankiewicz succeeded in putting NPR on the map, but he was unable to overcome its dependence on government support. After six years of his presidency, the organization faced a $9.1 million budget shortfall.[10] Mankiewicz was forced to resign, and the organization had to be bailed out by the CPB. Mankiewicz's fiscal mismanagement opened the doors to listener funding appeals with the "Drive to Survive." A *New York Times* article from August 2, 1983, reads: "National Public Radio went on the air today with its first fund-raising drive, four days after the network averted bankruptcy by negotiating an emergency loan from the Corporation for Public Broadcasting."[11]

The next president of NPR, Doug Bennett, wanted not only to pay off the debt to the CPB but also to double NPR's audience within five years. Radio veteran Thomas Looker argues that this announcement "affirmed the goal of increasing listenership as a valid and noble purpose for public radio[;] the genie that some have called 'creeping commercialization' popped out of its bottle and made a home for itself in public radio's air."[12] This transformation was made possible through the increased influence of marketing and audience research throughout the 1980s.

"LISTENER SENSITIVE"

Chronic government underfunding was exacerbated by budget cuts under the direction of the Ronald Reagan administration. In response to the increasing financial threat, NPR's local member stations, with insights from audience research firms, narrowed their focus to the audience most likely to donate. From 1979 to 1989, private funding went from about a third to well over half of contributions for public broadcasting. Sociologist Peter Nieckarz, in his dissertation on public radio affiliate stations, found that "declining tax-based subsidies, [along with] increased dependence on 'listener sensitive income,'" allowed market forces to creep into local-level programming decisions, a trend that accrued at the national level.[13]

Thus, as radio historian Jason Loviglio puts it, NPR privatized in part due to conservative threats and actions of government austerity. Such threats, combined with a savvy marketing campaign, mobilized liberal centrists to action. It is worth quoting Loviglio at length here:

> In 40 years, the politically inevitable solution of privatization has unfolded in a series of economic spasms within the network and political and cultural crises in the US. Modern public radio began in crisis and its growth from a marginal service to a truly national one is inextricably tied to its financial growing pains, technological change, and the neo-liberal logic that attended them.[14]

Listener-sensitive forms of funding continue to this day. Public radio is still a "public good" in the basic economic sense, in which the simplest definition is "a commodity or service that is provided without profit to all members of a society, either by the government or a private individual or organization." Economist and journalist Charles Wheelan explained how the provision of public goods can continue in the absence of robust government support on the public radio program *Planet Money*:

> One way that you can provide public goods is if you get a group of volunteers who are willing to tolerate the free riders [people who do not pay for the goods but may benefit] but there's enough purchasing power in that small, dedicated group to actually pay for the goods. We call that group the altruistic group that has enough purchasing power to actually do it. It's got a technical term. It's called a K-group.

The hosts of *Planet Money* drew on this interview in 2011 for an episode focusing on the public debate over whether NPR should receive any federal funding. Reporter David Kestenbaum presented Wheelan's explanation of a "K-group," then jumped in to say, "We call that group 'listeners like you.'" Later, he elaborated, "public radio exists thanks to a very large and enthusiastic K-group. It also borrows a bit from the commercial model, getting underwriting."[15]

Today, there are three main revenue sources for local public radio stations: (1) grants from the Corporation for Public Broadcasting and from institutional giving, (2) voluntary donations from "listener-members," and (3) corporate and institutional underwriters, or corporations and foundations that donate money to local stations in exchange for on-air announcements. The second and third of these sources are known as "listener-sensitive" funds; that is, they depend on a group of listeners who are (a) willing and able to financially support the station, and (b) attractive to corporate underwriters. But how did public radio secure a stable enough group of dedicated listeners such that it could rely so heavily on listener-sensitive funds?

Audience research, specifically the use of psychographic profiles created by David Giovannoni, played a key role in creating a loyal "listener-member" class, which public radio stations used as a financial boost to transition away from public funds. Giovannoni, an audience researcher and consultant for public radio, developed a type of audience research that augmented existing Arbitron (now known as Nielsen Audio) ratings with follow-up interviews, focus groups, and considerations of listener frequency.[16] He focused on the "core" 40 percent of NPR listeners who accounted for 80 percent of public radio listening hours, then created a psychographic profile of the "core 40": "middle-aged, college-educated, interested in social issues." Rather than trying to understand the entire existing audience, or reporting on how NPR might expand its base, Giovannoni focused on building insights about this core audience of donors. Others were welcome to listen in, but Giovannoni and his research team would be focusing on programming best received by this loyal base.

The construction of the listener-member, and its adoption by local stations, was not inevitable. It required a convergence of interests. Local station managers in the 1980s regarded audience research with suspicion and even derision. However, audience researchers successfully convinced these managers that these data were necessary to understand what the audience wanted, and importantly, what factors made them decide to contribute.[17] The internal emphasis placed on such psychographic profiles was a harbinger of a shift in priorities for local stations. When station managers of some local stations began to embrace audience research, they also tended to focus their programming decisions on the socially based audience segments Giovannoni designated as most likely to offer financial support.[18] Writer Tom McCourt quotes a station manager: "What good is a listener to public radio if they don't contribute[?]"[19] What made it on air was increasingly dictated by what station managers believed the "core 40" wanted to hear.

Thus, Giovannoni and his collaborators decided that they needed to figure out which programming made the core audience most likely to contribute. As recently as 2000, when Giovannoni was consulting for the local New York public radio station WNYC, he used extractive language to underscore the point: "Your challenge is to mine the existing audience. You want to support programming, right? It's hard to do that when nobody's listening. Or when nobody values what you do. The way to get more audience? The way to serve your public better? Lose what's on the periphery. Focus on a single audience and serve that audience extremely, insanely well all the time."[20]

COURTING UNDERWRITERS

Taken together, the category of public radio listener-member was created out of a combination of government budget cuts, a restructuring of the public radio system, and the rise of audience research. The listener-member class, mostly white, well-educated, middle- to upper middle-class Americans, is, in both aspirational and real terms, public radio's core listenership. This base is lucrative not only because they are more likely to donate, but also because they are the types of desirable consumers corporate underwriters want to court.

When NPR went through bankruptcy and restructuring in 1983, it allowed local stations to collect fees from corporate underwriters in exchange for mentioning their companies on air. Note that there is a legal distinction between *advertising* and *underwriting*. While advertising spots allow companies to make claims about their product on air, underwriting spots are prohibited from making quantifying statements, special offers, or calls to action. However, these underwriting spots have been creeping more closely toward advertising behavior over time. In a *New York Times* piece in 1995, Susan Harmon, vice president of member station KERA in Dallas, admitted this tendency: "Everyone knows we need to support our habit, and so, we're experimenting. We say as much as we can. We want underwriters to feel good."[21] Former *Planet Money* host Alex Blumberg put a finer point on it: "We call them underwriters. They're not advertisers exactly. But they have a lot of the same characteristics."[22]

To attract underwriters, the network's promotional material often emphasizes the NPR listener-member and the features that make this group a company's "best customers." As shown in figure 8, these desirable features include possession of an individual retirement account (IRA), ownership of a luxury car, high socioeconomic status, and attendance at museums and arts performances. As Gulf Coast Public Radio (GCPR) summed up, "Public radio attracts an audience notably distinguished by its educational excellence and professional success; listeners are choice consumers, savvy business leaders, and influentials who are active in their communities."

Figures 8 and 9, reproduced from local member station GCPR, are indicative of a larger trend.[23] In my review of twenty-five different underwriting packets, sixteen noted the affluence and high socioeconomic status of their listeners, eighteen noted that NPR listeners are more likely than the

NPR classical listeners are your best customers.

NPR classical listeners strive to get the most out of life. Compared with the U.S. population as a whole, NPR News listeners are:

- 443% more likely to attend classical/opera performances

- 348% more likely to purchase classical music

- 111% more likely to have an IRA account

- 77% more likely to belong to a civic organization

- 3% more likely to purchase a luxury car

Source: GfK MRI, Doublebase

Base: Total U.S. Adults

NPR News listeners are your best customers!

NPR News listeners strive to get the most out of life. Compared with the U.S. population as a whole, NPR News listeners are:

- 129% more likely to serve as an officer for some club or organization

- 145% more likely to write an article for a newpaper or magazine

- 124% more likely to visit museums

- 107% more likely to earn an annual household income o $150,000 or more

- 95% more likely to be involved in a charitable organization

- 90% more likely to have an IRA account

Source: GfK MRI, Doublebase 2013

Base: Total U.S. Adults

FIGURE 8: Gulf Coast Public Radio underwriting packet: "NPR listeners are your best customers!" Source: Gulf Coast Public Radio.

average American to have a graduate degree, and fifteen used statistics like those above to compare public radio's listenership favorably to a sample of average Americans.

An eye-opening twenty-two of these twenty-five underwriting packets, created by local stations but based on national-level NPR listenership data, claim that listeners have a more positive association with underwriters because of their association with public radio. Indeed, this is what NPR first identified as the sponsor "halo effect" in 2003. NPR's research manager for corporate sponsorship and development, Susan Leland, wrote about this dynamic in a 2011 post titled "Public Radio and Sponsors: A Win-Win Relationship." In it, she draws on research with a sample of 520 NPR news listeners to explain that the halo effect is "the positive association and shared values that NPR listeners attribute to the companies that sponsor us. Listeners have a higher opinion of those sponsors just because they support public radio."[24] Figure 10 illustrates the specific questions asked of respondents.

PUBLIC RADIO AUDIENCE PROFILE

Public radio attracts an audience notably distinguished by its educational excellence and professional success. Listeners are choice consumers, savvy business leaders, and influentials who active in their communities.

Demographics
55% Men
45% women

52% Aged 25 to 54
23% aged 18 to 34
36% aged 35 to 54

62% College degree or beyond
31% post graduate degree

75% HHI $50,000+
57% HHI $75,000+
Median HHI: $86,820

59% Married
25% never married

69% Employed
52% view job as a "career"
27% professional occupation
23% involved in business purchases of 1,000 or more
9% top management

Lifestyles*
93% Public activities
71% vote
23% fund raising

25% Consider self conservation or very conservative
33% liberal or very liberal
19% middle of the road

45% Theatre/concert/dance attendance
58% dine out
50% read books
33% went to zoo or museum

53% Regular fitness program
37% walk for exercise
19% swim

46% Own any financial securities
17% own stock or bond mutual funds

63% Household owns smartphone
43% own tablet or re-reader

68% Domestic travel in past 12 months
39% foreign travel over past three years

FIGURE 9: Gulf Coast Public Radio underwriting packet: "Public Radio Audience Profile." The misspellings ("conservation" rather than "conservative" and "re-reader" rather than "e-reader") are printed as in the original. Source: Gulf Coast Public Radio.

In 2013, the NPR Underwriting Research Project replicated the study and found that the halo effect still held, and at roughly the same rate. The main researcher on the project announced to public media directors that year: "You have something that money can't buy—your listeners trust in you so much that that trust transfers to the companies that sponsor you. Your credibility rubs off on your sponsors."[25] In short, not only is this listener-member class affluent and influential, but their opinions about a company

Listeners Have a Higher Opinion of Sponsors

How much do you agree or disagree with each of the following statements?
% Agree

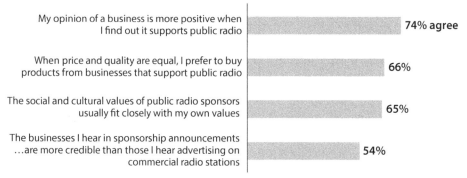

Base: 520 NPR News listeners

FIGURE 10: NPR Audience Insight and Research table: "Listeners Have a Higher Opinion of Sponsors." Source: Gulf Coast Public Radio.

are positively impacted by that company's sponsorship of NPR—companies can, in effect, purchase goodwill via NPR support. Local stations' development teams could hardly be more pleased by this configuration, so lucrative when converted into underwriting packages.

The small and elite K-group of public radio has become the main audience to serve should stations hope to receive donations and sell underwriting spots. The group is nearly always described in comparison with the general population—that broader group the public radio system was initially meant to serve.

LISTENER-MEMBERS AS AN OBSTACLE TO EQUITY

The reliance on a predominantly white, professional-class audience is a particularly lucrative dynamic for public radio; this core listener-member class that Giovannoni identified gives consistent financial support and is an attractive demographic to corporate underwriters.

At this point, some might wonder why it's an issue that stations have become dependent on the core listener-member class as a supplier of donations and lure for underwriting dollars. There was a gap in the funding model, and public radio successfully found an "enthusiastic K-group" able to step in. Certainly, this is Giovannoni's view. To him, critiques of listener-sensitive income are "sentimental," and his research program has data on its side, as it has enabled public radio to both survive and thrive financially. However, the public media system was meant to be an alternative to profit-driven commercial media systems.

To contrast with the "core" 40 percent of NPR listeners Giovannoni identified as "middle-aged, college-educated, [and] interested in social issues," he coined the term "cheap 90." This label refers to the 90 percent of listeners who have not donated to an NPR station. Rather than considering these listeners in programming decisions, station managers' plans to increase donations focus on overserving those listeners who fall within the core 40: the 10 percent of existing donors and those within the "cheap 90" likely to become donors. While NPR and its member stations remain nonprofit organizations, when we have a "public good" that is mostly subsidized by a small, elite group, and the small, elite group reaps the benefits because the programming caters to them, we can no longer claim that public radio is a viable palliative to commercial radio.

These dynamics of NPR's financial history have been well established in historiographies of public radio.[26] Further, Christopher Chávez's research on NPR's struggle to serve Latinx publics has turned attention to how NPR's economic history shapes and ultimately limits its enactment of its diversity mandate. Chávez demonstrates that while a narrow audience has provided the short-term benefit of financial sustainability, a rapidly diversifying American populace has changed this financial calculation:

> These practices are not sustainable. The baby boomers who NPR has long pursued are now reaching sixty-five and older, which means that NPR is finding itself in a position where its audience is becoming older and whiter, while the population at large skews younger and more ethnically diverse.[27]

Building off this scholarship, I ask how public radio's reliance on the listener-member class has shaped race- and class-based (in)equities within white racialized public radio organizations. Specifically, if there is, as NPR claims to this day, a "win-win relationship" among donors, station managers, and corporate underwriters, I am urged to consider just what happens to the employees who do not belong within that winning loop.

The existence of the listener-member class impacts employees of color at local public radio stations not only in mediated ways, such as in decisions about the programming best suited to courting white, educated, affluent listeners, but in personal, interactive ways, too. Employees at local public radio stations often take part in pledge drives and donor appreciation events, and greet donors during station visits. Throughout these interactions, employees of color express the need to perform diversity—a performance that serves as a solidification of whom public radio is for. For employees of color to perform diversity in direct interactions with the listener-member class requires labor that simultaneously makes these employees feel both tokenized and undervalued.

PLEDGE DRIVES

Pledge drives, broadly, are extended fundraising campaigns that ask for people to "pledge" or promise regular financial contributions. American public radio stations hold pledge drives about two to three times each year. Each usually lasts one to two weeks and consists of two main parts: direct calls to those who have donated in the past and on-air promotions.

Pledge drives, like so much else in public radio, focus on certain types of people who are "likely donors." This focus is consistent with Fatima's description of the audience at the beginning of this chapter, as well as Giovannoni's "listener-member" profile. As Jon, a Latinx reporter at a local station, pointed out, "Whenever we do public facing, marketing things, it's very much signaling to a college-educated, middle- to upper-class white audience."

A subset of my sample of employees of color regularly participated in pledge drives—that is, recruiting donations in one way or another was a part of their normal labor. When I asked whom they assumed they were making the appeals to, reporters of color often assumed that these were white, older, wealthy audience members. A Latinx host I spoke with described being surprised by the relative affluence of the donors compared to what she is used to: "I'm definitely not asking, like, my neighbors next door [to pledge]. We have a Special Circle,[28] which I think pay at least a thousand dollars a year. And that probably sounds like a small amount to some people, and it probably is in some sense, but I was like, 'Oh my God. Who gives a thousand dollars to public radio in a year?' That's awesome, but wow."

The details of each drive vary by station, but the requests for funds, either by direct call or by on-air appeal, are generally scripted. One reporter put it simply: "I was asked to take part in pledge drives: ring the phones and do promotions on air. There was a script. Think like working at a call center." The scripts are more important to follow at certain stations, as Jon revealed when telling me how deviating from the script got him removed from the pledge drives:

> I have been taken off two fund drives from pitching, because we have cards that we were supposed to read, and I would tend to freestyle a little bit so I sound like myself. I got pulled up halfway through my first shift the first time, and then when I was brought back on. [. . .] I was taken off after my first shift the second time. It's an example of authentic voice not being appreciated or valued or not sounding "public radio" enough.

Another reporter, Lila, recalled that there was a pledge drive in her first weeks at the station, and the script was indicative of the type of donor they sought:

> I got a script and it had Mike Birbiglia's name on it, but I didn't know who he was. "If you call and donate $5 or something, then you get a [chance to win a] copy of Mike Birbiglia's book." So, I didn't wanna mispronounce the dude's name, 'cause I don't know who the fuck he was. And so I asked the guys in charge of the fund drive, "How do you pronounce this guy's name? Mike Beer–" and he looked at me like, [imitates a surprised face and laughs] and I literally said, "Am I supposed to know who this guy is?" And he's like, "He's a really popular humorist." I'm like, "I'm so sorry. So, how do you pronounce his name?" Anyway. So, um, like shit like that where I'm like, I don't . . . I don't know. You know? Like, this is not my thing. I have no idea.

Lila noted that while she did not know who Mike Birbiglia was, she already knew it was "a white people thing." More specifically, it was another type of cultural reference she did not understand when she entered the primarily white, professional-class workplace, but she knew it was also one that the white people around her bonded over. When employees of the station take part in pledge drives or on-air appeals for donations to the station where they work, they often promise gifts like these as appreciation for donating to a local NPR member station. Employees of color participating in pledge drives noted that the presumed audience they are reaching out to is older and white.

There was a sense among some of the employees who participated in pledge drives that their identities were tokenized for the purpose of impressing listener-members. One reporter, Raymond, noted how he sensed this via how frequently he was asked to "pledge," or seek donations. "At one station, they had me pledging all the time, too. Um, which was fine, I was okay with it. But a lot of it was like, look at this dynamic person of color, and all the things they're doing—that's what you're paying for." It felt to Raymond and a dozen other employees in my study that they were trotted out as pledge-drive tokens, that their value was performative and not related to their actual work at their station.

This type of tokenization is consonant with other sociological research that spells out the ways that, as Ellen Berrey aptly puts it, "diversity is for white people."[29] Consider an analogous context: the university. As education scholar prabhdeep s. kehal argues, we must consider the ways that the flexible concepts of "diversity and inclusion" get applied differently over time and historical context according to an institution's needs.[30] As one example, Megan Holland and Karly Sarita Ford found that admissions websites of highly selective institutions are more likely to show-case underrepresented minority students, even while these institutions have fewer minoritized students than less-selective institutions.[31] These elite spaces seek to attract students from elite white families, who often value this performance of diversity. As we will see in the next section, the performance is present in public radio fundraising efforts, too.

MEETING THE LISTENER-MEMBER CLASS

Local stations sometimes opt to provide opportunities for listener-members to be more engaged with the station they support through donor events, station visits, and other events that provide points of access to employees, including on-air personalities.

Certain donor events take place in formal settings (or in virtual ones, as the COVID-19 pandemic required). A producer at one station described their yearly donor event as "a gala where they invite a bunch of people with money. And they hold a dinner, and a show, and a buffet and people are dressed up in suits and gowns and stuff, and they drink, and they donate." Employees at the station attend the event on a volunteer basis—meaning, they're encouraged but not required to go.

These events also take place at the station itself. As one Asian American reporter, Jenny, recounted, "I have seen the donor events that we've had in the office. They'll set up stuff in the atrium and you know exactly what it's like. Like super white, super old, people in suits drinking wine and [eating] cheese." At these events, Jenny told me, she felt undervalued as a reporter in comparison to her white colleagues:

They would often invite our funders, community people who donate $5 a month to come into the station. It was simultaneously pledg[ing] and [showing] funder appreciation, where they would come in and some of them would bring food for the station and others would just eat the food at the station. They would just gather in our atrium and volunteer. Try to get new members to sign up. They were incredibly racist. They would mistake me for being an intern constantly, for two years, even though I was pledging [which is an employee role].

If the space felt hostile to her, Jenny wondered, how might it deter different potential donor groups?

I just think that that was a really unfriendly environment for getting an audience that was more diverse in the way that they gathered in this cluster of extreme elite whiteness in our atrium. The whole station's idea was that you could just walk into our station on pledge week and meet the people who run the station and meet our friendly volunteers and you would want to sign up to support us. No person of color wants to walk into that, where [there are] a bunch of a vicious-looking white people who are about to ask you if you're the cleaner.

This space echoes journalism scholar Nikki Usher's account of an event for the *Washington Post* she attended; the event established an elite environment that distanced the journalism industry from some of the communities it is meant to cover.[32] Further, for my participants, direct interactions with donors often involved a very particular expectation to perform diversity. This performance could be prompted by a superior bringing up the employee's ethnic heritage.

I'd have to go to donor events. With me, all of a sudden, it became really fashionable to be, like, "J's great-grandfather was El Salvadoran." Which, like, I mentioned offhandedly. It's just, it's so disingenuous. I always trotted it out [the fact that my great-grandfather was El Salvadoran] at any station that dealt directly with donors.

Other requests to perform diversity were actively initiated by donors and facilitated by superiors. Elisa, a Latinx reporter at a local station, outlined a particularly odd request:

One time, our boss was like, "These donors want to meet you. They really like how you say your name [Elisa García]. Tell me what your schedule is, and we'll go to their estate." I was like, "This is a *Get Out* situation. This is my radio lady Latina version of *Get Out*."[33] I'm sure this isn't the first time that something [like] this has happened.

Elisa refused the request, and her supervisor accepted the refusal without pushback. But Elisa also had to explain to this supervisor, a white man, why the idea made her uncomfortable. The station had lots of student interns, and she wondered whether they would have felt able to push back against the same request.

Amanda, a Latinx reporter at a different station, recounted a time when a donor, who targeted their contributions toward diversity, wanted to meet someone who "did diversity reporting":

Somebody from development approached me, and they told me the story about how somebody donated money to go toward diversity reporting. [. . .] I don't know if they used the money or they didn't, but they wanted me—me specifically—to meet with these people and show them the work that I've been doing. That made me feel icky, because I'm not a diversity reporter. It was weird, and it made me uncomfortable. I was like, "I don't know. Couldn't it be the producer for the daily show?" She was like, "No, no, no. I talked to the content director, and she said that it has to be you. It would've had to have been you or Raquel [a person with Mexican grandparents], but since Raquel's not here anymore, it has to be you."

When the donor earmarked their donation for "diversity reporting," they expected to see a return on their investment. Amanda, racialized as nonwhite (and the only such reporter at the station at the time), was then used by those in development as proof of diversity reporting, regardless of her own reporting interests.

Across these three examples, diversity coverage and racially diverse staff get conflated, a common practice in the nebulous landscape of diversity, equity, and inclusion policy implementation.[34] Jay and Elisa both felt as if their presence was tokenizing, simply used as proof of within-station diversity for the benefit of liberal-minded white donors. At Amanda's station, when the donors wanted to see a commitment to diversity issues in reporting, she signified that commitment through her presence. This conflation puts greater labor on employees of color, who must perform their identity for their organization in ways their white colleagues do not.

PUBLIC RADIO'S POLITICAL ECONOMY

At NPR member stations, semiannual appeals to "listeners like you" are implicitly coded—fundraising appeals and materials distributed to woo corporate underwriters implicitly conflate "listeners" not only with white, well-educated, liberal-leaning audiences but with wealthy, philanthropically minded ones. They are the K-group identified by marketing researchers back in the 1980s and 1990s, now cemented in their status as the 10 percent of listeners—within the "core 40" percent of regular listeners—who *matter* for keeping NPR on the air (and in contrast with the "cheap 90" percent of listeners willing to be free riders). Of course this group is key: in the context of government underfunding, public radio stations have become, like many other nonprofits requiring regular donor support, privilege-dependent. Lucy, a Black producer at a local station, puts it this way:

> [The] mandate of public radio is to serve the entire public. There are things about [the funding model] that make it hard in a very ideological sense. The difference is, ideally, we are not beholden to the people who buy our things or [to] our advertisers. It is a mandate to be serving a broader audience than we currently are.

Naturally, this tunnel vision comes with costs, notably to the mandate of public radio to serve as a public good—to serve *everybody*—and to its non-white employees. This is because employees are often expected to participate in pledge drives, donor events, and other interpersonal exchanges with donors. Donors tend to match the model "listener-member" description: older, white, and affluent. Through these direct interactions, employees of color, already a minority presence in the workplace, are tapped to perform "diversity work" to satisfy donors in ways irrelevant to the content of the programming. Throughout this process, they are reminded of who public radio serves (and who does the serving).

Employees of color experience alienation through their interactions with station donors. When people of color enter white spaces where their presence is commodified, they are made to feel on display and uncomfortable. The "diversity" framework within white racialized organizations shapes this alienation.

Listener-sensitive funding sets up a workplace dynamic that, in the case of public media, inhibits the functioning of democratic public spheres in racially and class-exclusionary ways. Zooming out to where this workplace is situated in our public sphere, the economic model produces a privilege-dependence that is incompatible with multicultural social democracy. This overprivileging of the white professional class manifests in a way that is adverse for the inclusion of minoritized groups into the multicultural social democracy that the American experiment has purported to strive toward. A democratic public sphere is incompatible with a public media model wherein listeners opt into funding local stations, and local stations solicit corporate underwriting based on businesses wanting to attract a particular type of consumer.

PART II

People of Color in Public Radio Today

In May 2017, a Black teenager named Savanna Tomlinson shared her yearbook quotation on Twitter. It read: "Anything is possible when you sound Caucasian on the phone."

The tweet took off, met with a swell of recognition across Black Twitter. Once it extended beyond Black Twitter,[1] however, it received a more polarized reaction. Some critiqued the girl's "divisiveness." Commenters were soon discussing the "double standard" of being able to stereotype white English but not Black English. One prominent response accused Tomlinson of stoking "the race war." The divide across the color line manifested in these starkly different reactions to the teenager's tweet, but, as Tomlinson herself noted, "It's something that growing up African American you are thinking of and it is something that has relevance in today's world. It's a comical truth."[2]

A year later, the hit 2018 movie *Sorry to Bother You* premiered. Set in present-day Oakland, writer and director Boots Riley's film features a Black man named Cassius "Cash" Green working in a temp telemarketing position, trying to make ends meet. An older Black coworker, played by Danny Glover, advises Cash knowingly: "Use your white voice . . . I'm not talking about Will Smith white. I'm talking about the *real deal*." Presumably, this means that Cash should use a voice that can fully pass as white, revealing no vocal features associated with nonwhite communities. Crucially, this voice is one of a *wealthy* white person: "It's about sounding like you don't have a

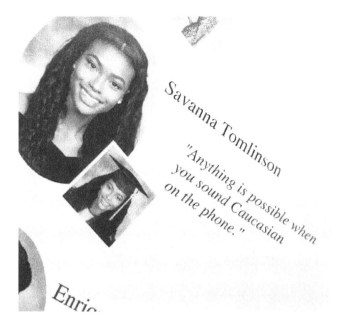

FIGURE 11: Yearbook quotation by Savanna Tomlinson, posted on Twitter on May 2, 2017. Source: BuzzFeed News.

care. Like your bills are paid and you're happy about your future and you're about to jump in your Ferrari when you get off this call."[3]

Heeding this advice, Cash, played by LaKeith Stanfield, moves up the corporate ladder, all the while using a voice dubbed by white actor David Cross (pictured in figure 12).

Soon, Cash has broken his class solidarity with his coworkers, happily leaving them behind on his way to the top of the organizational structure. Yet once Cash gains material success, he is invited to a party at the CEO's house, where he is asked to rap for the white crowd. Even as he perfectly performs a stereotypical white voice, the higher-ups project racialized expectations of voice onto Cash's body.

Tomlinson and Riley both hit on a common phenomenon in American society: first, the racialized evaluation of voice, and relatedly, the consequential rewards that come with performing a voice associated with whiteness. By contrast, the racialized evaluation of voices associated with the Black community comes with negative consequences in white institutional space. Tomlinson implies a world opening up for her when she speaks in a way associated with white-collar professionals in majority-white spaces, while Riley, himself exaggerating for comedic effect, shows this phenomenon in

FIGURE 12: Left: LaKeith Stanfield as Cassius Green. Source: Alamy. Right: voiceover actor for Cassius Green's "white voice," David Cross. Source: Alamy.

action, underscoring the role of white vocal performance as a marker of professionalism in the workplace and in the white-dominant world beyond.

Importantly, both Tomlinson's tweet and *Sorry to Bother You* discuss performing white voice in relation to a presumed white listener. This orientation reflects foundational Black sociologist W.E.B. Du Bois's conception of self-formation in a racialized world. The self is not a stable entity; rather, it is established through social interaction. If you live in a world where the dominant conception of beauty and intelligence is rooted in an ideal that excludes you, you are forced to measure yourself against an impossible standard.

Even if you form a positive self-conception within a community whose values differ from those of the mainstream, you still must contend with dominant standards in professional and bureaucratic settings. Savanna Tomlinson knows that it is still necessary to "talk white on the phone" to get what she needs; Cassius Green, albeit fictional, knows that to level up at his organization, he needs to abandon the voice he uses with his majority-Black community in Oakland when he enters his cubicle.

The discussion in the following chapters will not be an analysis of public radio programming itself, as I am more interested in the intersubjective meaning-making of what makes a voice authoritative, white, trustworthy, or otherwise. I follow Anamik Saha's cultural-industries approach to media, which encourages media scholars to focus on the cultural production *process* that creates racial representation via sound technologies. Rather than focusing on the programs produced by NPR and public radio affiliates, I focus on the makers and their processes, asking instead: How does the public radio industry "make race"; or, how do the industry's production practices play a role in shaping conceptions about race?[4] I look at the instances of mishearing and misrecognition in the process of making public radio stories as manifestations of a broader system of interpretation within the cultural industries. This focus brings to the fore the ways outsiders within such institutions make content more complex and contested than otherwise recognized.

The Work of Part II

In the first part of this book, I analyzed the white racial structure of public radio from its roots. I showed how the network was founded as a white racialized organization, inheriting the legacy of educational radio despite its aims to serve minority publics. I also explored how its distinctive sound expanded the media's voices of authority to include white women and new forms of speaking for white men, an expansion that nonetheless continued to sideline voices of color. Having gained a foothold in the mainstream American consciousness, the network nonetheless struggled from chronic government underfunding; this, too, came at the cost of serving minority publics as the need for funding encouraged public radio stations to focus their efforts on building loyalty among a core group of financial contributors—majority-white, professional-class listeners. In its founding orientations and through its financial imperatives, public broadcasting never deviated far from its narrow focus on the presumed interests and tastes of a predominantly white core listenership.

In this part of the book, I turn from the segmenting of listeners to the experiences of public radio employees of color and the consequences of these organizational orientations for the stories they tell. I interviewed eighty-three people of color working in the public radio industry to analyze the process of sourcing public radio stories. Using the case of voice evaluation in the public radio industry, I ask: How are voices subjectively evaluated in white institutional space? How do racial ideologies around race and voice shape the perceived value of a speaker's expertise? Looking at how cultural products are made offers a praxis-oriented approach; instead of decrying negative representations and suggesting more positive ones, looking at the production process offers us a map of where the representation-making occurs and thus, where it may be changed.[5] This line of inquiry shifts the focus from "What content upholds the sonic color line?" to "Who upholds or disrupts the sonic color line, and how?" Throughout, I theorize two concepts: "raciosonic disciplining" and "raciosonic resistance."

Raciosonic disciplining describes the suite of ideological and organizational practices that mark voices and sounds as partial, provincial, or altogether outside of an organization's sonic aesthetic. This analytic term is useful for identifying the different mechanisms that streamline an organization's final product meant to cater to a white audience at the expense of the voices—both literal and metaphorical—of minoritized workers and the communities they seek to cover. Raciosonic disciplining shapes and contributes to the mainstream white-dominant viewpoints and aesthetic that mark the news in the American public sphere. Readers might think of raciosonic disciplining as anything that *narrows* the voices and stories available on public radio.

Raciosonic resistance, by contrast, describes the strategies that workers who sense and/or experience such disciplining use to accommodate a broader range of voices—both literal and metaphorical—in the storytelling process. Whereas raciosonic disciplining results in narrative distortion, raciosonic resistance results in possibilities for transformation. When an employee pushes against the raciosonic disciplining they undergo in a white-dominant industry like public radio, they are making room for a more equitable and democratic public sphere. In this way, readers can think of raciosonic resistance as anything that *broadens* the voices and stories available on public radio.

In the next chapter, chapter 4, I ask how employees of color define themselves in relation to "public radio voice." I consider the voice performances of nonwhite speakers performing within a white institutional space—specifically, how "outsiders within" (defined by Patricia Hill Collins as people who hold historically marginalized identities while existing in elite spaces)[6] form an awareness of the ways their own voices are heard in white institutional space. Certainly, this is amplified in a broadcasting space, where voice is so key. Public radio broadcasters of color develop a unique relationship with their own voices through their interactions with existing public radio voice models, audience members, and coworkers. The dominant conception of public radio voice as a white, professional-class performance fosters three forms of raciosonic disciplining: self-disciplining, in which reporters work to adapt or amplify their own voices with regard to existing voice models; a reduction of their comfort on air; and the limitation of their sense of belonging within the network. Some broadcasters who do not fit the model public radio voice react by shifting their performance, but we meet others who reject both overt and subtle directives to conform. Still others, those "outsiders within" whose voices match the network, often find themselves questioning their own relationship to whiteness as external feedback marks their voices as unusual for their racial position. In reflecting on these experiences, employees of color across the spectrum exhibit collective awareness of the sonic color line—a "sonic double consciousness"—through their critiques of the racialized evaluation of voice in the public radio industry. It is through this awareness that they have the capacity to resist raciosonic disciplining.

In chapter 5, I dig into the process of pitching public radio stories. Station editors and managers, the midlevel arbiters of what makes it on air, describe chasing listeners (and, thereby, donors) via what are known as "driveway moments." These are the sorts of stories that become so engrossing that a commuter simply can't get out of their car before they hear the end. This subjective measure of a remarkable story, taken up and popularized as a shorthand phrase by NPR's audience outreach teams, relies on the assumption of a professional-class, likely white suburbanite on their commute. Thus, many employees of color I interview find themselves contending with the imagined white donor base even at the earliest stages of pitching and framing stories—the raciosonic disciplining starts well before a piece ever makes it on air, narrowing the types of stories reporters and their supervisors imagine as compelling for key audiences.

Chapter 6 reviews raciosonic disciplining and resistance in choosing sources for public radio stories. For many of the reasons already explored in earlier chapters, this process systematically excludes voices of color from public radio programming. For instance, when production teams evaluate a voice as nonwhite, they are more likely to question the guest's or interviewee's clarity and expertise. Here, too, we see employees of color counteracting these evaluative norms through practices of raciosonic resistance. These workers expand the voices that make it on air by developing arguments for nonwhite experts, conducting community outreach, and developing editing techniques aimed at making sources' voices intelligible to both existing and new audiences. Yet again, we see the toll that such resistance takes, placing a unique burden on individual nonwhite employees to expand the diversity of source lists and personally ensure the plurality of voices the network itself is supposed to feature and serve.

4

Sounding Like Myself

Devin's voice rose as he told me that he got listener emails focused on the way he talked "all the time." "That made me self-conscious," he admitted. "It was always like, 'We can't understand you. We can't understand what you're saying.' It was bananas, because I sound pretty much [like] this. I don't understand. What is the thing that makes me so hard to comprehend?" Dealing with it made him think, "Fuck this, I'm not doing these radio hits to get the grief from white people who I don't even want to talk to in the first place."

Devin is a Black broadcaster whose relationship to his own voice changed after regularly appearing on public radio's airwaves. He is not alone. Building on the previous chapters' understanding of public radio voice as a set of voices mirroring the comforts and tastes of predominantly white, professional-class listener-members,[1] this chapter considers how this iconic network voice impacts the self-perception of public radio broadcasters of color.

The broadcasters of color I spoke with had developed an ability to hear themselves both on their own terms and via the dominant listening ear of a white-dominant network. Over time, they began to anticipate the ways their voices would be received within the public radio industry. In fact, these broadcasters possessed a heightened awareness of the color line through their performances over time in relation to three different entities: their preconceived notions of public radio's model voice, their coworkers, and the network's audience, both real and imagined. By considering a pair of related questions—*How does the dominant understanding of public radio's iconic voice impact the way employees of color present themselves?* and *How*

*do their unique experiences as marginalized subjects shape their understand-
ing of what a public radio voice is?*—I came to understand that nonwhite
presenters form a racialized subjectivity, a sonic double consciousness, in
relation to their voices when they speak on public radio. This sonic double
consciousness arises out of their interactions with the white world, which
such performances entail.

My analysis in this chapter builds upon sociological understandings of
self-formation, particularly the idea that "the self" is not stable but socially
constructed through interactions. A foundational text in this regard is Erving Goffman's *The Presentation of Self in Everyday Life,*[2] which helps readers
embrace a "dramaturgical perspective." Put simply, this means understanding our selves as performances tailored to our context: the "audience" for
our performance, as well as factors like the setting in which our interactions
take place. Added to this is W.E.B. Du Bois's theory of double consciousness, which posits that, under the conditions of racialized modernity, this
self in relation to others is racialized.[3] This distorts relations between white
and nonwhite social actors and creates for the latter a specific form of being
in the world. Applying these frameworks to organizational life and racial
inequalities within public radio reveals a double performance, given the
very literal audiences of coworkers and listeners broadcasters of color must
always keep in mind.

I use the insights provided by my respondents to consider the sonic
color line. As a reminder, this concept refers to the enduring, historically
constructed set of relations that prevents white social actors from hearing
nonwhite voices in their full humanity.[4] This mechanism further shapes self-
formation and forms a particular twoness in relation to one's own voice
and relationship to white institutional space. Specifically, I analyze voice
performance as a site of racialized distortion between social actors, and I
consider the material and psychological toll it takes on nonwhite speakers
performing within a white racialized organization.[5] I follow the contention
that the subjectivity formation brought on by these performances allows for
the articulation of a unique sonic practice, known in sound studies as "sonic
subjectivity,"[6] which carries both the burden of raciosonic disciplining and
the promise of raciosonic resistance.

In broadcasters' complex considerations of self-presentation, they must
always examine their relationship to existing public radio voices, feedback
from audience members, and interactions with coworkers. But public radio
presenters of color also have different relationships to the network and to their
own voice based on how their voice is racially coded in their interactions with

the public radio industry—whether, that is, their voice is coded as nonwhite or nonnormative vis-à-vis the standard "voice of public radio."

Interactions lay bare the sonic color line for all broadcasters of color, and, in turn, that awareness creates possibilities for developing a sonic double consciousness that resists the sonic color line's reification. For these employees, to recognize the sonic color line is to begin seeing pathways of raciosonic resistance.

Self-Formation under the Sonic Color Line

Du Bois demonstrates that one's position with regard to the color line affects how one perceives race and society. His own experience of marginalization, he notes, awoke in him a particular consciousness that would have otherwise lain dormant: "Had it not been for the race problem early thrust upon me and enveloping me, I should have probably been an unquestioning worshiper at the shrine of the social order and economic development into which I was born."[7]

In *The Souls of Black Folk,* Du Bois gives a personal account, connecting his own embodied experience of being "a problem" to larger patterns of racism in society. A Black American, he realized his own difference as a young boy in school when he was rejected on account of his race and keenly felt his own separation from the rest of the world. He maps this feeling onto the metaphor of a veil that keeps him from being a full member of American society; while he is forced to live and participate in American society, he is excluded from having full humanity within it. This awareness creates a double consciousness in him, knowing that his own achievements as a Black man in America are distorted by whiteness serving as a dominant metric of success in society, constantly measured "by the tape of a world that looks on in amused contempt and pity."[8] In other words, "the racialized have no choice but to see themselves through the eyes of the racializing as reflected on the veil."[9]

Throughout the course of his life, Du Bois brought to this notion of double consciousness a deeper understanding of its global resonances and its multisensory nature. Through his engagement with global political movements, he further theorized that rather than stopping with the Black American experience, this notion of double consciousness could be applied to the broader context of the racializing and racialized in the larger world order. Furthermore, through his own engagement with radio, Du Bois began to theorize how the structural divide between the racializing and racialized can be produced through mishearing.

In *Dusk of Dawn*, Du Bois theorized beyond the visual veil into the realm of sound, writing of a "thick sheet of invisible but horribly tangible plate glass"[10] that kept the white world from hearing racialized voices in their full humanity. Racialized subjects, he explained, heard dominant narratives about themselves clearly and constantly, yet as they voiced their own experiences, the plate glass distorted the nonwhite voice to the dominant listening ear. Decentering the visual and focusing on the sonic dimensions of the color line, as Jennifer Lynn Stoever calls us to do,[11] opens up space to analyze how racial ideologies condition us to code the things we hear, such as a person's voice, as racialized entities.

Du Bois's insights have generated two relevant concepts in sound studies: the sonic color line and Black sonic subjectivity. Stoever developed the concept of the "sonic color line," which we've reviewed throughout this book. Sound studies scholar Alexander Weheliye, in his analysis of Du Bois's *The Souls of Black Folk* alongside contemporary practices of Black DJs, posits that Black DJs possess a particular "sonic subjectivity": an ability to pierce the Du Boisian veil through sonic practice.[12]

I build on Stoever's and Weheliye's explicit theorizations of the sonic Du Bois, setting my analysis in the context of white institutional space where cultural workers are grappling with their voices as they relate to the wider, white-dominant world. While Stoever theorizes the historical, macropolitical forces that structure how we hear one another, and Weheliye theorizes how Black DJs articulate their own sonic subjectivity, my analysis of the public radio industry sits between these two concepts to ask: How do racialized subjects come to recognize the sonic color line from their own experiences in white institutional space? How do they form or further develop a sonic double consciousness through workplace interactions?

I analyze this formation of sonic double consciousness through radio talk, which Goffman identifies as a speech form that reveals the deep complexity of the presentation of self by an announcer aware of a "generalized" audience less forgiving of minor mistakes than they would be listening to everyday speech.[13] Media scholar Helen Wolfenden specifically explores how broadcasters form on-air identities through their imagined interlocutors—the people they imagine judging their vocal style.[14] Here we grasp that the professional broadcaster is not solely a disseminator of norms but a social actor constrained by existing linguistic conventions. In a sense, when it comes to national broadcasters speaking to a broad audience, their interlocutor is a projection of who they consider to be the model audience member.

Public radio broadcasters are made aware of their racialization (and their coworkers' and sources' racialization) through interactions with existing broadcast voices, with audience feedback, and with coworkers. This trio of constituents that speakers must contend with while performing "radio talk" is revealing of how identity is produced by others' perceptions. I use my interview data to help draw out the ways public radio's broadcasters of color are (or anticipate being) perceived, and how such perceptions impact their relationships to their own voices.

Notably, many of the employees of color I spoke with were aware of the racism that shapes voice evaluation and how their own performance is mediated by racialized expectations of voice within public radio broadcasting as a profession. This awareness—this sonic double consciousness—affords agency amid the white dominance of their industry.

Nonstandard Voices and Vocal Color

As I noted in the introduction to this book, critical organizational research has found that the raced and gendered normative organizational form makes nonwhite and nonmale bodies *deviant*. In studying the British Parliament, for instance, scholar Nirmal Puwar notes that "the historical and conceptual weight of the ideal figure of leadership still pervades the allocation of authority and judgment."[15] That means that nonwhite, nonmale representatives, while they are legitimately operating within the position of parliament member, are in their very presence disruptive to the historical conception of the role. The disruption helps denaturalize unmarked white dominance and patriarchy in white, male-dominated organizations.

As Elia Powers notes in *Performing the News*, editors and trainers are more likely to give broadcasters subtle nudging rather than overt pushback on their voices. Indeed, as his interviewee Catherine Stifter noted, she was "never told as an NPR trainer to try to get people to sound a certain way." Instead, there were gentler directives to try again, and change tone, until they changed their voice to conform more with the prototype. This was corroborated by Celeste Headlee, who identified these nudges as "implicit racism where they don't realize what they're asking is for us to sound white."[16]

Broadcasters from nonwhite speech communities told me they often received feedback on their voices more explicitly from audience members, sometimes making their "vocal color" salient in a way that the broadcasters themselves had never noticed before. A Black reporter named Jillian explained, "I didn't have much of a relationship with my voice until I got on radio. And then I got a relationship with it. I never really thought about my voice or what it sounds like. I really thought that I was code-switching."

Prior to this on-air feedback, Jillian had gotten feedback from her own family, all Black, that her voice skewed "white" in comparison with how the rest of her community talked, particularly when she went on air. As she performs in this white racialized organization, however, it becomes clear that she is heard as Black by the white-dominant listening ear. Jillian then, due to her position in the organization, is consistently made aware of her own perceived "otherness" in relation to the primarily white audience.

Several broadcasters noted that the negative feedback stuck with them. For instance, a Black reporter, Aubrey, read a comment that her intelligence was being questioned because of the way she misspoke on air one day, when she said "cain't" instead of "can't." Citing the fact that she was employed in the public radio industry, the commenter said, "I assume you're smart enough to get this." The commenter still understood the content of the piece, and he knew that "cain't" was a variation on "can't." Yet his chastisement clearly connected intelligence to the ability to speak a standard English associated with the white professional class. Aubrey reflects that the comment "was not taking my intelligence as a given. It was making my intelligence a question, like, 'I *guess* you're smart enough to [work in public radio].' You do take it on a bit."

Similarly, a Latinx broadcaster, KK, told me about a listener calling in to scold her for mispronouncing the word "potent." He shamed her for dropping the middle *t*, pronouncing the adjective as "po'ent." Reflecting on this, she said, "it was a person saying how disappointed they were that I'm allowed to be on the radio when I can't say things, when I can't pronounce things 'correctly,' and that I should be a role model and I should feel ashamed of myself for not being able to pronounce things correctly." Again, using "po'ent" as a variation of "potent" did not detract from the listener's understanding.

Why did these pronunciations elicit such outsize reactions from audience members? Because these broadcasters' voices, in these examples, did not match the audience's expectations of public radio. As Aubrey made plain, "I talk the way my mom talks, my grandparents, the people around me talk this way. So [the commenter] is saying this about all these other people who talk just like me who are very intelligent." The audience feedback indicates that these reporters, by using words familiar to them and their communities like *cain't* and *po'ent*, do not live up to expectations set by the standard language ideology of *public radio voice*. This mismatch indicates an implicit assumption of the race and class upbringing of public radio professionals. Of course, employees of color are not the only broadcasters or hosts receiving feedback. However, Aubrey's and KK's nonconformity brought about a questioning of their intelligence and authority. The words, then, signal to the white-dominant ear what does not fit the mold of the network.

Listeners' questioning even extended to how reporters introduced themselves. Jay, a Latinx reporter, was told by an audience member how he should be pronouncing his own last name:

> I had one dude tell me I was saying my name wrong, my last name. He wrote an email to the news director, and I was asked to respond, and I was like, "How the fuck am I gonna respond?" [laughs] I try to be polite and stuff, and I came to understand that part of the job was educating white audiences.

Jay's reaction indicates that he understands several things about his job that are not explicitly laid out in its description. First, he is accountable within his role to the white listening ear. Second, there is a dissonance between how he expresses himself and the sort of expression the white listening ear deems appropriate. These glimpses of the sonic color line in action give us an idea of what it is for a nonwhite broadcaster to take to the air in the white racial structure of the public radio industry.

Devin, the Black reporter quoted at the beginning of this chapter, discussed how frustrated and baffled he was by listener comments that heightened his self-consciousness about his voice. He connected their complaints to a larger pattern in marking gendered and racialized voices as unintelligible or unpleasant in coded ways.

> This was around the time when people started talking about "vocal fry." They started coming up with all this coded language for voices who are not white men. Obviously, I wasn't getting vocal fry (although I did get that once). Anytime anyone didn't sound like these authoritative, news announcer voice[s], they would get some shit for it. I recognized that's gendered, that's racialized.

Devin's understanding of voice feedback as simultaneously gendered and racialized is crucial for understanding how broadcasters experience feedback. Devin explained that whatever feedback he got, it was way worse for his female colleagues. Across my sample, I would check in and ask about whether women face more feedback than men about on-air presentation. One woman looked at me with surprise, as if that were a given, saying:

"Yes, of course they do." This is a great reminder that it is imperative to consider the experiences of the workers of color I interview throughout this book through an intersectional lens,[17] which helps us focus on the ways the racialization of the soundscape is intertwined with processes of patriarchy and capitalism. The soundscape, and broadcasting as a profession, is always already gendered.[18] Thus, women and gender-nonconforming broadcasters of color tend to have compounded scrutiny on their own voice performances, even in a network known to champion female voices.

Further, when reporters born outside of the United States voice stories, editors often fear that the audience will not understand their non-American accents at all; at times they resolve this fear by keeping such accents off the air, reallocating voicing opportunities to American-born speakers. A Latinx reporter, Sabrina, recalled an experience in which a Chinese intern, who broke a news story, was not able to present it on account of her accent:

> Her English was good. It did sound like it was her second language, but you could understand every word that she's saying without any strain. And she reported this story that was on the front page of the morning newspaper in town. She produced a radio version of that story. The editor wanted this white man to retrack her voice because she had an accent. And I said, "There's no need. I'll coach her. I'll make sure that she sounds clear and that her intonations are good." And so I worked, we *both* stayed late that day to get her stories tracked and it sounded great. But then the next morning when the story, five minutes before the story aired, I found out that the white guy had retracked her story that morning.

Supervisors in this example denied this Chinese reporter the opportunity to voice her own piece. This denial is a notable hindrance to professional development in audio journalism. Desirée, a Black producer, witnessed the denial of airtime to multilingual reporters whose first language was not English. While their linguistic credentials were necessary to report the story, they were never able to voice those same stories on account of their accent:

> There are so many people who are doing translation work 'cause they know Russian, they know French, they know Farsi, they know all these things, and we can't put them on the radio? I know this one reporter, she does have an accent, but she is a reporter, and they would say, "I can't understand her well so she shouldn't be on the radio. She can file written reports." And I was thinking, "You sent her to Saudi Arabia. She has been interviewing people in ISIS, and she can't be on the radio?

You've endangered this woman for months, and like *now* you say you can't understand her. Why did you hire her?"

All these examples demonstrate a systematic preference for voices associated with the white professional class, which is seen by the audience as intelligent, clear, and trustworthy. Deviance, however slight, brings raciosonic disciplining from the audience and internal stakeholders alike.

In filtering out nonwhite broadcasters and reporters through the racialized evaluation of their voices by both audience members and editors, the industry produces content that reinforces existing voice standards associated with whiteness. In this evaluation process, broadcasters of color are reminded that their presence in the organization stands out; an unstated part of their job is a need to contend with and consider the dominant white listening ear whenever they perform.

MANAGING RACIALIZED EXPECTATIONS

The foregoing interactions with audience feedback give broadcasters an increased awareness of the sonic color line: their voices are called out for not conforming to the standard, and implicitly, so too is their otherness as a racialized body in a white institutional space. In this section, I highlight a few shifts in vocal performance that have arisen from the expectations of public radio voice, as well as examples of active resistance to such expectations.

Mark, a Latinx reporter, has seen through the years how his voice has shifted away from how he talks at home, even though he lives and works in the same region where he grew up. He notices it when others from outside of the industry react to his shift in voice performance off air:

> People have pointed that out to me. Just articulation with names and words and certain things . . . it's kinda hard for me to articulate. Words and pronunciation, where if I go home and I correct my parents or my siblings, they give me this look about it.

Devin, the Black broadcaster who pointed out the audience feedback he received as he began his career, has noticed a difference in his performance over time, and noted the tradeoffs of this shift.

> I get that that's a function of a jillion reps. A lot of it to me is a totem of my institutionalization. This is the thing that's marked me as being NPR-ified in this way that I want to resist in all these ways. It might be

beneficial to me in some immediate career ways—and also a little bothersome in terms of my self-conception.

While he no longer gets as much negative feedback on his performance, that in itself produces an ambivalence for Devin. What does his ability to forge a legibility to public radio listeners mean about his own voice and his relationship to a white institution? I will discuss this ambivalence and contingent belonging within the public radio industry further in a bit, but for the moment it is enough to recognize Devin's awareness that his changes to his vocal performance have served as a marker of his own discipline via the sonic color line.

Indeed, many broadcasters reported seeing similar shifts in their vocal performances over time, yet some of my respondents enacted raciosonic resistance, pushing to broaden the conception of "public radio voice" in two ways: (a) internalizing different voice models and (b) explicitly mentoring reporters and broadcasters to break away from dominant conventions. These strategies are an articulation of sonic subjectivity, yet they place the onus on individual broadcasters, reporters, and supervisors to recognize and actively reject dominant, unspoken voice expectations. Perhaps more plainly, these strategies are individual responses to a structural problem—and they represent additional labor tacked onto the work lives of public radio's "space invaders."[19]

People I spoke with cited listening to on-air personalities Sam Sanders, Shankar Vedantam, and Ayesha Rascoe and feeling encouraged to sound "less like the typical white voice." Some respondents even discussed making a very intentional shift away from conformity to public radio voice. D. B., a Black reporter, said that she started out by trying to sound the way a "public radio person" would. However, in the two years prior to our interview, she had allowed her own accent to show through:

> It was partial[ly] just confidence in myself and also hearing Ayesha Rascoe [a Black woman widely perceived to have an audibly Black southern accent] on air. She sounds very distinct in her voice. She felt like somebody I would just meet hanging out with friends. That made me feel a little bit more confident in embracing my voice and my voice being authentic to who I am.

Indeed, journalist Ariana Pekary wrote a feature on Rascoe, noting that her "route into public radio was unique compared to many of her predecessors. While they may have attended an Ivy League school or interned within public media, Rascoe graduated from a historically Black university and admits she wasn't familiar with the network before joining it."[20] Her current position as host of NPR's *Weekend Edition Sunday* has signaled to D. B. and others that Blackness and regionality *can* have a place in the network, and in some instances now do.

Other respondents cited examples of other voices on public radio giving them the courage to reject conformity to the dominant voice. An Asian American reporter, Derek, remarked how meaningful it was to hear a Latinx reporter using Spanish-language pronunciations:

> I was always amazed the way that other journalists of color were able to show their racial identity and be unapologetic for it and say this is who I am. I remember at a certain time, there's a listener who actually criticized a reporter because of the way she said Spanish names in her stories. She was like, "Look, as a Latina, this is the way I always say that. That's the way I speak. If you don't like that, then that's your problem." I was like, "That's great."

Derek continued:

> That really inspires me, in some ways, because when I say Chinese [proper nouns], then I'll say it in Chinese [pronunciation]. I don't really know what that means for the listeners. I hope that it shows that there are people in media who are proud of our culture and our language and want to make sure that's represented. That's really important to me. During this whole coronavirus thing, I wouldn't say "Wuhan" [American pronunciation]. I would say "Wuhan" [Chinese pronunciation]. I wouldn't say "Hubei" [American pronunciation]. I would say "Hubei" [Chinese pronunciation].

These reporters actively worked to shift their own relationships with their on-air voices. This strategy hearkens back to Kumanyika's vocal color manifesto, wherein he rerecorded his voice three times to "sound like himself" rather than an imitation of what he thought he was supposed to sound like. Reporters citing nonwhite voices as models for possibility, while powerful, also points to the work they must do to reclaim their own voices in the space. As a South Asian American producer, Noha, quickly reiterated after noting these exceptions: "Still . . . for the most part, it's a really, really white space." Individuals pushing back against voice standards recognized that they were doing so within a structure that more often rewarded conformity.

As some employees internalize these deviations from the norm as their new standard, leadership that encourages this type of thinking has a significant impact on how broadcasters and reporters feel about their own voices. One Latinx reporter, José, once self-conscious about trying to imitate his white colleagues, pointed to the difference that guidance from management makes: "The last couple of years, I've really been encouraged to sound like myself. That's what folks want, which is a really nice start, as far as inclusion and making people feel welcome [are concerned]."

A Black managing editor discussed her willingness to take a stand on behalf of her reporters:

> This one reporter . . . there *are* some words that she might say that you might go, "What did she say?" But for the most part, she's really solid as a reporter and finds the kinds of stories that I would just love to hear more of. But when she does stories covering schools, this one person would say, "I can't even understand what she's saying, and why didn't she talk right, blah, blah, blah." He's done it a few times. The first time he called, I tried to call him back but couldn't [trace the number]. But after that, when he called, I would say to him, "If you're a member, you're not the kind I want, I don't want your money."

This management-level support for voices that deviate from the unspoken standard is a welcome change for employees. However, this support is contingent on the discretion of individual managers actively resisting the feedback of frequent listeners. The strategy is therefore limited in its scalability and places the burden on individual managers rather than reprioritizing feedback in the industry more broadly.

The expansion of potential role models and the intentional mentorship and guidance to reject any preconceived notions help to slowly shift the boundaries of public radio voice. Further, they are manifestations of how outsiders within have taken notice of the sonic color line in public radio's dominant norms. However, as noted earlier, these individual acts are not adequate substitutes for a broader industry-wide shift away from the systematic privileging of white upper middle-class ways of speaking.

Nonwhite Embodiment of Public Radio Voice

What about when your voice *does* match the voice of the network? Another audience reaction is surprise when the voice they hear is deemed appropriate, yet the broadcaster turns out to be nonwhite. Former NPR host of *All Things Considered* Audie Cornish is a Black American woman who says that many listeners get confused when they meet her, because her accent is associated with professional-class white America.[21] Many of my nonwhite respondents with voices that could pass as white noticed a similar response. Jessica, a Black reporter, made it clear that non-Black audiences, particularly white people, seemed to have the strongest reactions:

> I *am* the NPR voice. I fucking embody it. And so it flips people out when they meet me. "Well, you don't sound, you know, South, so southern." And I'm like "South what?" I mean, yes. Black folks sound all kinds of ways. There are as many ways to sound Black anywhere as there are to be Black. And the only people who don't get this are white people. Black people are completely fine with it.

Another Black reporter, Jane, echoed this sentiment: "I'm very comfortable with my voice. But some white people, they just can't fathom that this is how I talk." These listener reactions are what Puwar has deemed a "disorientation," causing a double take that "occurs because authority is sedimented and naturalised in white bodies."[22] Sociologists have demonstrated these double takes across professional contexts; from Black women entering the professional arena of ballet to Indigenous Bolivians entering state bureaucratic professions, workers who do not fit the original demographic characteristics associated with a given profession reveal the unspoken expectations of what certain professionals look like.[23]

Jane's experience shows us how the dominant listening ear imagines the face of a public radio voice, and by extension, the white bodies associated with the voices of trustworthiness and authority. Upon hearing a voice that they associate with authority and white institutional space that is in fact spoken by a nonwhite broadcaster, listeners become incredulous and need time to process the collision of the racialized speaker.

Experiencing these ruptures provides broadcasters with a sort of clarity: the surprise that people express upon meeting the nonnormative bodies who broadcast with perceived authoritative voices reveals how authority is still coupled with the somatic norm of the white body. In this way, nonwhite broadcasters whose voices match the perceived sound of the network are still made aware of the disciplining process of the sonic color line, because it still elicits surprise from the listenership.

Ultimately, the expectations of the public radio voice bring career advancement for those people of color who are more willing and/or able to conform to the linguistic expectations associated with public radio.

However, this material advantage brings along with it several psychic drawbacks: namely, the experiences of being tokenized and, particularly in the case of Asian Americans, having one's racial authenticity questioned.

GRAPPLING WITH TOKENIZATION AND RACIAL AUTHENTICITY

Several respondents felt ambivalent about whether their voices offered them professional advancement. Evan, a Latinx reporter, pointed out his own privilege at being seen as bringing diversity but not making white people uncomfortable: "I don't think that I've ever been offensive to white people. [. . .] I have no doubts that a big part of the reason I have gotten to where I have in my career is because of the way I sound." Later in the interview, he noted that his absence of linguistic obstacles for the network, coupled with his ethnic identity, brings diversity without concerns around how to integrate it: "I'm an easy solution for them, you know?"

This type of hire brings value and moral authority to the network, particularly in recent years as NPR's focus on diversity has heightened. "There are always these moments in which we [nonwhite employees] become immensely valuable to other people. Like, right now, where suddenly NPR can hang its hat on the fact that we exist, even though they weren't supporting us, structurally or monetarily, for a long time." Sociologist Oneya Okuwobi has documented this pattern, showing in her book *Who Pays for Diversity?* how diversity programs have at times been counterproductive to racial justice, because they have commodified the identities of nonwhite employees to benefit white people and institutions.[24]

Certainly, the tokenization of nonwhite employees who conform to the standard voice may come at the expense of those with voices that do not fit the mold. For instance, while Jessica, a Black reporter, has embodied public radio's voice, she knows that her vocal performance has served as a rationale to exclude other nonwhite voices that do not conform to the public radio standard. She recalls how painful it was to realize that a fellow Black reporter, Cassandra, was instructed to sound more like her:

I have tried to do my best to support people who do not sound like me. We [in the public radio industry] seem to have a problem allowing any accents except British accents to be on the air. So, it's just a problem. People have somebody with a Latino accent, somebody with an accent from Asia, it's just, it's really hard for people [in the industry] to accept.

She remains vigilant about how the treatment of her voice impacts fellow women of color in the industry. Other reporters echoed this sentiment. Ali, an Asian American host, pointed out the difference between how Asian American (particularly East Asian American) voices are received versus how Black and brown voices are received:

> As an Asian American person, I also know what privilege that I have as compared to Black and brown people. I am not super surprised that I don't get the feedback that, say, some [other] folks do, because historically Asian people have tried to be white people so that we're not Black and brown. I don't know what to make of that besides, that is just a thing that we talk about.

One pitfall my respondents discussed was how those whose voices *do* conform to listener expectations can end up having their racial authenticity questioned by audiences and colleagues. Another Asian American reporter, Mindy, grappled with this question of her voice and identity during our interview in July 2020. "Compared to my peers, how I sound on the radio, I have less of an issue posing as white than other people do." A few months later, she followed up to amend and complicate her statement. She wrote via email:

> I was thinking about the question you asked me about my public radio voice. And I think I likely answered that it hasn't been as much of an issue for me compared to other journalists of color because I have a very white-presenting voice. But after our conversation I started to think about an odd conversation I had with a newscaster, a white man. We talked about how I don't sound that much different than a white woman and how because of that, I don't really add any diversity to the sound of the station.

Mindy's encounter with her white male colleague involved a claim that questioned her authenticity as a minoritized worker. He explicitly argued that her voice, in conforming to whiteness and thus to the overall sound of public radio, did not *count* as diversity. In this, he was implicitly questioning her authenticity as an Asian American. In her email, Mindy went on to reflect on why her voice is the way it is and its relationship to both whiteness and immigrant aspiration in her household:

> Second-generation Asian Americans like me are pressured to assimilate during childhood. I figured the more white I could be, the less people would impose certain stereotypes and damaging ideas on me—that was

of course before I realized that white people would instead see me as an exception to other Asians. This is also known as the "cool Asian" label. But I also used to tell people—rather proudly—that my father, who immigrated here in the seventies, has virtually no accent anymore because teachers/adults would often remark that they were impressed by how he presents himself.

She internalized through her own upbringing an aspiration to hide her differences from white families and white communities. However, over time, there was a change in her racial consciousness, and she began to see these childhood scenes differently. Upon reflection, Mindy says: "Now, I think about that and am revolted by it. Perhaps what I'm getting at here is that the pressure to 'whiten' my voice existed long before I ventured into a career in public radio and then working in public radio reinforced it." In other words, Mindy's practiced desire to hide any markers of difference later caused her regret and feelings of ambivalence about her own identity. While this dynamic predated her career in public radio, a reflection on what her voice signifies through her interactions with her colleagues has led Mindy to feel ambivalence about what her own ability to minimize her difference from whiteness has forced her to compromise.

Another Asian American reporter, Dana, commented that her own voice performance and self-presentation made her feelings of difference invisible to her white colleagues. Throughout our conversation, she emphasized all the ways in which she experienced nonbelonging, from feeling the need to adjust her workplace clothing and food choices to trying to catch up on white cultural references she did not understand because of her immigrant background. Despite these efforts, she was misrecognized as experiencing the workplace like everyone else:

> They're always talking about diversity in front of me. It's just uncomfortable. Being like, "We should hire more POC," and I'm sitting right there. Stuff like that just seems a little bit inconsiderate. I don't know how much of it is racialized, but I've always felt like, "I'm POC. I'm right in front of you. You should help all POC."

For Dana, this dismissal of her identity both hurt her and made her less trusting in her station's ability to tackle diversity issues.

> I get that I'm Asian and Asian American, and we're more embedded into whiteness and society, it just felt they ignored that I didn't see myself as white. They just treated me as someone who is like them or [whom]

they're used to being around. I don't know if that's an inappropriate thing to say, but it just felt like if you can't even treat a POC who's in the same room as you as someone that you want to bring forth and help along, how can you do that for people that you see as more nonwhite, on the further end of the nonwhite spectrum?

This presumption of whiteness extends beyond interactions with colleagues and can be felt in listener feedback. When Amin, a South Asian reporter at a local station, was coreporting on a community of color with his Black colleague, listeners questioned their ability to report on nonwhite communities:

Someone was like, "You got these two white reporters . . . How dare you guys talk about this," and it was this crazy thing. We're both immigrants, we're both people of color. It was an outlier, but it stuck with me because it was so weird. We sound like ourselves.

Marley, an Asian American reporter, noted this as a consistent pattern in feedback to her work, saying, "Honestly, the most crap I've ever gotten from my [white-passing] name, has come from other people of color who get angry that a person that they think is white, because of their name, is covering issues that have to do with people of color."

Overall, these mostly Asian American broadcasters are forced to grapple with their own racial identity as they consider their radio voice. The sonic color line puts them in a difficult position as their own voice performances translate into a silencing of their struggles in the racial hierarchy of public radio.

Hearing the Sonic Color Line in Organizational Life

Outsiders within public radio form a particular twoness in relation to their own voice and to the historically white institutional space. Their own marginalized status in their interactions with the network has fostered a deep understanding of the white racial character of *public radio voice*. Broadcasters of color, through their performances, form different relationships with the network and with their own voices. This relationship with the network is shaped, in part, by how their voices are racially coded in their interactions with the public radio industry.

Broadcasters of color whose voices are coded as nonwhite face challenges in getting their voices on air and enhanced scrutiny once they do. Many of these broadcasters noticed shifts in their performances over time, which some associated with their adherence to white-dominant institutional standards. Others have looked to nonnormative voice models in recent years to bolster their own legitimacy within the space.

By contrast, broadcasters of color whose performances *do* fit within the perceived standard public radio voice were more likely to understand themselves as a "palatable" asset to the organization. While these broadcasters receive less pushback on their voices, they nonetheless experience raciosonic disciplining in interactions with listeners who deem their on-air presentation appropriate for the airwaves but assume the speaker is white until shown otherwise. These broadcasters of color often feel conflicted about their linguistic credentials and the privilege they have been afforded, particularly as some face questions of racial authenticity from their audience and colleagues.

Despite the different ways their voices are racially coded, public radio's broadcasters of color have indirectly been made aware of the whiteness of public radio voice through example models. Their nonbelonging has been reinforced in their interactions with listeners and coworkers: either their voices are marked as a problem, or, when their voices match the voice of public radio, their experiences as people of color are discounted. While these two sets of experiences have markedly different impacts on broadcasters' careers, they both can be catalysts for the development of racialized subjectivity. Overall, these outsiders within public radio offer a unique vantage point onto the ways public radio broadcasting remains a white-coded profession through the racialized evaluation of voice. The next chapter documents how employees I spoke with use their insights to push for the inclusion of a broader set of public radio stories that include the perspectives of communities of color.

5

Chasing Driveway Moments

In 2017, the Knight Foundation produced a report assessing public media's past, present, and future. The report begins with Sarah Alvarez, former public radio reporter and Knight fellow, describing how employees conceptualize the model public radio listener: "In public radio, there's this person we consider, called 'Mary.' Sometimes, when people are pitching stories, somebody will say, 'Well, why would Mary care about that?' And Mary is in her 50s, she's well-educated, she's white, she's affluent. And Mary is not Maria, you know?"[1]

In the first section of this book, I laid out how these *Marys*, rather than *Marias*, became the core donors to public radio member stations and how this conception of the core listenership shapes the programming that public radio stations produce. Shows must always be framed in a way that is not too controversial for this audience, which is seemingly well intentioned but unwilling to be uncomfortable. But catering to this audience restricts the perspectives of journalists of color—if they make it into the newsroom at all. Bringing in nonwhite voices to public radio is important, but their simple presence in the newsroom does not necessarily change the white-dominant mindset that sets the standard for the medium. It is within the newsroom, where reporters pitch and pursue stories under the direction of station managers and news editors, that raciosonic disciplining and resistance play out to produce the suite of content that will eventually make it on air. Put differently, this chapter considers how *Mary* is prioritized over *Maria* and what happens when individual employees of color take it upon themselves to push back.

Gemma, a Black reporter at a local station in the Midwest, recognized limited journalism as a symptom and diagnosed the problem by saying:

> I think there is an idea that we want to be community led, and we want to be open for the community and of the public. But at the same time, we have to look at our funding structure, because we are largely funded by donors. Your donors often are older, rich, white people, frankly, and so I think that impacts the storytelling.

At Gemma's station, like many other local stations, individual contributions account for more than 40 percent of the budget. She is quick to clarify that tailoring stories to donors is not some sort of nefarious quid pro quo but notes that the awareness of *Mary* does shape which universe of stories the station leans toward producing:

> I don't think it's a thing where someone says, "Okay, we donated $1 million, so you need to do a story on our foundation." Absolutely not. But I do think [the funding model] sort of impacts the circles that we run in and the people who we think about as credible sources or as good talkers, and I think we have to really start to break away from that and realize that the donor part of it is, yes, it's strictly about the finances, and we need to start branching out and thinking a little more diversely about who's part of the stories we tell.

What Gemma is describing is not uncommon in the journalism field as a whole, which in the United States operates on a subscription and ad-revenue basis. In fact, the firewall between advertisers and journalists in this industry is particularly strong compared to commercial outlets. But it is worth recalling that *public* media is meant to serve as an alternative to this model, and there are different ways that journalists are reminded of a narrower listenership. Many state the characteristics of their station's model listener matter-of-factly, like Ben, a Black reporter at a local station in the South:

> For us, it's usually more progressive white audiences. I don't want to go off assumptions, but usually that's around our demographic and especially the demographic that the news media has adhered to and that is a lot of our own base. So, usually, it's those kinds of people that [are] the audience that we're either writing to or trying to speak on.

Rita, a Latinx reporter who worked at a local station in the Northwest, echoed this sentiment. She told me it was a "given" whom they were speaking to. Since the audience was presumed white, she said, there was no internal conversation about framing to the tastes of nonwhite people, who weren't listening.

The institutional practices that discourage voices and sounds from outside an organization's sonic aesthetic—here, a white, professional-class soundscape—serve one set of constituents over others, distort radio stories, and discourage employees of color from fully participating in the workplace. While the other chapters in part II highlight more literal voice qualities, this chapter emphasizes the political voice folded into a public radio story. Pitch meetings provide a forum to debate which story ideas to "voice," which stories get the thumbs-up, and which angles are most likely to provide those coveted "driveway moments" (a concept we will get to shortly).

Angela, a Black reporter at a local station on the West Coast, was frustrated by the narrow conception of the typical listener. If public radio was meant to serve a diverse set of publics, why would any one group take priority in storytelling? She had spent years puzzling through why her station served the people it did, and what this core audience actually wanted: "My station did their listener profile, and their profile skews older, skews white, and is college-educated. There's a tension: we're going to diversify staff and we're going to diversify sources, but we still are trying to make content that reaffirms our existing audience to itself."

What's in a Driveway Moment?

There is an industry-wide term for when a public radio story resonates with its audience: a driveway moment. Such a story "keeps you in your car after you've reached your destination, just to listen."[2] Jonathan Kern, former NPR trainer and author of *Sound Reporting*, focuses on the craft that goes into creating a driveway moment:

> Driveway moments are not born, they're created. And a lot of people have a hand in making them. But if I had to name one thing, I would say it is the ability of the reporter to connect with listeners in some intimate way.[3]

There are ways that a driveway moment could emerge from a journalist's personal understanding of a topic, sometimes from shared marginalized identity or lived experience. *All Things Considered* host Ari Shapiro, for example, has reflected on his own reporting on the mass shooting at Orlando, Florida's, Pulse Nightclub in 2016. Shapiro, a gay white Jewish man, had been to the nightclub while living in Florida over a decade prior, in 2004. He did not go to Pulse as a reporter; rather, he was there to participate in the scene.

He made friends with the bouncers and went out with them the following night. While other colleagues first heard of the place when it became the epicenter of a mass shooting, Shapiro knew its complexity and significance for the LGBTQ+ community in an embodied way that shaped his reporting on the issue. He explained what it meant to him to be able to cover the story from this closer perspective:

> I knew that any of my colleagues could have covered the tragedy. As a journalist, I understand that there can be value to approaching a story as an outsider. That's where I sit for lots of stories I tell: on the outside, looking in. But lived experience can be worth something, too. And I brought a unique set of experiences to this particular story.[4]

Yousef, a South Asian Muslim American reporter and host at a local station, spoke about his show embracing the unexpected in a story in an attempt to surprise its audience. At times, the surprise could come from covering communities generally overlooked in mainstream media. In that way, voices from marginalized communities could be welcomed when pitching: "Our show likes those things because they're surprising to most people and that's the fun." At the same time, Yousef acknowledges the flip side: these stories often require more hand-holding to get everyone on the same page. "It does take extra effort. You need to predigest things a little more when you pitch them so that people will receive them in the right way."

Both reporters are pointing to compelling storytelling that could fall under the rubric of the "driveway moment" as set out by Kern and other public radio industry experts. They describe connecting with listeners while centering marginalized voices and creating empathy across social differences, even if this requires additional communicative labor from the storytellers. Yet this is not always, or even typically, the case in making a driveway moment. Radio historian Jason Loviglio points out, "NPR's affective appeal has always been understood as part of a logic of equivalences between listener and speaker."[5] The narrator is often a stand-in for the model listener, whose subjectivity remains at the center of the framing. Thus, the vague and subjective term "driveway moments" more often than not offers comfort, rather than challenge, to the main audience it serves.

This affective appeal tracks heavily with social theorist Sara Ahmed's contention that "emotions do things, and work to align individuals with collectives—or bodily space with social space—through the very intensity of their attachments."[6] In the following section, I will elaborate on how the "driveway moment" invites the model listener into a relationship with the network, and by extension, with their fellow listeners.

THE SOCIAL WEIGHT OF THE "DRIVEWAY MOMENT"

Lots of assumptions are wrapped up in the term "driveway moment." To have a driveway moment, for instance, implies that you are listening to terrestrial radio (it can't be paused for later!) while in a car. It also implies that you have a driveway, presumably leading to a home you are returning to, presumably from something like work or an errand—maybe dropping your kid off at soccer practice. We live in a segregated society, and so this image and its cues further imply a white parent living within a nuclear family, often in a suburban setting. The color line lurks in the background of this image. Sociologist Victor Ray, in a tweet (see figure 13), has joked about the type of person who might experience a driveway moment, particularly one who laments that others make too many things *about race*.

In the conjured-up scene of a driveway, the sound of public radio can be read as a form of acoustic cocooning, or a way of unwinding within a protective shield from the outside world. Dutch historian Karin Bijsterveld describes the connection between car radios and a sense of separateness from the world beyond its borders, creating a controlled environment within the car where a more personalized soundscape can be produced.[7] As Loviglio notes, NPR has catered to this mindset and desire for a sense of separateness.[8]

Although the term "driveway moment" originated within the organization, it caught on with public radio's listener base. In 2003, NPR created

Victor Ray
@victorerikray
...

"Why do they make everything about race?" they asked, driving to their restrictive covenant, GI bill home, on a freeway bisecting a historically black neighborhood while listening to NPR.

8:20 AM · Dec 30, 2021

3,378 Retweets   **160** Quotes   **19.6K** Likes   **792** Bookmarks

FIGURE 13: Tweet by Victor Ray, December 30, 2021. Source: Twitter.

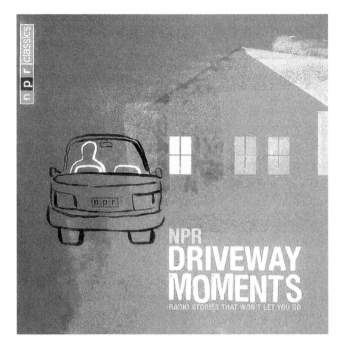

FIGURE 14: CD-ROM cover image from NPR's Driveway
Moments collection. Source: ©NPR.

a product series called NPR's Driveway Moments, a set of CDs (and later, books) featuring previously recorded NPR segments that were popular among its core audience, as seen in figures 14–18. The first CD cover is simple and to the point, picturing a person alone in a car, sitting in the driveway of a single-family home. An entire series followed in the subsequent decade, with collections centered around baseball, pets, and other tropes of white suburban Americana.

Intentionally or not, this branding further signals to the model listener-member, as laid out in the previous chapter, that the airwaves are emotionally resonant with their lives. Public radio, it communicates, *gets you*—it evokes a closeness with the model listener-member, and brings them into a collective.

The main difficulty that many of my participants had with the term "driveway moment" is in its operationalization, being directed toward the narrow segment exemplifying the prototypical listener. It isn't only about making a compelling story, that is, but about *who* is compelled to listen. How would these listeners like to feel, and how do programming teams evoke these feelings? As a Latinx employee in the industry pointed out,

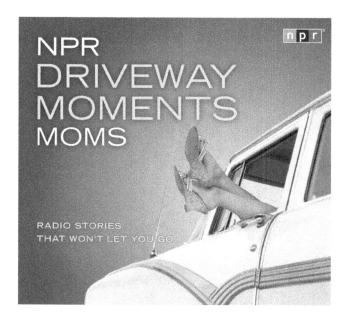

FIGURE 15: CD-ROM cover image from NPR's Driveway Moments collection. Source: ©NPR.

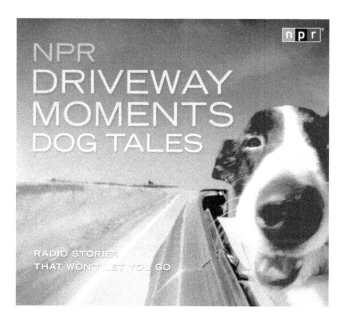

FIGURE 16: CD-ROM cover image from NPR's Driveway Moments collection. Source: ©NPR.

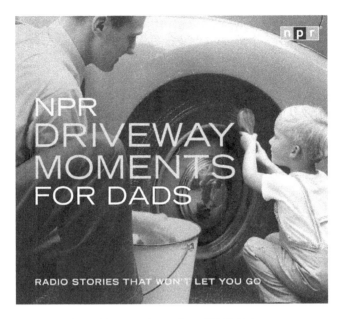

FIGURE 17: CD-ROM cover image from NPR's Driveway Moments collection. Source: ©NPR.

FIGURE 18: CD-ROM cover image from NPR's Driveway Moments collection. Source: ©NPR.

You're talking about a massive white audience, you know. And editors who are now part of the shows, whites [who] have a different way of thinking about things. And maybe are a bit more conservative in terms of their own willingness to push the boundaries, and force their own listeners to be uncomfortable, or to maybe put something in front of a listener that they might not understand.

Angela, whom we heard from earlier in this chapter, lamented how this treatment made reporters dumb down the content:

Public radio takes a lot of pride in being very cerebral. But then it's cerebral in a way where it assumes people are not that smart, in a way. You care about this random place and I'm going to tell you this story from this magical foreign land, but I'm going to tell it in two dimensions so then you can feel self-satisfied that you found out about what's happening in Djibouti, but you're not paying attention to the fact that none of the people who were called to speak on this topic are from this place, have stakes. Content is made to keep people comfortable.

If we draw a line between Sara Ahmed's argument that emotions *do things* by creating collectives of people who feel similarly in response to the outside world, we see here that driveway moments bring listener-members together through a feeling of comfort.

In *The Cultural Politics of Emotion*, Ahmed elaborates on how instructive the feeling of comfort is, telling readers to imagine themselves comfortable in a chair:

To be comfortable is to be so at ease with one's environment that it is hard to distinguish where one's body ends and the world begins. One fits, and by fitting, the surfaces of bodies disappear from view. The disappearance of the surface is instructive: in feelings of comfort, bodies extend into spaces, and spaces extend into bodies. The sinking feeling involves a seamless space, or a space where you can't see the "stitches" between bodies.[9]

Thus, the invocation of the driveway in a driveway moment, alongside the nuclear family, dogs, and normative American pastimes, is the insistence of a particular inhabitance of the world. We can see this playing out more clearly in my interviewees' experiences while pitching and framing stories. As they did not feel this same seamlessness and comfort, the shared assumptions of a driveway moment surface through their reflections.

Pitching and Framing Stories

THE PITCH PROCESS

The orientation toward listener-member comfort manifests when reporters are pitching and framing stories in the newsroom. In the pitch process, many producers and reporters run story ideas by their editor; in turn, the editor chooses whether to reject the piece, ask the reporter to revise their pitch, or green-light the story, sending the reporter out to make it. The pitch process solidifies the focus on stories that most resonate with public radio supporters. If "the audience" won't like or understand a story, the pitch is typically a nonstarter. "The audience" is invoked vaguely, but when named it tends to be white and middle-aged or older—*Mary*, not *Maria*. Employees who do not keep this core audience in mind often hear that the ideas they pitch don't match the tone the station wishes to set. Editors have told the reporters who work under them to consider an audience listening on the way to work or with their kids in the car. What about a woman listening in the suburbs? Will she understand or relate to the story?

I asked Nadia, a mixed-race Asian American reporter, to what extent she thought such pushback was about the editors' own viewpoints versus their estimations of core listeners' viewpoints. She explained: "It lives at the intersection of those things. I think, for the most part, when you walk past our senior editorial meetings, it's mostly white people, right? They center themselves."

There is no standardized pitch process across local member stations, or even across programs at the national organization. Some employees mentioned that they did not need to pitch; given the size of their network, they simply needed to make sure they had enough stories each day, and they pursued stories without much oversight. Pitch meetings are, on the other hand, more regular and include the whole team for the more popular national shows. A reporter of color who worked as an intern on a prominent show in the 1990s told me that pitch meetings were intimidating: "The thought of pitching—it was just going to be impossible. I'm an intern. Nobody there gave me any sense of power, and I'm sitting in the back. I'm an intern. I'm going to get trashed in a pitch meeting."

More generally, however, there has been a trend toward encouraging interns and low-level employees to pitch stories, especially at local stations. Sofía, a Latinx reporter, assessed her own pitch process fondly:

> At [my first station] they were really, really great about making their interns feel a part of the news team. Weekly, they have these pitch

meetings where everyone's talking about story ideas. Everyone's on the call, and they have a pretty big newsroom. You had the opportunity to say, "This is something interesting that I would like to work on," or hear what other people are talking about. If the room was quiet, then I'd be like, "That's something I'm interested in."

Even in spaces that encourage pitching, some employees pointed out that there was a "hidden curriculum," or untaught rules. Without explicit directions when it comes to how and what to pitch, employees felt trepidation about speaking up. Wendy, a South Asian producer, described it this way:

> It's very daunting, sitting in the pitch meetings with thirty of your staff; the costaffers and the hosts are all there. You're around this big table, and you're expected to bring ideas. Honestly, it's funny because you have to pretend to be an expert, and no one's an expert. [. . .] If someone didn't like what you were saying, or if you had a stupid pitch, you definitely got schooled. No one talks to you about how to pitch, and pitching is still something I struggle with verbally. I'm much better with my written word.

Over time, and as they gained more experience, most employees I spoke with found that pitching became a smoother process. Aidan, an Asian American reporter at a local East Coast station, reflected on his own progress: "I think the 'accept' to 'reject' rate went up, so more of my projects got accepted over time. I guess that's because I maybe learned what sorts of things get accepted and rejected." Notably, this shared socialization process includes getting a feel for "what sorts of things" lead to green lights—acquiring knowledge of the kinds of stories and framings about communities of color that are more likely to be accepted. Many employees of color like Aidan learned through trial and error over time. However, the rejections or suggestions to reframe stories reinforced a general maxim: never forget the white, well-educated, civic-minded, and professional-class public radio listener. What's *their* driveway moment?

RACIOSONIC DISCIPLINING IN PITCHING

While pitch rejections can happen for stories on any topic for a variety of reasons, my participants got the sense that stories about nonwhite communities brought more scrutiny. Wendy, an Asian American reporter at an East Coast station, recalls: "For the first six months, I pitched really bland stories about nothing in particular. They were super easy to get through. And then I started pitching some more racially charged stories, and [my editor] would not support me at all." Similarly, Leila, a Latinx reporter, reflected on her tenure at a local station in the South:

> I went from being this star that they had recruited—like, the diversity red carpet was rolled out to me. The first couple of months were good, and as soon as I started questioning our coverage, as soon as I was questioning why certain people were not getting opportunities, as soon as I found my voice, I was completely marginalized until I had to leave to protect my mental health. It was so sudden. It was horrible.

Wendy and Leila spoke generally about their trajectories when challenging the status quo of stories. Several Black employees I spoke with named more specific rejections that pointed to anti-Black racism on the part of the editor. One producer recalled a meeting in which her coworker pitched a piece about the significance of hair: "It was a Black woman pitching a story about Black hair. I remember we had to explain to the editors why it mattered. There was this idea of, 'it's just hair, who really cares?' That stands out to me as a lack of understanding of the depth of racial history."

Ken, a Black reporter at a local station in the South, suggested discussing the controversies over Confederate monuments in the region in 2017. When the host argued that people wouldn't be interested, the reporter countered, "*I'm* interested in it. If we were looking at this [story from the perspective of those of us around] this table, this is why diversity matters—I'm [here, and I'm] Black and from the South. This story matters to me." His editor leaned in and challenged, "How does this matter to you? You were never a slave."

Clearly, raciosonic disciplining was imposed when potential stories threatened to make white people feel uncentered or uncomfortable. Producers and reporters learned through rejection (their own or others' they witnessed in pitch meetings) that any pitch "the audience" might not like or understand was typically a nonstarter. Deana, a Black reporter on a global affairs show, got frustrated with the constant pushback her pitches received. She declared that, in public radio:

> We have so many opportunities to represent the world, but there are these few people who are very white, and they close off to hearing those things. Where they're like, "The audience won't understand this language. The audience doesn't know what this is. That audience doesn't care about Puerto Rico anymore."

She told me that she heard from a top executive, "Audiences don't care about border stories anymore. Those make them sad." These rejections, too, fell within the category of raciosonic disciplining, in that they insisted a story be both legible and light enough for the model listener. Editors and managers rejected stories that communicated the realities of nonwhite communities.

This is not to say that public radio wholesale rejects stories about communities of color. Indeed, in subsequent sections of this chapter, I will show how stories about communities of color are present in the soundscape. However, the pattern of rejections demonstrates that the pitch process is subject to distortion toward what the model listener is presumed to be willing to hear and engage with at any given time.

RACIOSONIC DISCIPLINING:
FRAMING BEHIND THE MUSEUM GLASS

Pitches centering nonwhite communities may face an uphill battle, but many still make it into production. There, too, employees of color must contend with raciosonic disciplining, only now in the framing of their stories. As Rita reminded me, public radio's "assumed white audience is people who love the diversity stories, too."

The phenomenon of public radio framing stories about communities of color in an exoticizing way might be best encapsulated in a 2015 episode of a podcast called *Morning Program* by former public radio reporter Stephanie Foo. The episode takes "a satirical look at the way public radio often treats 'exotic' holidays—and appl[ies] that voice to Christmas."[10]

Foo asks her guest about Christmas as if it were a holiday unknown to herself and her audience. Throughout, she returns to other reference points to help her audience out. Comparing Jesus with the character Neo in the *Matrix* films is a common theme, as Foo asks for clarification: "Help us understand . . . Christmas is sort of like Neo's birthday?" After listening to her guest's thick descriptions of the holiday, she relates it back to other holidays and summarizes it as "kind of like Diwali on steroids with *The Matrix*!" A listener calls in and says that he adopted an American child and wants to celebrate their beautiful heritage; the call is meant to drive home the point that public radio stories, in their unsatirized form, tokenize ethnic holidays for the benefit of educating a white American audience.

Thus, some, like Anna, an Asian American reporter, were less worried about the *proportion* of stories that covered communities of color at their local stations than about the way such stories were meant to be packaged for the core white professional-class audience:

> So, you could say that even though a lot of our coverage was about minority communities and the disparities, those stories were meant to highlight those problems for the white people in power, for sure.

In other words, even stories about communities of color must have some specific relevance for the model listener. Tina, an Asian American producer, thought,

> There's not actually a problem in covering the stories of people of color, Black people, Asian people, all these other things. That's actually public radio, bread and butter . . . but we do it with a false idea of empathy and an idea that kind of actually buys us, um, buys away our guilt.

It is notable that Tina says "our" white guilt despite her identity as an Asian American woman. Her analysis of the issue demonstrates that she, as a worker, understands herself as implicated in the larger institutional tendencies of story production that cater to white guilt. Gillian, an Asian American reporter, echoes this sentiment. She laments the focus on the suffering of communities of color at the expense of stories that showcase their joy:

> The only stories that get accepted are where we're suffering. You're putting out all this Black and brown suffering on the airwaves to make us out to be victims instead of strong people. And you don't hire people to demonstrate Black joy. Why don't we get to tell those stories? We have to constantly be the victim and that's the white savior, "I'm a good white person" thing, at play. Super unconscious, but real racism.

Tina goes on to describe how these stories emerge:

> Editors would come up to me to say, "My friends down the street are talking about a lot of homeless encampments cropping up and it's really making them scared. I think you should report on that." And I'm like, I should report because your homeowner friends are worried that there are homeless encampments—that's what I should report on? So, I mean, there was definitely the attitude that "this is the thing that's bothering the people that I know and they've complained to me about it, so maybe that's where the story is."

Her example points to the intended audience being the listener-member in a way that fits with comments from Nadia, the mixed-race Asian American reporter quoted earlier in this chapter:

The refrain would be, "What about a white woman listening in [a wealthy county in our coverage area]?" It was said to me on more than one occasion as a way to continually center whiteness in our stories when I tried to decenter it.

When I asked Nadia to give me an example, she told me about reporting on unofficial block parties put on by Black and brown communities, and having to explain why they mattered beyond their stereotypes:

> I was doing stories about [these parties, which] became racially profiled as this horrible property destruction event when actually they started off as this gathering, particularly for young Black people who had nothing. Throughout, my editor kept saying, "What about the white woman in [a wealthy nearby county with high listenership rates]?" And I'm thinking, "Why is she the person we care about?"

A Black producer from the Northeast, Grace, remarked upon how much the framing depends on the ease and comfort of the model listener.

> It would be like, so infantilizing to the audience, I thought. "Old people don't know anything," or "White people would be offended," or "White people wouldn't understand this thing, so you need to explain it."

Even as stories got past the pitching and framing stage, other factors revealed the stations' editorial priorities to employees of color. Angela spoke about how blatantly her manager, in scheduling the news, deprioritized a story about a marginalized community:

> Our executive editor of news was like, "No, that's right that the farm workers should be second." In my head I was like, "Great." And then she was like, "Because I don't care about farm workers. Why should I? I don't. And I just don't feel right if it was at the top of the hour."

This interaction was revelatory to Angela. It was just so plain whom her station set out to serve—and it was not a working-class, mostly Latinx constituency. She was hurt by the implications: "I'm one generation out of a village. My dad grew up on a farm. His whole side of the family are farm workers."

Further, she recalled, "there were thirteen people in the room, and no one else said anything." The conversation not only affected Angela's story in the moment, but it helped set the tone for the rest of her working group, none of whom spoke back to this manager. She continued, noting, "this is something that this person feels empowered to say, because they don't think it affects anyone in the room. So, what is being said in rooms that I'm *not* in?"

Various practices of raciosonic disciplining affect not only whether stories about nonwhite communities get airtime, but also *how* they get airtime. Considerations in the production process center the feelings and subjectivities of the white professional, allowing assumptions about the preferences of this constituency to take precedence over the complexity of the stories. And, in the process, the stories reinforce the neoliberal ideologies that public radio has become increasingly known for since the 1980s.[11]

Benjamin, a Latinx reporter, offered this critique of why the framing of nonwhite stories around struggle is always, to him, so unsatisfactory:

> The framing has always been so off. It's always been in the personal, it's always been in the cultural, and it's always actually about the emotions of the white people who are listening. Nine times out of ten, that's your driveway moment—a moment produced to [make listeners] feel catharsis, so that maybe you don't have to do what you might have to do or give up what you might have to give up.

Communications scholar Michael P. McCauley writes that "NPR airs many stories and programs about [disenfranchised] groups, phrased in a manner that speaks to the sensibilities of its core listeners." The argument that follows in McCauley's book, however, diverges from my own. He contends that leftist critics view this overserving of an audience as a problem that can be solved by offering a wider array of programming, a logic he finds flawed. He cautions, "If NPR stations offered something for everyone in their daily schedules, their overall appeal for current listeners would drop markedly."[12]

This warning might be true in terms of market research wisdom. Yet, the experiences of the people of color working in public radio have highlighted for me the urgency of finding a new path forward. It is my contention, and that of many of my respondents, that we can think more creatively about this roadblock set up by the fraught financial relationship that has emerged between NPR, its loyal donors, and its corporate sponsors.

While McCauley argues that "[t]here is no reliable evidence that disenfranchised Americans who do not like NPR have somehow become 'underserved' or have stopped listening to radio altogether,"[13] I counter that this misses the point of *having* a public broadcaster. Why should a national, noncommercial broadcasting system meant to be an alternative to commercial media *exclusively* serve a group of people—primarily white, well educated, affluent—that is already quite well served?

Beyond the ethical dubiousness of accepting that another public system is catering to the people who arguably need it the least, this focus on a narrow audience may not actually benefit the model listener-member who proclaims civic-mindedness. A few employees of color I spoke to had, to an extent, internalized the messages they received in response to their story pitches and framings and begun to curtail their creativity and the complexity of the stories they brought to editorial meetings. Will, a South Asian American freelance reporter, began to regard his pitches as formulaic and transactional:

> You're specifically wondering about pitching to public radio news? Motivations are not always pure. Sometimes I find something interesting that I think people should hear about, and that's where the story comes from. But sometimes I just want to buy something, and I want $600 to buy it with. So I'll just come up with some crap.

A Black producer, Stacey, had a similar understanding of how she would pitch, given the types of Black stories a core audience would understand and accept:

> I subconsciously absorbed the fact that I'm a Black girl [at the organization] and it's a bunch of liberal white people. They say their goal is putting diverse stories on the airways. I can leverage my Blackness.

Some of the people of color I spoke to *cannot* do their best work under these strictures. They end up giving something more formulaic than creative. And this ultimately compromises the stories available to public radio audiences, a disservice to all.

RACIOSONIC DISCIPLINING: WHAT'S LEFT UNSAID

About a third of those interviewed said that they had restricted their own efforts when it came to pitching stories that might run up against these tensions. Over half of my interview sample gave examples of concrete resistance they encountered when proposing stories that made white people feel uncentered or uncomfortable.

Jon, a reporter from a local affiliate, indicated a direct causality in this shift, remarking, "I withdrew from trying to pitch anything, because I didn't feel valued or seen." A Latinx reporter named Sandra explained that she shifted away from any topics that would engage with racism, migration policy, and power, in order to preserve her energy. "The more I fought for . . . doing something that really mattered to me, the more pushback I received. I got tired, and I stopped pitching those stories. I don't have the energy to argue about so many different pieces. And, so, I started pitching lighter, less controversial pieces about the arts."

When I asked Lora, a Black reporter, whether there were story ideas she did not pitch because she felt she would have to explain too much, she responded:

> Yeah, and that's not just me. That's a lot of the reporters of color that I work with. All the time, we'll be like, "That'd be a good story. Not for here. We can't do it here. Someone else will do it."

Alongside the pitches that are rejected or reframed, then, we see that great story ideas end up redirected or shunted to another moment (or, tellingly, to another network). Sometimes public radio stations, in their effort to serve what they think the model listener would want, lose out on the opportunity to tell a story altogether.

Raciosonic Resistance in Story Pitching and Framing

Raciosonic disciplining resulted in workers limiting their pitches, reorienting them toward *Mary*, or taking their pitches elsewhere. It also resulted in employees of color finding innovative ways to resist. In my interviews, three main strategies emerged: tailoring the audience for their pitches, reframing pitches in ways that didn't compromise the main point of the story, and, in a few cases, pushing back against raciosonic disciplining directly.

A common refrain across my interviews was the need to find (and leverage) allies higher up in the newsroom. Ismelda, a Latinx reporter who noted feeling incapable of pitching in larger sessions, found another way to get her ideas out there. She shared one experience in which she thought, "I know I'm going to be trash in a pitch meeting, because I don't have the chutzpah right now, but I have to do something. So, I go to the newsroom, which is where they put together the newscasts." Ismelda walked up to a woman she knew from before her days in public radio and pitched the story directly to her. She felt safe in doing so, in a way she didn't at the pitch meeting.

Alonso, another Latinx reporter at a local station in the Northeast, opted to pitch to a different programming team than the one with which he worked directly: "It was easy [there] to get my pitches that I thought would tackle issues on race in a very insightful way or off-center way. There are some shops that do a really good job of having those nuanced conversations. I really focus my attention on those pitches."

Coworkers of color were also excellent resources, able to act as peer mentors and share strategies for pitching and framing stories successfully. Gaby, a Latina reporter, explained to me how useful it was to be welcomed by a colleague of color who had already been at the station for a year:

> He has helped me think about these things a little bit more and [is] someone to share and talk about that with. That's been important—to have someone [. . .] to navigate the space in. I don't know how people who are totally on their own do that.

She spoke about running pitches by her colleague, another reporter of color with a few more years of experience at the station, before sharing them more widely:

> I feel you need to bounce ideas off of each other or have someone that, on a work level, [I can ask,] "Could you read the script? Does this make sense? Is this idea bad? Here are the qualms I have with this. I'm worried I'm doing X, Y, or Z." I know he'll get what I'm saying and feel it's more of a collaboration. I feel I can be less professional and more frank.

Connections like these, with trusted colleagues, helped the employees of color I spoke to in gaining confidence to pitch ideas. Gaby said,

> Because as you're probably finding [across conversations], people diminish a lot of what they do, and having that other person say, "Actually, you did all these things," it's important.

Beyond peer support, employees of color expressed specific strategies with regard to pitching. One was to practice the pitch extensively, aiming to reach a threshold where everyone would understand the specificity of the context. RR, an Asian American reporter, explained: "There's a higher threshold to explain something that is a minority perspective or a minority experience. Those pitches need a little more hand-holding."

Tyler, a Black reporter at a local station in the South, usually met this threshold of legibility and universality by tying issues relevant to Black residents to the economic health of the station's city in general:

> A lot of my fallback, in terms of just trying to make it "relevant," is tying it to money and the fiscal impact. Usually I say, "This is an issue affecting Black residents in the city, but it also has this much financial impact on the city, or it also is part of why there's this income disparity in the city." So that's usually how I try to take some of my story topics or pitches and

adjust it in a way that makes it broader and makes it seem more tasteful for a broader audience.

Tyler does not need to tell his story differently; he does, however, need to justify the larger relevance of the story. Deanna, a Black reporter at a local Northeast station, says that she also pushed for these types of stories, finding she was frequently told to edit out key elements.

> There'd be moments where you try to push for things, but also it has to get through the editors who are also not in the mood necessarily to be pushed against. He might like a piece, but then there'd be these moments that he'd want to take out and change. We would be like, "That's the thing that's really culturally really important and beautiful," but there was this pressure for universality.

Thus, while these strategies of raciosonic resistance bring more stories to air, reporters still risk raciosonic disciplining in the editing phase.

DIRECT PUSHBACK

Sometimes, employees of color recalled moments when they more directly challenged conventional wisdom in the newsroom. Antonio, a Latinx reporter at a local station in the Midwest, rejected the editorial suggestion to include white perspectives in a story that was not about white people. He held firm, noting that both the station and journalism in general need to "step back from this idea that our stories on Black and brown communities are meant to change hearts and minds of white people." In other words, rather than the narrator becoming a stand-in for the model listener, Antonio imagined the narrator speaking to a far broader audience.

Lucia, a Latinx reporter, told me that by the end of her time reporting for a local station in the South, she had become more insistent on allowing sources to express the urgency of stories to the audience. By way of example, she recalled her time covering the experiences and mistreatment of migrant farmworkers.

> She interviewed a guest that had witnessed these migrant farmworkers having to strip down and remain in cages as they were being disinfected. And my guest said, "It looked to me like Nazi Germany." And my boss wanted to take that out.

Lucia, however, insisted on including this quotation, which was necessary to reflect the guest's understanding of the event to the audience.

> And I was like, "No, he said it. That's what it looked like to him. Why can't we deal with that?" So, we delayed the publication of the piece for weeks because I was arguing that I will not take it out. "And if you take it out, I will not run the piece."

There is a tension between the concerns of public radio's editors and managers and a maxim of media storytelling: some of the most acclaimed stories take narrative risks or operate outside the conventions of the genre. Public radio was once known for its experimentation. Its very first broadcast of *All Things Considered* was a twenty-three-minute recording of Vietnam War protests in Washington, DC.[14] In part, the willingness to experiment in those early years reflected the fact that no one was listening yet. As the medium became more professionalized and the audience was secured, greater risk aversion arose. Once there was an audience to lose (and a budget to cover), few wanted to risk actually losing it.

Diana, a Middle Eastern American reporter, talked about her editor's resistance to covering a Muslim holiday, even though their station had covered other, similarly prominent Judeo-Christian holidays:

> I wanted to cover Eid al-Fitr, and I got a lot of pushback, which is weird. I was surprised by the pushback that I got. She [the editor] was like, "No, why do you want to cover this?" I was like, "If we're covering Purim and we're covering [Ash Wednesday], why wouldn't we cover a Muslim holiday?" I'm like, "You have no problem telling me to reach out to [the Muslim community] during an instance of a hate crime."

Diana was frustrated that she was told to interview community members about Islamophobia but got pushback on trying to cover an event that would showcase the end of Ramadan, a more joyful experience. When she went ahead with the story despite her editor's reservations, "it was the story that did really, really well on our social media platforms." Diana noted, with palpable annoyance, that the editor "was gushing over the pictures and she was showing everybody the story."

Diana was not the only person of color who felt their ideas were undervalued within the organization, despite receiving validation external to the organization. Gavin, a Black reporter, noted the dissonance between flack he got at his program and validation he received elsewhere.

I loved that, the month that I quit, I won [a prestigious award] for investigative reporting. The thing that they had made it out to be, my boss was giving me stress because she was like, "You didn't tell us where you were." I was working on a documentary, but still doing my job or traveling. Part of what made me a "deficient" reporter was I was working on a documentary that got us one of our biggest awards and it landed.

Nate, a Black reporter, talked about how for months he was not able to do any in-depth reporting, citing a lack of time and resources. Yet, when the opportunity came to report on a story in a community of color when his editor was away, he forged ahead.

My editor went on vacation for two weeks, and I got a tip-off. I'm calling up people and there's obviously this thirst in the community for some sort of investigation. I ended up doing this story without permission, on my own.

Nate felt forced to circumvent standards—and was vindicated when he and his program were subsequently awarded several investigative journalism awards, bringing prestige both to him and to his organization.

In addition to pushing for their own storytelling, some employees of color I spoke with pushed back on the standard framing of stories in general. Dave, an Asian American reporter, told me that the practice he most often resisted was the use of the vague term "community" during a specific news report. He told me,

Often the word "community" gets attached to groups of people of color. You don't really hear, "Leaders in the white community are talking about this . . . ," but you'll hear it all the time: "Leaders in the Asian American community are talking about . . ." I've heard stuff like that on our radio and then I will call it out.

While not directly about his own reporting, Dave's reminders to his colleagues about this practice have led them to be more specific about which group they are speaking of, rather than using the blanket term "Asian American community" or "people of color" when the topic and the person speaking about it represent a much narrower group of people. Another simple form of raciosonic resistance, his notes help ensure that guests are featured in ways that are more accurate to the issue being covered in any given story.

THE ROLE OF EDITORS AND MANAGERS

Editors, I was told time and again, can "make or break" a story. When I asked reporters and producers what might improve conditions at their stations, many said without hesitation that more people of color need to be in management and in editorial positions.

Jamie, an Asian American editor, affirmed this importance, lamenting that there were so few editors of color at her organization, where "the direct editors are almost all white." She saw this manifest in whether her fellow editors would green-light a piece and in what they were willing to count as "proof":

> They have standards for what makes a story green-lightable. You could say they're higher, but you could also say, like, in a way, relying on documents and data and things that are very provable already puts the stories of people of color at a deficit, because a lot of experiences are hard to prove. Or data is not available or even the way that data is collected can have bias within it.

It was not uncommon for Jamie to end up in debates around such issues. "Sometimes, when we're debating a pitch, the kind of feedback I hear . . . I can tell that people don't have a lived experience of marginalization." And, of course, reporters and producers need to cater to those perspectives in pitching and framing their stories. Leila, a Latinx reporter quoted earlier, told me that "you really develop an intuition kind of about what each editor wants. Each editor wants different things, and you have to figure it out. You have to pitch to the editor that you're pitching."

Keith Woods, NPR's head of newsroom diversity from October 2010 to May 2025, spoke of a pattern experienced by reporters of color in both public and commercial newsrooms wherein "an issue arises so close to the surface of their lives, the impact of which is sometimes not shared by their white colleagues. That's a reality of being in this profession. There's this wrestling over whether or not a quote or an anecdote or an adjective gets put into a story; it can hinge on whether or not the editor has the ability to stand in the shoes of the reporter and understand."

Woods noted that in any newsroom,

> you can easily find yourself, as an editor, not certain whether this value that you're wrestling with a reporter over is a function of a more universal sense of what is news, [or] whether it's a function [. . .] of your understanding of the news. For the thoughtful editor, [. . .] the arena for

growth as leaders is to figure out when you're defending a true, legitimate journalistic value and when you're defending an unexamined and narrow definition of news.[15]

Jamie takes seriously her responsibilities in shaping public radio stories. During the beginning of the COVID-19 pandemic's spread, she was assigned as an editor on a piece about care workers in assisted living facilities and the exploitation of their labor.

When a white reporter sent her the original edit, it did not unpack that all of the workers and many of the managers in this context were Filipino.

And so, to me telling a story about this industry and not talking about the history between the U.S. and the Philippines. It was an incidental fact to [the reporter] whereas for me, we couldn't tell the story without acknowledging that.

Jamie was able to intervene in the story to contextualize how colonial history had shaped the labor force.

Unfortunately, editors of color are even more underrepresented than producers and reporters. In general, editors are less likely to be entry-level workers. They are usually promoted from another position or have editorial experience elsewhere. Given that journalists of color, particularly Black women, tend to leave their workplaces due to the racism in their work environment,[16] the barrier to recruiting editors is higher.

Afflicting the Comfortable

A driveway moment is meant to encourage listeners to finish a captivating story even after they have reached their destination. But some stories are uncomfortable, and they require us to continue listening even when it would be more convenient to turn away. Jessica, a Black woman who has been a public radio reporter for decades, summed it up this way:

Sorry, you're uncomfortable. But right now that old journalistic maxim—which is "to comfort the afflicted and afflict the comfortable"—must be applied to liberal white people. People who think well of themselves right now, the certitude has to be smashed.

She continued to note that this cannot happen gently: "If we're not extra loud, you'll never hear anything." To me, her words again recalled Du Bois's sonic metaphor for racialization, introduced at the very start of this book, in which Black Americans struggle to be heard as if from behind a thick glass barrier. Passersby "either do not hear at all, or hear but dimly, and even what they hear, they do not understand."[17]

This barrier, a structured societal divide, shapes both how people can be heard in institutional contexts and the amount of communicative labor it takes to exist in white-dominant space. The next chapter will delve into how this barrier shapes which sources make it onto public radio's airwaves.

6

Their Accent Is Too Much

"Just because someone isn't a great talker doesn't mean they don't have something great to say," pointed out Grace, a South Asian American producer. Yet it became clear through my interviews that, as stories bubbled up from ideas to pitches, as reporters and producers began to source interviewees, and as higher-ups gave their input, being a "good talker" is a crucial part of getting a voice on air. And, as might be expected, this sorting is highly raced and classed.

When a public radio story is approved for production, the producer or reporter must line up voices to speak on air. This process is known as sourcing. There has long been a widespread bias toward white male sources in broadcast journalism,[1] and sourcing practices in the public radio industry are no exception. National Public Radio conducts a yearly audit on the organization's weekday newsmagazine programs. In fiscal year 2018, the voices on air were "83% white and 33% female."[2] While the organization has made a concerted effort to improve these statistics, the bias persists. As one respondent within the national organization recalled, "There was a brouhaha at NPR [in spring 2020] in which one of the weekend shows, for an entire hour, every voice on it was a white dude. How does that even happen? You have to try."

This bias toward white male experts holds across the public radio industry, and it has been documented through self-audits conducted by local stations like Philadelphia-area WHYY.[3] Attempts to change these statistics have involved encouraging employees to track their own sources to promote accountability and self-reflexivity in their own practices; some local station respondents noted that this source-tracking could be effective in reducing the bias toward white male experts. Erin, an Asian American reporter, noted, "Forcing yourself to audit your sources definitely makes me feel I should work harder to get more diverse sources." But as we've seen elsewhere in this book, the practice puts the burden of change on individuals, leaving organization-wide practices unchanged.

There is also a sonic dimension to sourcing that cannot be adequately captured by demographic tracking: a public radio guest or interviewee still needs to be deemed a "good talker." Who's generally excluded from this coveted category? Guests without media training and voices associated with communities of color.

While the previous chapters highlighted how stories and reporters get chosen for public radio's airwaves, this chapter considers how sources—the people from outside the workplace—get selected and evaluated. Once again, the process is suffused with raciosonic disciplining, here the exclusion of voices and perspectives that are outside the white organization's sonic aesthetic, and it is met with acts of raciosonic resistance in which reporters and producers work to broaden the range of source voices that make it on air. Employees of color enact their resistance by training guests, conducting bilingual reporting and interpretation work, and even working to protect sources from the whiteness of the public radio space by acting as cultural brokers. As my respondents in this chapter reflect on their own experiences trying to get sources on air, they propose alternative ways of listening to sources and evaluating which voices are worthy of airtime.

Racism in Voice Evaluation

The role of race and racism in producing and evaluating cultural products comes as no surprise to scholars of race and ethnicity. Work in racial theory across decades has demonstrated how racism structures American life[4] and the white spaces that are designated as "universal" in American society. Attending to the processes of cultural production moves us beyond the question of whether a cultural product is racialized toward a better understanding of *when* and *how* cultural products are impacted by racism and race relations.[5]

As discussed earlier in this book, racism does not necessarily operate overtly within the cultural industries. In fact, racially exclusionary norms are often invisible (and inaudible, for the purposes of this book!) even to those who enact them.[6] Further, because racism is so ubiquitous and continually enacted in American life, race is understood as a real social category, naturalized to the point where we forget that racism is the root cause of inequalities along perceived racial lines.[7] Over time, racial inequality, as an outcome, has thus been ascribed not to racism but to racial difference, cementing the idea that race itself has inherent meaning.

All this makes it hard to spot racism. Recent work in the sociology of evaluation demonstrates that racism and sexism shape things such as whether and how cultural figures get consecrated[8] and how cultural genres get legitimated[9] and reviewed.[10] Yet even organizations actively seeking to remedy histories of racial exclusion through workforce practices and hiring have trouble identifying ongoing processes tainted by racism, like the evaluation of public radio's workers of color and their stories.[11]

If raciosonic disciplining is the suite of ideological and organizational practices that mark certain voices and sounds as partial, provincial, or altogether outside of an organization's sonic aesthetic, it is, in large part, what creates the public radio voice—and everything that is *not* the public radio voice. And it is systematic. When voices evaluated for broadcast, through racist practice, are coded as nonwhite, their clarity and expertise are more likely to be questioned. These patterns are uncovered through the insights of outsiders within, like Arvand, quoted in this book's introduction, who enter public radio with different practices of evaluative listening. The discrepancy between his hearing and that of his white colleagues has been socially conditioned over time, and it is integral to understanding the negotiation and enforcement of the sonic color line.

Finding Good Talkers

The majority of those I asked defined "good talker" through two features that made a person's voice "easy to understand": media savvy, which is associated with people in the professional class (i.e., white-collar professionals), and a "standard" American accent, commonly understood by editors and by the perceived audience. Together, these features cement white, professional-class American voices as the standard for evaluation and mark foreign, often nonwhite accents as deviant.

As a Black reporter named Sammy pointed out, "a good talker can toe the line between being a friend and an academic." In other words, the ideal good talker brings expert-level analysis and is relaxed while doing so. Karla, a Black producer, said to think of "your smart friend on an HBO show who can tell you about, like, a crisis in another country," while Devin, a Black broadcaster, summed up, "When they mean 'good talker,' they always mean somebody who works at fucking think tanks. You end up with the same institutional white voices." Note the key part of Devin's claim—these are not simply *white* voices, but white voices representing white-dominant institutions. This conception of good talker often prioritizes institutional expertise over lived experiences of the same topic. Angela, a Black producer, told me:

> I grew up listening to NPR, and it would be like, "There's a famine. Oh no." And they would talk to someone who was starving. And then they'd be like, "Let's talk to this expert from Oxford." What if you talk to people in the country?

Pablo, a Latinx producer, commented on the racialized patterns involved in determining who was a "good talker" and deserved airtime:

> It seems very implicit. I think it's, [. . .] the rest of the producers and the rest of the senior producers and staff, I don't think they recognize it as such, but it's like, "Oh, well that person was great, they're a great talker on the show, we should have them back on again," and it's like, [laughs] it's a very white accent, very American white accent, very enunciated.

While Pablo was attuned to the white Americanness of the voices, their racial character remained unmarked for the rest of the producers. To them, "very American white" voices were the standard and racialized voices the deviations—but the process was so normalized that even they were unaware that it was racist. The exclusion of nonwhite voices becomes clearer when we trace the path for sources who do not hew to these expectations. For instance, Grace, a producer of color, received negative feedback for bringing a guest with limited airtime experience to the show, who did not have the same level of comfort on air as the "good talkers" described above:

> We looked for the voice of a protester, and we brought this [Black] guy on, and he was not . . . He wasn't a professor, you know? He hasn't been trained in how to speak to the media. He had really interesting things to say. He was just a little bit more clunky when it came to saying them. And [the host] was unhappy with him. But my team was like, "No, he's really good." Like, just because someone isn't a great talker doesn't mean they don't have something great to say.

In this example, the host was frustrated by a guest who was not entirely prepared for a live, free-flowing discussion. The burden was on the guest to be a good talker, instead of on the interviewer, who might adjust her questions to connect with the guest, or on the station, which might provide basic media training for the protester. This orientation toward guests' styles runs counter to research that has emphasized the value and expertise of Black witnessing: as noted by journalism scholar Allissa V. Richardson, Black activists and bystanders have often been the first responders in communicating injustice, doing so outside of the confines of formal knowledge-producing institutions such as media outlets or higher education.[12]

Some respondents pushed back against hosts who urged producers to find people who were already comfortable on air, noting that clunkiness or reticence on air, while associated with inexperience or not being a "good talker," can actually *enhance* the emotional resonance of a story. Esteban, a Latinx reporter, explained to me how his source's unpolished responses were revealing a deeper emotional truth:

> One of my sources was a [Latino] guy who was very shy, had never been on radio before, but he had this beautiful story [about how he had turned to music to learn to communicate with his family]. [. . .] The hesitance and reluctance in his voice, in and of itself, is part of why he is that way.

In these examples, Grace and Esteban managed to get sources without media training on air—they resisted raciosonic disciplining and enacted raciosonic resistance. However, bringing these voices on air entailed more labor for these employees, who enacted individual solutions to a systemic problem. Grace had to defend bringing on the protester as a guest; Esteban had to do a more extensive edit of his piece. Extra work like this is not compensated, and often not even recognized. A Middle Eastern American reporter, Lila, was exasperated by the process of pushing back: "It's *so* much more work. No wonder it's all white! I get paid too little [to do this extra work]."

REGIONAL ACCENTS AND AUTHENTICITY

Whiteness is not a static set of observable empirical features but a conceptual category. White accents and speech patterns, then, do not form an empirically stable monolith. As articulated by linguistic anthropologists Sara Trechter and Mary Bucholtz:

> [C]ertain tropes of whiteness "compete" and are reformed in context, and, depending on the contextual circumstances, "win out" or are

highlighted in opposition to others. Thus, contextual, semiotic associations can index different concepts or identities of whiteness, which are "marked" to varying degrees, while not necessarily challenging the overall hegemony of whiteness.[13]

In other words, language can still be marked as white *and* as "other" within the public radio industry. Linguistic anthropologist John Hartigan's 1999 ethnography of white "hillbillies" in Detroit, for instance, finds that despite their very apparent whiteness, "hillbillies" are racially marked because of their linguistic and cultural distinctions from professional-class white Americans. Through their forms of speech, that is, Detroit's "hillbillies" are classified into a "degraded form of whiteness" when compared to locals from professional-class white communities.[14] Rather than separating race and class and comparing them, I follow sociologist Mo Torres's theorization of race as a "resource signal";[15] a voice associated with the professional class is often coded as white, because historically the race category was constructed as a means of material resource allocation.

In the production process, American regional accents brought mixed reactions. I talked to a white reporter, Lance, who noted that there could be a lot of currency in white regional accents, which were marked as "authentic" in contrast to the standard, unmarked language of broadcasters and hosts on public radio.

> My very first radio feature had this man in it who was a fisherman who had, like, a really strong, [rural region] accent . . . that was like gold. People were like, "Ooooh!" You know, like, white-people accents are considered very valuable. And I was good at going and getting that kind of people as a white person. I can roll up in those places and, like, get these people talking to me who have these, like, white-people accents.

At first, this made Lance keen to search out such voices, but over time he realized, "It's very tokenistic and I don't like it anymore." Janice, a Black reporter, notes the problem with the term "authenticity" being tokenizing:

> They'll say, like, "That person sounds so real." Like, "That's such a real person that you got, that was a good get," and it'll sometimes be someone with a southern accent . . . it will just be like, "That was a real person with a real story."

Janice noted that this "authenticity" comes with a false bifurcation between "realness" and "expertise."

Depending on the region of the member station, southern accents shift in value. While in the above examples, southern accents were tokenized, in some regions, like the Northeast, these same accents become problems. Jackie, who produces stories in the Northeast, found that when she interviewed "older Black women that have really thick southern accents, [. . .] there's always, uh, a little bit of pushback there." Similarly, on the West Coast, Angela, a Black reporter originally from the South, said, "I try to get immigrants on the air, accents of every stripe, especially southern accents." But "there is a very heavy assumption that if you have a southern accent, you must be dumb and probably also racist. That's not the case."

The regional variability of the reception of southern accents as either "dumb" or "authentic" (what Lance calls "public radio gold") points to the shifting and unstable understandings of regional accents in white institutional spaces; the evaluations correspond with whether the normative white professional-class communities of the region are expected to connect—or not connect—with certain regional accents. As we have seen throughout the previous chapters, the specter of the model public radio listener looms large.

Respondents also told me they could not get distinctly Black voices, even if they had local regional accents, on air. Jackie noticed how differently she and her editors heard some sources:

> Guys that sound like they're from the city [in the Northeast], if they sound like they're from my [predominantly Black] neighborhood, I'm like, "Oh, this, I want to hear what you have to say because you sound familiar to me." But for them [the editors], it was like, "I can't even listen to the story, because I can't get past their accents."

Around the country, American accents associated with Black communities are more likely to be met with misunderstanding and derision than are white regional accents. Among those American accents that do not hew to the professional class, there is a raciolinguistic hierarchy of whose voices make it on air. This raciolinguistic hierarchy maps onto accents from immigrant communities as well.

NON-AMERICAN ACCENTS

Respondents noted how their editors put extra scrutiny on guests or features from immigrant communities of color. Certainly, and as I address below, these designations of "nonstandard" are racialized; among "foreign" accents, European voices endure less pushback than do accents from Asia and the

Global South. Reporters struggled to get sources with Chinese accents on air, for example, even when the source's perspective was highly salient. Sammy, an Asian American reporter, recalled, "I was instructed to pick someone without too heavy of an accent because then people wouldn't be able to understand them. That really stuck with me, actually, because there are so many credible sources that I know that have terrible accents when speaking English."

Producers and reporters of color cited clips of sources that they could understand without strain but that were considered by white editors to be unintelligible. Arvand, the Middle Eastern American broadcaster cited in this book's introduction, was blunt: "It's always a white person that's standing on the other side being like, 'We can't book this person because I don't understand them.' Well, we [people of color on the team] all understand them."

Pablo, the Latinx producer who noticed a pattern of success for white American accents, understood that he needed to preempt pushback by putting extra scrutiny on Latin American accents he could readily understand:

> I think I've been more cautious about it than maybe some of my colleagues, just because I'm nervous—if I book a Latin American reporter I always am second-doubting, because I can understand them perfectly, because they speak like my dad speaks, they speak like my mom speaks, they speak like my cousins speak. I can understand clearly, and it's perfectly fine, but I'm worried that, I always worry that, "Okay, is this accent too thick for English-speaking Americans?" And so, um, I tend to actually be overly cautious, more so than the other folks.

Pablo's caution has proven well founded. Once, he recalled, he tried to bring on a Latin American reporter who had been reporting on his own region:

> There's . . . this just absolutely stellar, stellar reporter for a Latin American outlet, and I wanted to book him, uh, for the show, and I was, you know, very nervous about his accent. I showed the executive producer a clip of him speaking. I could understand everything perfectly well, but she goes, "Oh, no, no, that . . . that accent, that's, yeah, that's too much." So, we ended up not booking him, and we went with a, you know, a, [laughs], an American white reporter, who was covering Latin America, to discuss the story.

Pablo's knowing laughter points to a predictability that he pointed out elsewhere in the interview: when in doubt, the most common practice was to get a white reporter as an expert on a region rather than someone with an

accent from the region itself. Amelia, a Latinx reporter, similarly internalized editors' reactions to previous interviews she had done in English and
conducted her subsequent interviews in Spanish:

> I even started policing myself in that sense. There were definitely times
> that I was like, "I understand this person fine, but, like, they have an
> accent as thick as my mother's, which I don't think my editor would
> actually like." I imagined him saying, "They're tough to understand, we
> shouldn't include this."

Anticipating her editor's comments encouraged Amelia to conduct her interviews in Spanish and translate them into English. Of course, this shift creates more work for Amelia without additional compensation, and it further
excludes nonstandard-English foreign accents from her station's airwaves.
When station employees anticipate such reactions, they may preemptively
restrict the range of accents they include in stories to increase the probability
of their recordings being approved for air.

Although in some instances, the rejection of an accent as "too much"
is chalked up to the need for clarity on air, differing reactions to different
accents show there are even racialized notions of clarity. For instance, consider Black international reporter Mara on African versus Italian accents:

> We were covering stories in Africa, and editors would be like, "Oh,
> that audio's unclear." And I was like, "These are the only people who
> have internet access. You can definitely hear what they're saying . . .
> the audio is fine." And, and they were like, "OK, well, their accent is
> like . . . their accent is really hard to understand." The contrast to that
> for me was the Italian soccer team when . . . they did this whole speech.
> And everyone was like, "That's beautiful. Let's play the speech in Italian
> for a really long time." And these were the managers who were usually
> like, "I can't understand this Japanese language . . . It's not clear to
> me." Or like, "It's just [a] bad connection," when it wouldn't be a bad
> connection.

Black producer Karla also called out a "hierarchy on certain accents":

> Just the other day, I produced a story with this African [content expert].
> I could understand everything he was saying. I had an editor who
> told me, "Oh, come on, his accent is so thick." And I'm like, "Really?
> I understood everything he said." I asked a few of my friends afterward,
> [and they could all understand it]. I've also produced interviews with

this French academic who had a heavy French accent. But you know, this guy's French and he has a French name. And . . . that's never a problem.

Both Mara and Karla saw a gap in the way European accents were evaluated more favorably than African accents. This racialized valuation can absolutely inhibit valuable sources from getting on air. The best possible option for a radio piece, according to a few employees I spoke to, is to use people's original voices as much as possible. However, when conducting interviews in English (no matter how proficiently it is spoken) with people who have thick accents, there is a risk that the editor will reject the original interview due to perceived lack of clarity—an evaluation that seems, on its face, beyond reproach but is, in fact, deeply racialized.

Overall, the industry's unspoken definition of "good talkers" creates raciosonic disciplining in story production. The preference for speakers who are comfortable on air leads to the greater use of experts from white-dominant institutions; the preference for "commonly understood" accents reflects the perceptions of both editors and audience members, disproportionately excluding foreign accents. Further, employees of color noted that foreign accents associated with white ethnic groups, such as Italian and French accents, were reviewed more positively than accents of Congolese and Sudanese sources. In filtering out nonwhite voices through the racialized evaluation of sources, the industry produces content that reinforces existing white voice standards.

Marta, a Latinx reporter who has worked at five local stations, expressed her frustration about these ongoing difficulties, particularly amid broader organizational discussion of the *need* to diversify sourcing practices.

> I am so tired of public radio people hiring me to help them diversify their audience or to help them diversify their sourcing and then not letting the sources that I found on the air. "We can't understand them," or "they're going to turn off the white people."

White institutional space structures the work of sourcing for public radio employees. When designating whose accents are appropriate for air, the ultimate test of intelligibility is whether the typical public radio listener would hear it without strain—that is, will "the white people" get it? Still, within these constraints, my respondents have found ways to expand sources beyond the traditional white American accents associated with "good talkers."

Raciosonic Resistance

Whereas raciosonic disciplining results in narrative distortion, raciosonic resistance results in possibilities for transformation. When an employee pushes against the raciosonic disciplining they undergo in a white-dominant industry like public radio, they are making room for a more equitable and democratic public sphere—often at some personal expense.

Within the public radio industry, respondents of color pushed to broaden the conception of "good talker" in two main ways: spending more time preparing and editing sources and conducting interviews in foreign languages with an English translation. These strategies opened up space for a wider diversity of sources while still producing work that reached the (white) standards of the industry.

Some respondents agreed that if guests, sources, or experts were not used to speaking into a microphone, they were less likely to be deemed "good talkers." A little preparation and patience often helped get past the stiltedness of inexperience. I spoke to Patricia, a Black editor who was committed to expanding the notion of a good talker. She had a mentor early on in her career who guided her through how to prepare guests on a live show. She recognized that "good talkers" are made, not found, but that it is not a typical part of a reporter's training to elicit "good talk" from folks who don't have comfort speaking to media:

> It's not *really* about being a bad talker. It's about making people comfortable, helping them to explain things, and I think that, when we look at diversity, it's like, certain interviewers work to make people comfortable . . . which makes for better talking.

Another producer had strategies to ensure the clarity of English-language learners on air, suggesting, "Let's actually listen to people and what they're saying and what they're trying to say and come back to them. 'Is this what you mean? Did I understand you correctly?'" Meanwhile, a Black editor, Jane, told me how a mentor had guided her through preparing guests for a live show.

> Sometimes when I hear someone bomb on a live show, it's like, I wonder how they were prepped. Did they understand the parameters? . . . I don't think that producers are trained . . . on the responsibility that they have to prep guests and that they, like, make the show in that way.

In addition, I heard frustration over the speed with which white editors would dismiss voices as incomprehensible, even if they added to the story. This producer developed a list of editing techniques she could use to help make the accent "work":

> I would often bring back tape, and I said I'd spoken to an Asian American man. He has an accent. I say, "Maybe we can present it this way." Instead, you would get, "This person isn't going to be comprehensible"; or "How much Spanish are you going to put on the air?"; or "People will tune out when they hear Spanish" or whatever the language is. I say, "No, no, no. We can put it on, and then we can summarize."

Both examples above showcase that the voice standards in broadcasting can be shifted to ensure clear enunciation and speech that is interesting and dynamic, *without* excluding guests who lack training and experience within dominant institutional spaces. However, producers, reporters, and editors are not systematically taught to guide their guests on how to ensure that their voices come through clearly and compellingly on air.

Journalists can also diversify the sources and voices eligible for broadcast by conducting interviews in foreign languages and translating them. However, newsrooms often undervalue the labor of translation work by their multilingual employees. Deirdre, a multilingual reporter of color, walked me through the added labor that goes into this process:

> Let's say I conduct an interview in Spanish. It's an hour-long interview in Spanish. Now, I have to transcribe that interview from Spanish [audio] to [written] Spanish and then from Spanish to English. And then I have to pull the important parts in English into a *separate* document to then organize it into a story. So, even in the production of that story, you're adding two extra steps. You have to really be committed to wanting to do it, because otherwise it's not worth the time.

When I asked Deirdre whether her extra work was compensated, she explained that most of this labor remains in the background, invisible to her editor:

> [My editor] doesn't recognize the amount of work that I'm doing on the back end. I resorted to having to pay somebody [online] to transcribe my Spanish stories into Spanish . . . and then I can just transcribe whatever I want into English, but then I need [help from colleagues or friends] sometimes, because I wanna make sure that I got the translation exactly right.

Sometimes, bilingual producers of color must do this translation and interpretation work for (mostly white) monolingual English-speaking reporters. A bilingual Latinx producer, Javier, felt put upon at being used as a translator to help report immigration stories, when he is trying to build his own portfolio of immigration stories as a freelancer on top of his producer position:

> As one of the only Spanish speakers at my station, I have been thrust into this role of interpreting and translating for reporters who are doing immigration work. I'm not compensated for it. It just gets exhausting doing this work for reporters who are very talented, who I adore and admire as colleagues, of course, but who kind of rely on our labor to translate and listen to the interpretations so that they can get the story right. That takes away time [with which] you could be doing your own story on immigration stuff.

These examples point to a racialized double standard when it comes to *which* linguistic competencies hold enough social currency in the American radio context. Translation and interpretation work remain undercompensated and undervalued as a journalistic credential, even when the work is necessary for producing a story about a non-English-speaking community. While the practice allows for a broader range of sources, it increases the labor (but not the recognition) for translators and interpreters. Any pushback puts their own jobs at risk. Michelle noted that, as a lower-level reporter, she was less able to resist these extra duties:

> It was always very explicit: "This is why we're not going to do it. This person is not going to be comprehensible." And I said I disagree, and I was overruled and I didn't have a lot of political power in that job. So, I often would lose, and sometimes I would push back, but I didn't have the power that I have now to push back in the same way. I needed my job.

At times, journalists of color found themselves acting as cultural brokers between fellow journalists and communities of color. Maria, a Latinx reporter, put it plainly: "All the nonwhite voices—All the nonwhite people are bringing them to the station." Even transplants to new locales are looked to for help finding "diverse sources." Amber, a Black reporter, pointed out this dynamic, stating, "I'm not from here. There's no reason for me to know these communities of color any better than anybody else." Yet it was incumbent upon her to build trust and relationships with communities of color, not just Latinx communities, because the source list was otherwise overwhelmingly white.

Amber's experience building contacts at a new station indicates that sources are hard earned across communities of color. She explained that she did not see the same effort by her mostly white colleagues. "I was the only one intentionally trying to do it on a consistent basis. I really did try to intentionally sit down with communities that I'm not a part of, like the Asian American community, and just to get a sense of what's going on for them and how we can do better. I don't feel that was an across-the-board effort." This dynamic is consonant with research by sociologist Melissa Abad, who shows that nonwhite workers are often assigned tasks at work because of assumptions about their racial and ethnic knowledge,[16] rather than being allocated tasks based on their official role in an organization.

PROTECTING MARGINALIZED SOURCES

Even as respondents have developed strategies to include a more diverse array of sources, there are additional considerations for bringing these sources into white institutional spaces. Producers who bring in guests from marginalized communities recognize that even if guests and sources are approved, they would still be subject to the pressures of performing within a white institutional space.

Angela indicated that there was a crucial second consideration after getting her sources green-lit: "I'm constantly thinking about diversifying our sources. I'm thinking about how we keep those folks safe." Producers work with hosts of radio programs and podcasts to ensure that their scripts are both accurate and true to the host's voice, as well as creating a list of relevant questions to ask guests and sources. Some producers have quite positive and close working relationships with their hosts. Others find that a host's own racial ignorance can stifle what types of conversation will make it on air. For instance, Angela reflected on how a host's whiteness matters when writing questions for them, because it often shapes the host's comfort in talking about race and identity.

> To some extent, you're using the host as a tool and, especially for our listeners, they tend to skew older and whiter. [The host] was a pretty good stand-in for our audience as it was when I started. Writing for [the host] and getting him to be comfortable talking about race, identity, and gender have been uphill [battles].

Respondents who produce reports for white hosts often think twice before inviting a community member of color onto the program. One producer recalled dealing with this by "apologizing for the shit that [guests of color] would have to endure for actually coming on and sharing their story."

Valerie, a Black producer, lamented that

> there are stories that I just won't do, because I know that they won't do it in a way that is fair to the interview subject. A lot of the times, I'll stay away from these stories with white hosts or reporters, because they can be very patronizing. There's a lot of explaining that you have to do ahead of time on really basic things that I feel I shouldn't have to be explaining.

Another Black producer, Brianna, noted how she would try to write the script for the white host of her program to encourage him to ask questions about race and identity. However, particularly when speaking on the subject of police brutality, the white male host would water down the script to avoid the subject directly:

> Instead of asking so directly, he'll change it and say, like, "How are you feeling right now?" And the guest will be like, "What do you mean?" Like, "Uh, this is an awful moment, I don't know how you want me to answer." And they'll be so clearly offended, but I had written the question so directly.

The host's discomfort negatively impacts the experiences of Black guests, and it makes Brianna reticent to bring on activists of color. The work she must do to smooth out interactions between guests and hosts is consonant with sociologist Jelani Ince's ethnography of an interracial parish. He finds that in order to promote diversity and inclusion in historically white organizations, people of color in the space must make efforts to smooth over uncomfortable interactions.[17] This work of "smoothing" manifests in the public radio industry in the complex considerations and interpersonal work required when producers of color bring in sources from marginalized backgrounds.

The Ethics of Listening

I have elaborated in this chapter, as well as in previous ones, that there is a substantive consideration of the white professional class's comfort and ease in public radio story production. One reporter often heard that "you have to be able to understand [the accents] while you're driving down a highway or on your morning commute." The "you" presumably belonged to the imagined white, professional-class public radio listener. This consideration reifies the sonic color line because it centers white sensibilities within the public radio soundscape. As Jennifer Lynn Stoever expresses in her description of the segregated American soundscape:

> Without ever consciously expressing the sentiment, white Americans often feel entitled to respect for their sensibilities, sensitivities, and tastes, and to their implicit, sometimes violent, control over the soundscape of an ostensibly "free," "open," and "public" space.[18]

This consideration of whether white Americans would understand particular story lines and accents has caused frustration for public radio employees from communities of color, who have been raised outside of these white institutional spaces. Seema, a South Asian American reporter, pointed out that her own ability to hear accents from marginalized communities came from experience and exposure.

> Our white colleagues aren't as familiar with accents as we are. And, so, I personally feel like the more exposure to accents you've had, the better you are at understanding accents. And me and the other reporters have just a really high tolerance. And then we really like hearing accents as well. Um, so this is a very ongoing frustration with us, because the editors will just be like, "I don't understand them." And lately that's been a really big thing with Chinese people.

Their own sense of responsibility to listen to different accents has been structured not just by "exposure," as Seema rightly notes, but also by their own racialized subjectivities. If public radio caters to the white professional class, there is not much dissonance for those white employees raised in white-dominant spaces, their whiteness remaining unmarked throughout. However, as "outsiders within," public radio employees of color are better able to hear the whiteness of public radio's auditory filter and to consider how it categorizes voices that diverge from ways of speaking associated with whiteness as "other."

Daphne, a Black reporter, identifies the effort made to listen as a key component beyond "exposure":

> We never say [their accent is really hard to understand] about someone who has a British accent. Ever. And, so, yeah, and I get it, like our vernacular is maybe a little more attuned to be able to comprehend those things. But sometimes it's also about just maybe listening a little harder or something.

This comment fits with research in linguistic anthropology on how the perception of race and ethnicity shapes listening practices. For instance, Jonathan Rosa's ethnography of a Chicago public high school demonstrates how the white hegemonic listening ear erased the language proficiencies of Latinx youth at the school, marking them as "limited English proficient" despite their bilingualism, due to processes of racialization that mapped onto the institution's dominant language.[19] Once the social actors of the school, at all levels from student to principal, were primed to believe that the speaker was a racialized subject, that person's intelligibility as a speaker diminished.

The sonic color line has inhibited recognition across axes of racialized difference because of the way that race has structured our society. Many of my respondents, however, feel a responsibility to hear the narratives of potential guests and sources that fall outside immediate legibility in white institutional space. Thus far, their sense of responsibility has manifested as translation work from sources to hosts to presumed audiences, due to the constraints of the white institutional space in which they are embedded. But the reflections that public radio employees of color offer provide insight on what it might sound like to upend the white racial structure of the public radio industry. In an interview with Anna North for *Vox* in 2019 (notably, prior to the racial reckoning of 2020), Lourdes "Lulu" Garcia-Navarro offers a glimpse of how she enacted this in her show on NPR at the time:

> One of the things I've really tried to do on my show is try and retrain the audience about what to expect. For so long, we've been taught that a certain type of person has authority, and that person has to speak in a certain way; they have to have a certain pedigree, a certain background. And that's because that's all we've been given.[20]

What if, instead of bringing nonnormative voices to white American legibility, the white American listening ear was decentered, even challenged throughout the industry? I consider some structural mechanisms that could make this more of the norm in the conclusion that follows.

Conclusion

RECKONING WITH PUBLIC RADIO

The tension between the mission of public radio and its failure to serve marginalized publics has plagued the institution from its very formation. Public radio's founding technical standards, hiring networks, and programming priorities resulted in a predominantly white workforce and audience, both of which solidified in subsequent years. As the network was finding its footing, a group of well-credentialed white women came to define the network's sonic aesthetic. When the network faced budget cuts, it responded by increasing its reliance on corporate underwriters and affluent, civic-minded donors—the white audience it had cultivated both intentionally and unintentionally in earlier years. Together, these elements have entrenched a divide between the pluralism that public radio espouses and its orientation toward the prototypical listener-member. And lately, particularly in the wake of 2020's racial reckoning in the United States, this divide has become far harder to square.

The stakes of creating a more inclusive media ecosystem have taken on new urgency since June 2020. In the wake of George Floyd's murder at the hands of police, there was a broader racial reckoning in how the news gets covered. This reckoning made its way into workplace production processes, laying bare the uncompensated and enormous extra work taken on by employees of color. Their labor is used to evidence diversity; this limits the potential for their work to be fully harnessed toward the goal of an expanded soundscape. I ended my fieldwork in spring 2021, and at that point, public radio journalists of color I spoke with were expressing a range of emotions—most notably exhaustion, skepticism, and hope.

Some were exhausted and frustrated that the conversations that had been deemed irrelevant by management months earlier were coming to the fore again:

> We had a whole meeting about a racist headline [that had appeared before this racial reckoning], and [another] story that [appeared to use a criminal mugshot]. So we talked about that for an hour today, which they didn't do [when the earlier story came out], because now we're in a period of racial reckoning. So that, like, shows me the difference of like, audience feedback [that] happened months ago. And now we're talking about it today. It's been exhausting. It feels really late. I feel like I'm not actually part of the conversation, and that I'm witnessing a lot of people catch up. Oftentimes it feels like a waste of my day to go to a Zoom meeting about racial equity that I feel like I've been in eighty times already.

Some were suspicious about whether the shift toward supporting Black lives was a passing phase:

> I have conversations with my [white] colleagues, it's so weird to see them jumping so hard toward the Black Lives Matter vibe. I've talked to my Black colleagues about this, because on the one hand, you want to be like, okay, the progress, but on the other hand, you cannot help but eyeroll because where was this six months ago? It was not the vibe at all six months ago. It was much different. And so what I'm trying to say here is there's a lot of virtue signaling. It's a lot of people who want to publicly appear to be woke.

Some wondered whether there would be a few initiatives that signal progress without introducing deeper institutional change:

> I'm very skeptical of white liberals. I feel like they have a history of, like, they will give us just enough so that we don't burn the whole thing down, and I feel like that's a conversation that we're having.

Another reporter noted that this skepticism will not abate without larger-scale changes in the industry. She remarked, "We must change the structures in order for any of these good ideas to succeed. And I believe [there are] people who really want change. But yeah. It's not enough."

One thread of common experience is the fatigue that public radio employees of color felt during this reckoning. As one of my respondents, a Black journalist, put it in late 2020:

Journalism has always said that it holds people accountable, that it sheds a light, you know, where it needs to be shed. But I feel like people of color are really the ones who are pushing and defining what that really looks like, because journalism has for so long been subjected to the status quo in many ways, especially around policing, especially around white supremacy. And so I am grateful to be in this conversation in this moment. I also think it's incredibly exhausting. And that we're not getting paid extra to do that work, you know, but it's so important and that's where it's messy, because it's like we all, we want this to get better, it needs to work better. Because there are literal lives on the line. Damn. It gets tiring. It's so tiring.

Despite all this exhaustion and cynicism, there were still paths of possibility that kept reporters hopeful:

Public media is in such a unique position to actually provide public service. I do hear from other people that a lot of their pushback from the editors and stuff [. . .] has been, our audience wouldn't this or our audience wouldn't that. They're worried about the donation dollars because otherwise, how can they do what they do, which is important.

But there's so much value in just embedding, taking time to just be out in these communities that are not being reported on. That's something that I try to do; I really don't have time, but maybe if things calm down, maybe I will be able to just be there. Being mindful of reaching those other audiences and providing a service to other audiences is something that I would love. The thing that I really love about this particular industry, at least in my station, we have time to get the stories right. It's not like the newspaper, the television cycle. We have more time to get in depth.

The journalists of color I spoke with were deeply invested in the mission to serve a diverse set of publics that might not be the target audiences in commercial broadcasting. Their critiques of their industry originate in their belief in its possibility.

Where Do We Go from Here?

Throughout this book, I have systematically laid out what public radio employees of color have told me, pulling the threads of common experience to better understand the issues of the industry. At the end of most interviews, I asked participants what they would change about public radio if they were in charge.

Here are some of the diagnoses of the industry as told by public radio employees of color themselves. Each of these suggestions connects back to tackling the foundational issues of public radio I have identified throughout the book: its formation as a white racialized organization, the feminized white voice as the network's dominant mode of speaking, and its dependence on both individual contributions and corporate underwriters in lieu of genuine public funding.

BREAK PUBLIC MEDIA'S MORAL CERTITUDE

I have established that public radio was formed and developed as a white racialized industry. To address this structural issue in the industry, leaders must confront the gap between public radio's moral certitude and the way that many of its employees from marginalized backgrounds have felt within the space. Tomasa, a Latina broadcaster, told me that she questioned how reformable public radio is because of its self-image as being better than other news organizations.

> It's the worst thing about [public radio] because they are so convinced of how great they are, because everybody has always told them how great they are, that they believe how great they are. And then you're the greatest, so you don't have problems. That's why it's going to be really challenging to change the culture.

Linda, a Black reporter, echoed that sentiment: "There was so much certainty that what we were doing was good and right." Connie, an Asian American producer, discussed how her white colleagues had a sense that they could not be racist because of their association with a good nonprofit and mission-oriented media organization.

> They think that they are good people. They are the good white people who took the pay cut and worked all those years and plowed through this for nothing so that there would be the good people making the good media. That makes it very hard for them to see that they could be racist, or that they could have unconscious bias.

This certitude is linked to how public radio got its start as a white racialized organization. When white male founders who had experience in educational radio and government bureaucracy built the network, they did so with marginalized publics in mind, but not with genuine consultation of the groups they imagined serving. Because they thought their intentions were good, they were surprised to receive a scathing review from the Task Force on

Minorities of 1977. Because minoritized listeners and creators were never given a seat at the table, the founders did not get the pushback that would have been required to make the network racially pluralistic in practice.

Sasha, a Black broadcaster, noted a similar certitude among the mostly white management structure she has worked under for decades. When I asked her what legacy she would like to leave in the industry, she told me, "My goal is to knock holes in their certitude and make them realize that the structure is what's fundamentally flawed. They have great intentions. The road to hell is paved with good intentions." Sasha continued to note that now is the perfect time to do this work to make the industry realize its shortcomings. They have experienced the racial reckoning, and "now they're uncomfortable."

CHANGE PRODUCTION PRACTICES

The bulk of part II of this book has focused on raciosonic disciplining: institutional practices that mark voices and sounds as partial, provincial, or altogether outside of an organization's sonic aesthetic. Deeply held beliefs in journalism on "good talkers" and what counts as a valuable story cannot be dismantled by changing organizational policy on production processes alone. That said, there are ways that public radio's leadership can ameliorate these ills by listening to "outsiders within" the industry. This suggestion builds on journalism scholar Chelsea Peterson-Salahuddin's work in defining intersectional journalism. She identified thirteen creators of news who used an intersectional approach and interviewed them to ascertain how such journalism was operationalized. Taking their responses seriously as a roadmap toward a more inclusive and multiperspectival journalism, she concluded that sourcing from marginalized communities and considering intragroup complexity in journalistic analyses are two key features for operationalizing intersectionality in news content.[1]

My interviewees offered me rich insights by telling me of not just their challenges, but the ways they resist raciosonic disciplining. Based on how they articulated the story production process, people of color in public radio have revealed to me a roadmap for raciosonic resistance that offers alternatives in storytelling. First, skills like translation and expanding source lists need to be made visible as additional labor and compensated accordingly, because, as I have shown, public radio employees of color are often left in charge of this without considering the disproportionate workload that it leaves them with.

In addition, there are a lot of ways that production teams can consider and define more precisely what vague and subjective terms such as "our audience" and "listeners like you" and "good talker" mean. These are still useful terms of art if they are explicitly defined with more precision and can lead to generative conversations. Some employees of color I spoke to belong to teams like these, and they feel more empowered to tell stories that speak to communities that extend beyond the stereotypical, presumed listener-member. For instance, Javi, a Latinx reporter, noted that he and his team are able to have nuanced conversations about communities of color because they do not center whiteness in their pitch sessions:

> It was great to be in pitch meetings where we could flesh out stories together. The editors, producers, and the host are asking good questions. And that's only possible because of the diversity of the team. Black people, mixed-race people, children of immigrants. We are explicitly having clarifying conversations across difference, but we know we want to get into the nuance and specificity of the community being covered.

Javi went on to note that this enabled him to create more interesting stories about communities of color rather than one-dimensional pieces that, even if positive, are unsatisfying to him.

Key to the changing production practices is an investment in training and mentorship that encourages a more inclusive and multiperspectival approach to audio journalism. Even if my participants were fatigued and cynical about the institution of public radio itself, they cited key moments in their careers that made the difference, mentioning people who took the time to coach them on technical skills or to help them navigate white institutional space.

Although many of these mentorships developed informally, a notable initiative to institutionalize this support is a program called NextGenRadio. Housed under NPR and run by Doug Mitchell, this is not a diversity program. Rather, it is a one-week training program in digital-first audio storytelling. It was founded in 2000 to foster a range of perspectives in the public radio industry.[2] The program is inclusive: no university training is needed, nor is there a requirement to have journalism experience.[3] Further, the program is free. Participants gain both technical skills and community. Many alumni of the program note keeping in touch with both Mitchell and the rest of their cohort, and looking out for one another as they work to secure jobs, keep jobs, and do pathbreaking work in the industry. Mentorship and connection through programs like NextGen have been key to keeping people motivated to work toward a more equitable public media.

PUBLICLY FUND PUBLIC MEDIA

Through an analysis of public broadcasting archives and marketing materials, I have shown throughout this book that public radio has become reliant on a set of mostly white, affluent donors for financial survival. To resolve the fundamental tension between public radio's mission to reflect and serve all Americans and its entrenched white dominance, it is necessary to rethink the public radio industry's funding structure altogether. Underfunding by the state leads to a dependence on donors, which promotes personal attachments to public radio. It might sound daunting and perhaps overly ambitious to completely change this model, since it's been in place for fifty years at the time of this project's writing. But then when we look at any other democratic nation with a public broadcaster, it becomes clear that this model is both uniquely American and not an inevitability.

The United States, with respect to NPR, relies on a more variable and thus more tenuous system of philanthropy and member patronship than do Great Britain, Australia, and Canada with respect to their peer institutions: the BBC, ABC, and CBC.[4] As Victor Pickard notes, our media system is dominated by oligopolies that are lightly regulated and predominantly commercial. On the global scale, "[w]e currently have a weakly funded public system that is highly susceptible to political and economic capture."[5] I join Pickard and other media historians in the insistence that the way forward is a new structure of public media that is fully publicly funded. As he argues, "[f]ree from the economic imperative of appealing to wealthy owners, investors, advertisers, and high-income audiences, media outlets could abandon various forms of redlining to include entire classes and communities previously neglected."[6] Such a move would not completely remove the pressures of elite capture, as it is clear that more robustly funded alternatives such as the BBC and the CBC has been charged with their own political and aesthetic biases that stem from their association with government bureaucracy. Still, the change would be a necessary first step in ameliorating the reliance on public radio's older, white donor base, thereby reducing the need to appeal to the constituency that has been overly catered to in this industry.

As it stands now, NPR is in a cycle of crisis.[7] Every few years, right-wing legislatures and politicians spread rhetoric about seeking to "defund public media." There is a common counter to this rhetoric: that public media is allocated only a drop in the bucket from government funding and is supported mostly by donors and sponsors. This variety of counter is often coupled with pledge drives: "We rely on 'listeners like you'" to save public radio. This cycle keeps public media in a defensive position; rather than seeking more government funding, defenders of public radio call for legislators to not *further* chip away at the meager public funding, then turn to private donors and sponsors for help. And again, this cycle has consequences for who has influence in public media. According to a 2024 study published by the Center for Study of Responsive Law authored by legal analyst Michael Swerdlow, "public media's governing boards consist mainly of representatives from corporate donors. This financing and governance model incentivizes public media to reflect the interests of professional, affluent listeners mainly in coastal urban centers."[8]

Recently, media professionals and analysts have argued that a reliance on donors can be effective so long as media organizations seek out a racially and ethnically diverse set of donor listeners.[9] Indeed, recent studies in the sociology of culture and philanthropy have demonstrated a growing non-white donor base in the nonprofit cultural industries.[10] However, we must consider inclusivity through an intersectional lens. If all the solutions to this fraught relationship between public radio audiences and workers of color involve the creation of a more racially diverse donor class, we ignore the need to serve working-class audiences.[11] This dynamic—the emphasis on looking for a racially diverse set of donors—is particularly concerning in the public radio industry, as public media might be the only way to reflect a working-class public because of the prevalence of corporate interests in the commercial media space.[12]

It might sound unfeasible to completely change this model, as public radio reflects back on its first fifty years. But when we look at any other democratic nation with a public broadcaster, it becomes clear just how exceptional this funding model is. This exceptionalism may give us hope—other nations provide clear financial models, ready for study if we are ready as a populace to begin to treat media and information as a public good. This preoccupation has only become more salient in the twenty-first century, as an emerging podcast industry has ushered in a new "golden age of audio." While podcasting was at first considered a potentially democratizing force, this optimism was tempered by how the industry quickly became commodified,[13] and as public radio personalities brought their social capital to the private sector.[14]

Toward an Equitable American Soundscape

This book has demonstrated the utility of centering sound in how we think about organizational life and racial inequality. I have offered an account of the dominant American listening ear through an analysis of the public radio industry. By analyzing how race and sound are conaturalized in the public radio industry, this book provides insight into the media's role in upholding the sonic color line through its perpetuation of an ideal standard language.

This analysis of voice as a site of racialized evaluation shaped by institutional processes has resonance in other organizational contexts. As noted previously, sociological research on inequality has begun to identify some of the material consequences of linguistic discrimination, a mechanism by which landlords, teachers, and employers exclude nonwhite applicants. In analyzing the sonic construction of racial difference within organizations, networks, and nations, the book complements these studies of how linguistic discrimination functions, explaining how linguistic discrimination is *formed* and maintained through institutional processes.

This book's analytic frame combines insights from the concept of racialized organizations and the concept of the sonic color line. The framework could be applied beyond the case presented here to understand the role of voice performance in reifying inequalities within white-dominant organizations. As more and more organizations face a "racial reckoning,"[15] this framework is timely, as it moves us away from simple measures of surface-level progress toward understanding the deep cultural shifts needed to transform the experience of employees of color in historically white organizations.

Beyond the industry under study, these findings seek to shift the public debate regarding workplace racial equity and inclusion. Revealing the patterns of racial exclusion in public radio also exposes the more complex, historically constructed cultural barriers to racial inclusion such as language standards and technological access. Highlighting and recognizing the communicative labor taken on by employees of color makes audible some of the cultural work that has gone unrecognized because of its invisibility within racialized organizational spaces.

These findings have parallels to the experiences of racialization in other professional spaces such as higher education, the aviation industry, tech organizations, and governmental organizations.[16] The sustained focus on how employees of color make sense of themselves in these professional contexts, coupled with the insight that the Du Boisian color line is complex and multisensory in impact, can offer us a way to move beyond listing barriers and toward a focus on the agency of racialized subjects. The impact of this excavation is twofold.

First, in recording the experiences of workers of color in a particular industry across organizational contexts, the research of this book creates a rich dataset that provides a different perspective from that of the institutional archive. Attention to nonwhite voices within these organizations corrects the organizational archive to consider the experience of nonwhite workers in a predominantly white field. This analysis offers a new path forward on how to study inequality in racialized organizations.

Second, in making the unheard heard, this research enables employers to begin to acknowledge and reckon with the work their employees of color do that has largely gone unrecognized due to existing organizational structures. As organizations work to transform their structures to become more racially just, they have a responsibility to consider the current impact on employees doing uncompensated work in navigating these spaces.

The Politics of (Mis)hearing and (Mis)recognition beyond Organizational Life

At the base of my sociological inquiry are these questions: Who gets heard in public space and why? How do some voices get amplified and coded as authoritative, while others get excluded or relegated to side characters?

While I set my research project within the particular industry of public radio and the production that occurs there, this book is ultimately concerned with a larger phenomenon haunting American society: that of testimonial injustice. According to philosopher Miranda Fricker, testimonial injustice occurs when "a speaker receives an unfair deficit of credibility from a hearer owing to prejudice on the hearer's part."[17] Fricker notes, for example, that a listener may presume the speaker's race, class, or gender, indicating a social charge. Crucially, the social charge carries with it an *epistemic charge*, as the presumption of these sets of identities plays a role in inflating or deflating the credibility of that speaker.[18]

As Tanja Dreher writes on listening across difference, it is not a simple shift of being able to hear and receive knowledge from a racial "other," who normally have to hear and know intimately the dominant white voice due to its power in institutional life. Instead, it is to "gravitate towards understanding networks of privilege and power and one's own location in them."[19]

What might the world sound like if we began to dismantle the racialized valuation of voice, especially in institutions that hold material resources? How would we all relate to the world differently if we opened up what the voices of authority and importance sound like?

When I asked Rodrigo, a Latinx reporter at a local station, about how his station conceives of their audience, he echoed what you've heard throughout this book: "I think they see them as very, uh, white and English speaking. Very American-centric . . . and it's, well, obviously very much reflected in the reporting, right?"

Crucially, he ponders on what could be otherwise:

There are these dumb, juicy stories about the Latino community in my area, whereas you only hear a few stories from my neighborhood. It's very unfortunate. Because there's just a wealth of stories there. I live in a Latinx neighborhood, you know, and our office is right on the border of it. There are a wealth of stories and beautiful people whose stories deserve to be told, but nobody's telling them, because there are no [other] Spanish speakers at the station and they've thought that audiences maybe wouldn't want to hear that.

When I hear Rodrigo say that, I feel a deep yearning: I want to hear those dumb, juicy stories! And I do not want it to be a struggle to push stories through from pitch to air because of where those neighborhood residents sit in the US social order.

In a 2019 interview with Rachel Toor of the *Chronicle of Higher Education*, Tressie McMillan Cottom discusses how the norms of writing can inhibit one's full voice from coming out:

Voice is the deviation from norms. And I am very committed to my intellectual ideas' sounding as much like my natural voice as possible because part of my personal political project is naturalizing the sound of expert information in a Black American woman's voice. And I want you to be able to hear that through my syntax as a way of naturalizing that syntax.[20]

McMillan Cottom is speaking about the written voice here, but one can easily see how that spills over from the page to the airwaves. One can also see how her voice, like Ayesha Rascoe's voice, can be heard as a Black American woman's voice of authority from the southern United States. These are professionals who offer insights from their own vantage point and expertise, in their own voices. They bring us a broader bandwidth of voices of authority, and they open up bandwidth for others to sound more like themselves.

Dave, a Black manager, has worked for decades to bring in a diverse set of public radio professionals. His reaction to an on-air voice, presumably Rascoe's, is both proof of individual voices making a difference *and* of the work ahead of us:

> I heard a young lady on last week reporting from the White House. She sounded young and she sounded Black. I remember thinking, "Finally." The fact that I remembered that . . . it still sticks out. Still, everybody else still sounds the same. I was trained to sound public radio–like. What's happening is, there's finally getting some acceptance. People can attune their ears because they should be interested in the story.

As Dave notes, the voice gave him hope and reminded him of the norm. These hopeful breaths of fresh air are still heard as reminders of the broader atmosphere. Or, a voice breaking the mold is proof that the mold is still there. It is that same mold that Chenjerai Kumanyika, whose insights were laid out in the introduction to this book, had to break through to sound like himself.

Consider, for a moment, the stories lost when employees of color do not feel comfortable pitching or voicing stories from their own perspective. Consider all the insights that don't push through to make it to the status of authority, all the voices that do not get the chance to make waves. The people I spoke with for my research are largely still in media. But I think a lot about those who left before I got a chance to speak with them.[21]

I have identified some of the complex barriers that keep all these voices from making it through without struggle. We must remember that the point of dismantling barriers is not only to ameliorate inequalities—although that is a plenty good reason in and of itself. It is also to get to the point of truly listening across difference, breaking down institutional barriers so we can fully experience the depth and richness and juiciness that public radio stories can have. There is still a wealth of stories yet to be told in all their complexity on our public airwaves, and unless we attend to these institutional hurdles for people of color, we will all continue to miss out.

ACKNOWLEDGMENTS

I am grateful to the many people and communities that have made this book possible. I'll start with my dissertation committee, who helped make the research for this book a reality. As I spent the first few months of my graduate program trying to figure out what sociology was, I was fortunate to have had the guidance of José Itzigsohn, Michael Kennedy, and Dan Hirschman. I had heard of graduate school as a site meant to "break you down to build you back up." But from these mentors, I got quite the opposite: they built with me, and they took my ideas seriously even as I questioned whether my inquiries "fit" into sociology. This was lucky, because I likely would not have had the patience to stick around if I weren't able to pursue my ideas as freely as I had! José told me to never worry about whether something was "sociological" in the mainstream sense, and he pushed me to think through the theoretical implications of my ideas until I, too, could see their importance to the field. Michael offered and continues to offer endless generosity, an open door, and an open ear; from day one, he displayed by example the importance of community in intellectual pursuit. Dan taught me how to be a thoughtful scholar and colleague; I looked to him to learn how to publish, how to coauthor, how to offer generous feedback, and how to navigate graduate school and the years following.

Thank you to Susan Smulyan and Paja Faudree. As I moved beyond the department, Susan expanded the scope of my imagination through her insights on radio history, communications, and archival methods, all while encouraging me to keep writing through doubt. Paja's rich understanding of how to talk about and think about language profoundly shaped my data collection and interview process. Together, all five committee members were essential to shaping this project and to supporting me throughout the graduate school process. I would also like to thank mentors Nic John Ramos, Josh Shepperd, and Jennifer Stoever for their support and guidance from the early stages when this book was still just a vague idea. Thank you also to the

National Science Foundation and the American Association for University Women, who helped to fund the data collection and writing process.

I am lucky to have entered graduate school with a cohort of four hilarious and caring women: Chinyere Agbai, Amanda Ball, Danielle Falzon, and Ieva Zumbyte (love also to Thomas Marlow, whom I consider an honorary fifth cohort). I deeply appreciated learning from and alongside the rest of the graduate student worker community at Brown University, especially Tina Park, Amy Chin, Ricarda Hammer, and Syeda Masood.

In my current role, I am grateful to my colleagues at the University of Minnesota for offering their enthusiastic support, especially Kathy Hull for her leadership as chair of the Sociology Department and my mentoring team: Awa Abdi, Michelle Phelps, and Michael Walker. I am glad to have found a wonderful home with colleagues who are intellectually curious, supportive, and kind. And my relocation to the Midwest was made infinitely less lonely because I had two of my most important thought partners and friends nearby: prabhdeep singh kehal and Marquel Norton. Thank you for surrounding me with love, sharing your brilliance with me, and letting me ramble to you about this and all things.

I had a tremendous team helping me to mold my project into a book with a clear throughline. Princeton University Press has been a joy to work with. Meagan Levinson, thank you for your faith in the book at its proposal stage. Thank you to the editing team Erik Beranek, Eric Crahan, and Rachael Levay for guiding me through the entire publication process, providing clarity at each step. Thank you to Norman Ware, whose detailed copyedits offered me a feeling of peace as the book went out to production.

Many thanks to Letta Page for her edits on the full first draft of the manuscript, making the final product much more streamlined, organized, and accessible. To the anonymous peer reviewers, for their wise suggestions in peer review. To Marceleen Mosher for her excellent insight into the donor relations process and assistance on research. And to Angela Garbes and Shereen Marisol Meraji, whose feedback helped me strengthen how the manuscript would reverberate beyond the academy.

Thanks to the Franconia Sculpture Park and the University of Minnesota's Center for the Study of Race, Indigeneity, Disability, Gender, and Sexuality, who each provided funded writing retreats as I completed the manuscript. This book benefited greatly from feedback at conferences and reading groups from 2017 to 2023—to name a few, the Society for the Study of Social Problems, the Black Sociologists Association, the American Sociological Association, the Social Science History Association, the Media

Futures Hub at the University of New South Wales in Sydney, Australia, codirected by Tanja Dreher, the NEH Radio and Decolonization Seminar led by Andrea Stanton, Rebecca Scales, and Alejandra Bronfman, Juho Korhonen's workshop on historical sociology, and the International Sociological Association. Thank you to my various writing groups that offered both encouragement and smart ways to strengthen my writing. These interlocutors include Jenn Lena, Rachel Skaggs, Gillian Gualtieri, Phillipa Chong, Tania Aparicio-Morales, Jess Feldman, Hannah Baron, Rithika Ramamurthy, Dennis Hogan, Matthew Ellis, Claire Grandy, Laura Doering, John Robinson, Kim Pernell, Alicia Sheares, Dunja Antunovic, and Carolina Velloso.

I am grateful to family and friends who knew me well before I embarked on this project and were willing to read draft presentations, chapters, and proposals, ensuring that I sounded legible outside of sociology: Noha Ahmed, Chris Baumohl, Whitney Braunstein, Lilly Fisher, Grace House, Kwame Obimpe, Catherine Roseman, and Martha Wydysh.

Thank you to my family, especially my mom, Kathleen Garbes-Persse, and my dad, Isosceles Garbes, who have always encouraged my curiosity and offered unconditional love as I pursued this path. Gratitude beyond measure to my partner Sofía Pacheco-Fores and our dogs Biscuit and Raskol for being a sounding board and a dream support system.

I would like to acknowledge the hard work of archivists who have made this research possible: the team at the National Public Broadcasting Archives, in particular Laura Beth Schnitker, and at NPR's Department of Research, Archives, and Data, in particular Julie Rogers. Finally, I would like to thank the people to whom this book is dedicated: the "squeaky wheels" of public radio. I was inspired to undertake this project because of the critiques coming from outsiders within the industry. My requests to interview, to visit, and to bear witness to this world from their vantage point were met with open arms. The public radio workers of color I spoke with form the intellectual bedrock of the project. I am indebted to them for having the courage to speak up and to imagine a more ethical soundscape.

This book's analysis of public media organizations combines insights at the intersection of race, culture, and organizational theory to understand how organizations, as meso-level structures nested within fields that orient their action, are shaped by histories of racial exclusion. I have two main methods. Primarily, I conducted interviews with employees of color. I supplemented this with archival analysis and secondary data from the work of media historians of NPR, to help contextualize the experiences that my respondents tell me about and determine the larger forces that shape common experiences of employees of color.

Archival Research

I have offered a brief contextualization of noncommercial radio in the United States to show: (1) its underdevelopment in the media ecosystem as compared to European models of noncommercial broadcasting; and (2) within this comparatively small space in the ecosystem, its white dominance. To do so I analyzed existing histories of radio broadcasting and conducted a close listening of a government-sponsored radio program, *Americans All, Immigrants All*. Once this was established, I analyzed NPR's organizational meeting minutes, external reports, oral histories, and founder memoirs from the period 1967–1977 to explore how institutional actors made founding organizational decisions shaped by both larger fieldwide precedents and their own white subjectivities. To understand the conditions of racialized minorities employed and served by public broadcasting by 1977, I drew on political histories of NPR cited throughout the text, and on the Task Force on Minorities report of 1978, an assessment of how public media fared in addressing the needs of minoritized publics. The findings of pervasive racialized inequity in station ownership, workforce composition, and programming oriented my exploration of NPR's institutional archive, with a focus on how these inequalities emerged. The National Public Broadcasting Archives

(NPBA) at the University of Maryland, College Park, was my principal data source. Established by the original authorizing legislation of the Corporation for Public Broadcasting, the site contains official documents, collections of informal intraorganizational and interorganizational correspondence, oral history interviews by institutional leaders in public broadcasting, and papers of interest from former employees at NPR and the CPB dating back to the earliest days of the public broadcasting system.

From the NPBA, I digitized and analyzed the personal collections of five key leaders in public broadcasting governance: two NPR presidents, one CPB president, and two public media consultants who originally set up the national public broadcasting system. Further, I analyzed the papers of Susan Stamberg, cohost of NPR's *All Things Considered* from 1971 to 1986; CPB and NPR employee Elizabeth L. Young's papers, which include both NPR's articles of incorporation and the meeting minutes of the NPR Board of Directors from 1967 to 1972; and the work of two researchers, Burt Harrison and Christopher Buchanan, who conducted qualitative interviews and oral histories with founding members of public broadcasting. In laying out a history of the larger racialized organizational field of radio broadcasting, I used the NPBA's John Macy Files to understand the policy studies that motivated NPR's formation. To expand the breadth and depth of my description of this organizational field, I drew on historiographies analyzing radio broadcasting and race in the twentieth century, consulting the work of William Barlow, Barbara Dianne Savage, and Jennifer Lynn Stoever. To understand the founders' perspectives in decision making, I used accounts by professionals in the public radio field at the time from research by Harrison and Buchanan as well as employee memoirs. Through organizational handbooks and policy change memoranda, I identified policies and practices that had a direct impact on each of these inequalities. I analyzed meeting minutes to identify moments of organizational choice and how founders made and justified decisions at those junctures, to understand the process by which founders and employees translated the norms of the larger organizational field of noncommercial radio into NPR's policies and practices. Institutional archives give a rich sense of the logic of decisions to adopt certain practices in real time. Histories and memoirs written by those connected to NPR illustrate the stories that the founders themselves tell about such decisions in retrospect.

In approaching the development of a donor class, I reviewed the secondary literature on financial histories of public radio to demonstrate the tension between public radio's ambitious aims of pluralism and its chronic underfunding issues. Next, I outlined how a focus on NPR listener-members emerged in the 1980s in part as a solution to this tension, and how this focus has remained a consistent source of growth for the network. Specifically, I reviewed public radio's successful use of marketing firms to help them adapt to the financial crises they faced. In particular, I analyzed the success of *Audience 88*, a landmark report in the public radio industry that prompted a shift in long-term audience development strategies. *Audience 88* found that most public radio listeners "are professionals and managers, live in affluent neighborhoods, and are very concerned about their society." The report declared "that public radio is sitting on a demographic gold mine. With college degrees and corresponding high incomes, public radio listeners are attractive to many prospective underwriters." The report marks an increased focus on attracting corporate underwriters by showing that public radio's core audience is a lucrative market. I coupled this with a review of twenty-five underwriting packets during my 2020–2021 fieldwork, as shown in table 1 following the methodological appendix.

Interviews

Once I established the racialization of the organizational field and the larger market of public radio, I turned to the contemporary experiences of people of color in public radio. Between January 3, 2020, and April 19, 2021, I interviewed eighty-three people with current or previous experience in the public radio industry in the United States: of these eighty-three respondents, thirty identified as Black or African American; twenty-six identified as Asian, Asian American, or Pacific Islander; twenty identified as Hispanic or Latinx; five identified as being of Middle Eastern descent; six identified as mixed race or biracial; one identified as Native; and two identified as white. The total exceeds eighty-three (totaling ninety identifiers) because I allowed the designation of biracial/mixed race and invited participants to identify with more than one racial category.

While I conducted in-person interviews in January and February, the remainder of interviews took place via Zoom videoconferencing due to COVID-19 travel and meeting restrictions. Interviews ranged from 45 to 240 minutes in length. Typically, I asked participants to set aside 90 minutes, and over half of the interviews fell within the range of 65–80 minutes. I recruited respondents at the Third Coast International Audio Conference in October 2019; reached out to individuals via their institutional email addresses; sent invitations to LadioNYC and PubradioNYC via their Google

Groups pages; and posted a call for participants on my own Twitter page. I asked all respondents to share this call for interviews with other people of color in the public radio industry who might be willing to participate. Respondents proceeded to share this call for participants in workplace Slack channels, Journalists of Color groups on Facebook, private WhatsApp groups, and individual colleagues via email.

I interviewed these participants about their experiences at the station where they work, or the stations where they have worked, since many people work at multiple stations over the course of their career. I sampled from a wide array of member stations—high- and low-resourced stations, and community- and educational-based stations—as well as from all regions of the continental United States. This sample also included employees working at the national organization, both NPR in Washington, DC, and NPR West in Culver City, California. From there, I identified patterns of experiences that emerged from the data. Ultimately, I found that in pitching, sourcing, and voicing stories for public radio, not only is #pubradiovoice in the minds of production teams, they also must contend with their idea of who the listeners are and make decisions based on these assumptions.

I followed a semistructured interview script designed to explore several themes, including: early exposure to public radio, professional training, workplace production processes, and diversity and inclusion initiatives. I focused on respondents' discussions of the voice and sound of public radio pieces, particularly as they relate to workplace training and production processes. All interviews were transcribed and coded using NVivo 12 qualitative analysis software. I analyzed interviews with contemporary employees of color in public radio to consider how listener-members constrain and shape dynamics within the public radio workplace today. I also traced the storytelling process, coding for emergent themes such as "unintelligible," "too much," "white," and "professional" in participants' answers to key open-ended questions such as "What is your relationship to your voice?" and "How do you find your sources?" I then layered onto these codes key mechanisms that elicit discussion of these themes, such as "editorial feedback," "audience feedback," and "unspoken modeling."

My own positionality shapes both the data I was able to collect and my own understanding of the collected data. I share several key experiences with the bulk of my respondents. Like the majority of the participants in this project, I am a person of color who is making her career by producing knowledge in a white institutional space. These similarities, at times, engendered trust, or at the very least a comfort among my respondents in revealing workplace racial inequities to me. I was able to signal this by validating common experiences, particularly for those respondents who fell into roughly the same (millennial) generation as me. As I continued via snowball sample, some respondents noted that they felt they could trust me because a friend or colleague who had also interviewed with me confirmed that it had been a good experience for them. In other words, the amount of overlap in common experience made it so that these respondents felt I would understand what they were telling me.

Data collection and analysis were overlapping and iterative. I began coding the data before I had finished collecting it all, which enabled me to understand the terms of art and more closely align myself as someone who understood narrative and storytelling. I also invited respondents to remain in touch over time, sharing anything else they found relevant to the project. Several respondents followed up via email, either reflecting upon an experience they had already shared in a new light or sharing a new one they had experienced in the intervening months. These ongoing relationships have made the project a richer one.

There were times, however, when this "insider" status fell apart in terms of age and time in the workforce. Some respondents, particularly women of color who had been in the workplace for decades longer than I had, would stress that there are things that I do not understand about how much worse it *was*. However, this tension is useful and brings to the fore the need to contextualize how institutional norms have shifted over time.

As an Asian American cisgender woman, my own gender presentation shaped the way that respondents shared experiences with me. My freelance transcriptionist, Stacey Tran, another Asian American cisgender woman, agreed to give impressions of patterns in the data along the way. She was struck by how long men's responses were versus the responses of women and nonbinary respondents. When we discussed this contrast, though we could not be sure of the root cause, I speculated that the tendency for men to speak without pause for much of the interview had to do with a combination of their own socialization and my own presentation as a woman.

All names in the project are pseudonyms. I do this to protect the respondents, as each workplace and programming team within the industry is sufficiently small so that coworkers can make identifications. Each quotation in this project has been vetted by the respondent to ensure (a) accuracy; and (b) anonymity, such that the respondent could not reasonably be identified by the quotation.

TABLE 1: Underwriting Packet Tracking

Link	Associated station	Location of station	Emphasis on high income / wealth	Emphasis on halo effect	Emphasis on educated listeners	Emphasis on "cultured" listener or "influential" listener
https://gulfcoast.edu/campus-life/wkgc/documents/underwriting-packet2.pdf	WKGC	Southport, FL	Yes	Yes	Yes	Yes
http://mediad.publicbroadcasting.net/p/kasu/files/underwrite_kasu_0.pdf	KASU	Jonesboro, AR	Yes	Yes	Yes	Yes
https://krtu.trinity.edu/sites/krtu.trinity.edu/files/krtu_underwriting_media_kit_11.2017_pdf-2.pdf	KRTU	San Antonio, TX	Yes	No	No	Yes
https://npr.brightspotcdn.com/legacy/sites/ksor/files/JPR_Underwriting_Packet_2014.pdf	JPR	Jefferson City, MO	Yes	Yes	Yes	Yes
https://www.wqcs.org/become-a-wqcs-underwriter	WQCS	Fort Pierce, FL	Yes	Yes	Yes	Yes
https://www.wnmufm.org/sites/wnmu/files/MasterMediaKitWebWNMUFM_0.pdf	WNMU	Marquette, MI	Yes	Yes	Yes	Yes
https://www.wamc.org/become-underwriter	WAMC	Albany, NY	No	Yes	No	No
https://www.knau.org/underwriting	KNAU	Flagstaff, AZ	No	Yes	No	No
https://www.peoriapublicradio.org/discover-underwriting#stream/0	WCBU	Peoria, IL	No	Yes	No	No
https://www.wuky.org/underwriting#stream/0	WUKY	Lexington, KY	Yes	Yes	Yes	Yes
https://kchu.org/underwriting/	KCHU	Valdez, AK	No	Yes	Yes	Yes

URL	Station	City				
https://www.kamutvfm.org/support/underwriting/	KAMU	College Station, TX	No	Yes	Yes	Yes
https://www.vpr.org/post/underwriting-vpr#stream/0	VPR	Colchester, VT	Yes	Yes	Yes	Yes
https://www.upr.org/underwriting	UPR	Logan, UT	Yes	No	Yes	Yes
https://www.ypradio.org/business-support	YPR	Billings, MT	No	Yes	No	No
https://www.wkms.org/become-business-sponsor#stream/0	WKMS	Murray, KY	Yes	Yes	Yes	Yes
https://static1.squarespace.com/static/57c87e0346c3c4fc1ca67410/t/5cf54a7b80cc67\00]646bbe/1559579261828/mediakit.pdf	NCPR	Canton, NY	Yes	Yes	Yes	Yes
https://www.cpr.org/become-a-sponsor/	CPR	Denver, CO	No	Yes	Yes	No
https://www.wunc.org/sponsorships	WUNC	Jackson Hole, WY	Yes	Yes	Yes	Yes
https://www.nhpr.org/underwriting-business-support#stream/0	NHPR	Concord, NH	Yes	Yes	Yes	Yes
https://www.wabe.org/wp-content/uploads/2020/11/WABE-Media_Kit_New_and_Small.pdf	WABE	Atlanta, GA	Yes	Yes	Yes	Yes
https://www.capradio.org/support/corporate-support/	capradio	Sacramento, CA	No	No	Yes	Yes
https://www.wboi.org/business-and-corporate-underwriters#stream/0	WBOI	Fort Wayne, IN	Yes	Yes	Yes	Yes
https://www.kdll.org/sites/kdll/files/kdll_underwriting_flyer.pdf	KDLL	Kenai, AK	No	Yes	No	No
http://files.hawaiipublicradio.org/pdf/2020/hpr_media_kit_Oct2020.pdf	HPR	Honolulu, HI	Yes	Yes	Yes	Yes

Introduction

1. A list of discussion questions for reading groups and book clubs can be found on this book's website.

2. Throughout the book, I use the term Latinx, a relatively new ethnoracial identification when compared with the terms Hispanic, Latino, and Latin@. The term is not universally accepted in academic circles or in communities of practice, and it has variable usage, particularly across generational cohorts. See G. Cristina Mora, Reubén Pérez, and Nicholas Vargas, "Who Identifies as 'Latinx'? The Generational Politics of Ethnoracial Labels," *Social Forces* 100, no. 3 (March 2022): 1170–94, https://doi.org/10.1093/sf/soab011. However, I follow Salvador Vidal-Ortiz and Juliana Martínez in their framing of Latinx as a contested term that offers possibilities of inclusion, particularly in the term's shift beyond binary conceptions of gender. See Salvador Vidal-Ortiz and Juliana Martínez, "Latinx Thoughts: Latinidad with an X," *Latino Studies* 16, no. 3 (October 2018): 384–95, https://doi.org/10.1057/s41276-018-0137-8.

3. Throughout this book, I capitalize Black and lowercase white. This capitalization is in recognition of Black as an inclusive ethnic category; as Alexandria Neason of the *Columbia Journalism Review* argues, "I view the term *Black* as both a recognition of an ethnic identity in the States that doesn't rely on hyphenated Americanness (and is more accurate than *African American*, which suggests recent ties to the continent) and is also transnational and inclusive of our Caribbean [and] Central/South American siblings." I lowercase white because, by contrast to the demonstrated need to do so for the Black diaspora, who often cannot trace their ethnicities due to the institution of slavery, the category of white has been used to subjugate rather than reclaim. See the *Columbia Journalism Review*'s announcement of their style shift at Mike Laws, "Why We Capitalize 'Black' (and Not 'White')," *Columbia Journalism Review*, June 16, 2020, https://www.cjr.org/analysis/capital-b-black-styleguide.php. Like the use of the term "Latinx" throughout this book, I adopt this practice knowing that linguistic meaning is relational; I acknowledge that as the political context shifts, I may change this practice over time based on shifting processes of communal identification.

4. Roman Mars is the creator and host of the popular public radio podcast *99% Invisible*; as he notes on his personal webpage, he is known as the "Ira Glass of design"; https://www.romanmars.com/. Sarah Koenig is a former producer of the public radio show *This American Life* and creator of the Peabody Award–winning podcast *Serial*; https://barclayagency.com/speakers/sarah-koenig.

5. The research project this book is based on was published in 2022 and is publicly available on ProQuest: Laura Garbes, "Racialized Airwaves: Tracing the Sonic Color Line in the American Public Radio Industry" (PhD diss., Brown University, 2022), https://www.proquest.com/docview/2784391272/abstract/6EA38864C974528PQ/1.

6. Pierre Bourdieu, *Language and Symbolic Power*, ed. John Thompson, trans. Gino Raymond and Matthew Adamson, 7th ed. (Cambridge, MA: Harvard University Press, 1999), 199.

7. Rosina Lippi-Green, *English with an Accent: Language, Ideology, and Discrimination in the United States*, 2nd ed. (London: Routledge, 2011).

8. Margaret Sullivan, *Ghosting the News: Local Journalism and the Crisis of American Democracy* (New York: Columbia Global Reports, 2020).

9. Nikki Usher, *News for the Rich, White, and Blue: How Place and Power Distort American Journalism* (New York: Columbia University Press, 2021).

10. Christopher Chávez, *The Sound of Exclusion: NPR and the Latinx Public* (Tucson: University of Arizona Press, 2021), 5.

11. I want to acknowledge that Chávez conceptualizes NPR in his analysis as white space. I agree with his assessment. For the purposes of my analysis throughout this book, I am building on the work of organizational sociologists and sociologists of race who have used the term "white institutional space."

12. Jason Loviglio, "Public Radio in Crisis," in *Radio's New Wave: Global Sound in the Digital Era*, ed. Jason Loviglio and Michele Hilmes (New York: Routledge, 2013), 34–52; and Jack W. Mitchell, *Listener Supported: The Culture and History of Public Radio* (Westport, CT: Praeger, 2005).

13. Jason Loviglio, "Sound Effects: Gender, Voice and the Cultural Work of NPR," *Radio Journal: International Studies in Broadcast and Audio Media* 5, nos. 2–3 (July 2008): 67–81, https://doi.org/10.1386/rajo.5.2-3.67_1.

14. Tom McEnaney, "This American Voice: The Odd Timbre of a New Standard in Public Radio," in *The Oxford Handbook of Voice Studies*, ed. Nina Sun Eidsheim and Katherine Meizel (New York: Oxford University Press, 2019), 96–123.

15. Mitchell, *Listener Supported*.

16. National Public Radio, "Diversity in Action at NPR," https://www.npr.org/diversity; and Corporation for Public Broadcasting, "Diversity," September 25, 2014, https://www.cpb.org/diverseaudiences.

17. Wendy Leo Moore, *Reproducing Racism: White Space, Elite Law Schools, and Racial Inequality* (Lanham, MD: Rowman and Littlefield, 2008).

18. George Lipsitz, *How Racism Takes Place* (Philadelphia: Temple University Press, 2011); and David L. Brunsma, Nathaniel G. Chapman, Joong Won Kim, J. Slade Lellock, Megan Underhill, Erik T. Withers, and Jennifer Padilla Wyse, "The Culture of White Space: On The Racialized Production of Meaning," *American Behavioral Scientist* 64, no. 14 (December): 2001–15, https://doi.org/10.1177/0002764220975081.

19. Amanda E. Lewis and John B. Diamond, *Despite the Best Intentions: How Racial Inequality Thrives in Good Schools* (New York: Oxford University Press, 2015).

20. Deirdre A. Royster, *Race and the Invisible Hand: How White Networks Exclude Black Men from Blue-Collar Jobs* (Berkeley: University of California Press, 2003).

21. Adia Harvey Wingfield and Renée Skeete Alston, "Maintaining Hierarchies in Predominantly White Organizations: A Theory of Racial Tasks," *American Behavioral Scientist* 58, no. 2 (February 2014): 274–87, https://doi.org/10.1177/0002764213503329.

22. Joan Acker, "Inequality Regimes: Gender, Class, and Race in Organizations," *Gender and Society* 20, no. 4 (August 2006): 442, https://doi.org/10.1177/0891243206289499.

23. Victor Ray, "A Theory of Racialized Organizations," *American Sociological Review* 84, no. 1 (February 2019): 26–53, https://doi.org/10.1177/0003122418822335.

24. Eduardo Bonilla-Silva, *Racism without Racists: Color-Blind Racism and the Persistence of Racial Inequality in America*, 4th ed. (Lanham, MD: Rowman and Littlefield, 2013).

25. Imani Perry, *More Beautiful and More Terrible: The Embrace and Transcendence of Racial Inequality in the United States* (New York: New York University Press, 2011).

26. Danya Lagos, "Hearing Gender: Voice-Based Gender Classification Processes and Trans-gender Health Inequality," *American Sociological Review* 84, no. 5 (October 2019): 801–27, https://doi.org/10.1177/0003122419872504; Russell K. Robinson, "Perceptual Segregation," *Columbia Law Review* 108, no. 5 (June 2008); and Bourdieu, *Language and Symbolic Power*.

27. Douglas S. Massey and Garvey Lundy, "Use of Black English and Racial Discrimina-tion in Urban Housing Markets: New Methods and Findings," *Urban Affairs Review* 36, no. 4 (March 2001): 452–69, https://doi.org/10.1177/10780870122184957.

28. Thomas Purnell, William Idsardi, and John Baugh, "Perceptual and Phonetic Experi-ments on American English Dialect Identification," *Journal of Language and Social Psychology* 18, no. 1 (March 1999): 10–30, https://doi.org/10.1177/0261927X99018001002; and Richard C. Doss and Alan M. Gross, "The Effects of Black English and Code-Switching on Intraracial Per-ceptions," *Journal of Black Psychology* 20, no. 3 (August 1994): 282–93, https://doi.org/10.1177/00957984940203003.

29. Sara Trechter and Mary Bucholtz, "White Noise: Bringing Language into Whiteness Studies," *Journal of Linguistic Anthropology* 11, no. 1 (January 2001): 3–21, http://escholarship.org/uc/item/78b5t2xq.

30. Nelson Flores and Jonathan Rosa, "Undoing Appropriateness: Raciolinguistic Ideologies and Language Diversity in Education," *Harvard Educational Review* 85, no. 2 (Winter 2015): 149–71, https://doi.org/10.17763/0017-8055.85.2.149.

31. As of this writing, the concept of raciolinguistic ideologies has begun to be adopted by sociological researchers. A clear example of this work appears in a special issue of *Ethnicities* edited by Stephen May, which showcases a collection of empirical work in the social sciences focusing on the phenomenon of linguistic racism. See Stephen May, "Linguistic Racism: Origins and Implica-tions," *Ethnicities* 23, no. 5 (October 2023): 651–61, https://doi.org/10.1177/14687968231193072.

32. Jane H. Hill, "Language, Race, and White Public Space," *American Anthropologist* 100, no. 3 (September 1998): 680–89.

33. Alison Martin, "Plainly Audible: Listening Intersectionally to the Amplified Noise Act in Washington, DC," *Journal of Popular Music Studies* 33, no. 4 (December 2021): 105, 111, https://doi.org/10.1525/jpms.2021.33.4.104.

34. Shilpa Davé, "Racial Accents, Hollywood Casting, and Asian American Studies," *Cinema Journal* 56, no. 3 (Spring 2017): 142–47.

35. Madhavi Mallapragada, "*The Problem with Apu*, Whiteness, and Racial Hierarchies in US Media Industries," *JCMS: Journal of Cinema and Media Studies* 60, no. 1 (Fall 2020): 148–52.

36. Hari Kondabolu, *The Problem with Apu*, Apple TV, 2017, https://tv.apple.com/us/show/the-problem-with-apu/umc.cmc.79ccp9drj3lwqvctz77ct5eie.

37. Hank Azaria has used the voice of Apu outside of the cartoon for laughs, most promi-nently in a Tufts University commencement speech in 2016, even at the height of public critique by South Asian intellectuals. See Mallapragada, "*The Problem with Apu*, Whiteness, and Racial Hierarchies."

38. Nancy Wang Yuen, *Reel Inequality: Hollywood Actors and Racism* (New Brunswick, NJ: Rutgers University Press, 2017).

39. Jennifer Lynn Stoever, *The Sonic Color Line: Race and the Cultural Politics of Listening* (New York: New York University Press, 2016).

40. W.E.B. Du Bois, *Dusk of Dawn: An Essay toward an Autobiography of a Race Concept* (New York: Oxford University Press, 2007), 66.

41. Jennifer Lynn Stoever, "'Doing Fifty-Five in a Fifty-Four': Hip Hop, Cop Voice and the Cadence of White Supremacy in the United States," *Journal of Interdisciplinary Voice Studies* 3, no. 2 (November 2018): 115–31, https://doi.org/10.1386/jivs.3.2.115_1.

42. Nirmal Puwar, *Space Invaders: Race, Gender and Bodies Out of Place* (Oxford: Berg, 2004).

43. Tsedale M. Melaku, "Black Women in White Institutional Spaces: The Invisible Labor Clause and the Inclusion Tax," *American Behavioral Scientist* 66, no. 11 (October 2022): 1512–25, https://doi.org/10.1177/00027642211066037.

44. Ray, "A Theory of Racialized Organizations"; and Joan Acker, "Hierarchies, Jobs, Bodies: A Theory of Gendered Organizations," *Gender and Society* 4, no. 2 (June 1990): 139–58, https://doi.org/10.1177/089124390004002002.

45. Aileen Moreton-Robinson, Maryrose Casey, and Fiona Nicoll, *Transnational Whiteness Matters* (Lanham, MD: Lexington Books, 2008).

46. Adia Harvey Wingfield, "Are Some Emotions Marked 'Whites Only'? Racialized Feeling Rules in Professional Workplaces," *Social Problems* 57, no. 2 (May 2010): 251–68, https://doi.org/10.1525/sp.2010.57.2.251.

47. Louwanda Evans and Wendy Leo Moore, "Impossible Burdens: White Institutions, Emotional Labor, and Micro-Resistance," *Social Problems* 62, no. 3 (August 2015): 439–54, https://doi.org/10.1093/socpro/spv009.

48. Patricia Hill Collins, "Learning from the Outsider Within: The Sociological Significance of Black Feminist Thought," *Social Problems* 33, no. 6 (December 1986): s14–s32, https://doi.org/10.2307/800672.

49. Elijah Anderson, "The White Space," *Sociology of Race and Ethnicity* 1, no. 1 (January 2015): 16, https://doi.org/10.1177/2332649214561306.

50. Moore, *Reproducing Racism*.

51. David G. Embrick and Wendy Leo Moore, "White Space(s) and the Reproduction of White Supremacy," *American Behavioral Scientist* 64, no. 14 (December 2020): 1941, https://doi.org/10.1177/0002764220975053.

52. Laura Garbes, "Sonic Double Consciousness: Public Radio Voices of Color," *American Journal of Cultural Sociology* 12, no. 4 (December 2024): 677–97, https://doi.org/10.1057/s41290-024-00215-x.

53. When I use the terms "white collar" and "professional class" throughout this text, I am doing so as shorthand for a group of people who perform salaried labor in an administrative, clerical, or office-based setting rather than performing manual labor for wages. I landed on these terms as approximations of a group of people public radio has become associated with, because it offers a descriptor of the group's typical work life, as white-collar occupations and occupations in which workers refer to themselves as "professionals" often require formal education in white institutional spaces. I will also use the terms "middle class," "upper middle class," and "professional-managerial class," but more often when they are mentioned by participants and secondary literature.

54. Nick Couldry, "Commentary: Rethinking the Politics of Voice," *Continuum* 23, no. 4 (August 2009): 580, https://doi.org/10.1080/10304310903026594.

55. Tanja Dreher, "Listening across Difference: Media and Multiculturalism beyond the Politics of Voice," *Continuum* 23, no. 4 (August 2009): 445–58, https://doi.org/10.1080/10304310903015712.

56. Sara Ahmed, *Complaint!* (Durham, NC: Duke University Press, 2021).

57. Claire Jean Kim, *Asian Americans in an Anti-Black World* (Cambridge: Cambridge University Press, 2023).

Part I. Public Radio's White Racial Structure

1. Adrienne LaFrance, "How NPR Tote Bags Became a Thing," *Atlantic*, April 16, 2016, https://www.theatlantic.com/business/archive/2015/04/how-npr-tote-bags-became-a-thing/390657/.

2. Alexandra Dane, "Cultural Capital as Performance: Tote Bags and Contemporary Literary Festivals," *Mémoires du livre / Studies in Book Culture* 11, no. 2 (Spring 2020), https://doi.org/10.7202/1070270ar.

3. Elizabeth Currid-Halkett, *The Sum of Small Things: A Theory of the Aspirational Class* (Princeton, NJ: Princeton University Press, 2017).

4. Michael P. McCauley, *NPR: The Trials and Triumphs of National Public Radio* (New York: Columbia University Press, 2005); and Mitchell, *Listener Supported.*

5. Loviglio, "Sound Effects."

6. Lisa Napoli, *Susan, Linda, Nina, and Cokie: The Extraordinary Story of the Founding Mothers of NPR* (New York: Harry N. Abrams, 2021).

1. To Serve All Americans

1. Thomas R. Schmidt, "Challenging Journalistic Objectivity: How Journalists of Color Call for a Reckoning," *Journalism* 25, no. 3 (March 2024): 547–64, https://doi.org/10.1177/14648849231160997.

2. *The Takeaway*, "Reckoning with Race in Public Media," July 9, 2020, https://www.wnycstudios.org/podcasts/takeaway/segments/reckoning-systemic-racism-public-media.

3. Richard F. Shepard, "Public Broadcasting Assailed on Race," *New York Times*, November 26, 1978, https://www.nytimes.com/1978/11/26/archives/public-broadcasting-assailed-on-race-recommendations-sought.html.

4. Gloria Anderson et al., "A Formula for Change: The Report of the Task Force on Minorities in Public Broadcasting," November 1978, https://eric.ed.gov/?id=ED172269.

5. Bill Siemering, "Radio with a Purpose: Bill Siemering on NPR's Original Mission Statement," National Public Radio, May 7, 2021, https://www.npr.org/2021/05/07/993569986/radio-with-a-purpose-bill-siemering-on-nprs-original-mission-statement.

6. Stella M. Nkomo, "The Emperor Has No Clothes: Rewriting 'Race in Organizations,'" *Academy of Management Review* 17, no. 3 (July 1992): 487–513, https://doi.org/10.5465/AMR.1992.4281987; and Jane Ward, "White Normativity: The Cultural Dimensions of Whiteness in a Racially Diverse LGBT Organization," *Sociological Perspectives* 51, no. 3 (September 2008): 563–86, https://doi.org/10.1525/sop.2008.51.3.563.

7. Ray, "A Theory of Racialized Organizations," 20.

8. Ellen Berrey, *The Enigma of Diversity: The Language of Race and the Limits of Racial Justice* (Chicago: University of Chicago Press, 2015).

9. Wendy Leo Moore, "The Mechanisms of White Space(s)," *American Behavioral Scientist* 64, no. 14 (December 2020), https://doi.org/10.1177/0002764220975080.

10. Moore, *Reproducing Racism*, 200.

11. Kimberlé Williams Crenshaw, "Toward a Race-Conscious Pedagogy in Legal Education," *National Black Law Journal* 11, no. 1 (1988): 1.

12. Mitchell, *Listener Supported*, 43.

13. For more on this system and its creation, see Josh Shepperd, *Shadow of the New Deal: The Victory of Public Broadcasting* (Urbana: University of Illinois Press, 2023).

14. Hugh Richard Slotten, *Radio's Hidden Voice: The Origins of Public Broadcasting in the United States* (Urbana: University of Illinois Press, 2009).

15. Dolores Inés Casillas, *Sounds of Belonging: U.S. Spanish-Language Radio and Public Advocacy* (New York: New York University Press, 2014).

16. Dan Shiffman, "A Standard for the Wise and Honest: The 'Americans All . . . Immigrants All' Radio Broadcasts," *Studies in Popular Culture* 19, no. 1 (October 1996): 99–107.

17. Michael Omi and Howard Winant, *Racial Formation in the United States: From the 1960s to the 1990s*, 2nd ed. (New York: Routledge, 1994).

18. From 1925 to 1934, the association was known as the Association of College and University Broadcasting Stations. Later on, it was renamed the National Educational Radio Network (NERN). For the purposes of this chapter, we will use the name National Association of

Educational Broadcasters, as this was the name for the majority of its operation before merging with National Public Radio.

19. National Association of Educational Broadcasters, "Constitution of the Association of College and University Broadcasting Stations," 1930, https://archive.org/details/naeb-b101-f02-45.

20. William Barlow, *Voice Over: The Making of Black Radio* (Philadelphia: Temple University Press, 1999); and Barbara Dianne Savage, *Broadcasting Freedom: Radio, War, and the Politics of Race, 1938–1948* (Chapel Hill: University of North Carolina Press, 1999).

21. Neil Fligstein and Doug McAdam, *A Theory of Fields* (New York: Oxford University Press, 2012).

22. Eduardo Bonilla-Silva, Carla Goar, and David G. Embrick, "When Whites Flock Together: The Social Psychology of White Habitus," *Critical Sociology* 32, nos. 2–3 (March 2006): 229–53, https://doi.org/10.1163/156916306777835268.

23. Bourdieu, *Language and Symbolic Power*.

24. McCauley, *NPR: The Trials and Triumphs*.

25. A field is "a community of organizations that partakes of a common meaning system and whose participants interact more frequently and fatefully with one another than with actors outside the field." See W. Richard Scott, *Institutions and Organizations: Ideas, Interests and Identities* (Thousand Oaks, CA: SAGE Publications, 1995).

26. Paul J. DiMaggio and Walter W. Powell, "The Iron Cage Revisited: Institutional Isomorphism and Collective Rationality in Organizational Fields," in *Advances in Strategic Management*, vol. 17, *Economics Meets Sociology in Strategic Management*, ed. Joel A. C. Baum and Frank Dobbin (Leeds, England: Emerald Publishing, 2000), 149.

27. Tim Hallett, "The Myth Incarnate: Recoupling Processes, Turmoil, and Inhabited Institutions in an Urban Elementary School," *American Sociological Review* 75, no. 1 (February 2010): 52–74, https://doi.org/10.1177/0003122409357044.

28. Melissa Wooten and Andrew J. Hoffman, "Organizational Fields: Past, Present and Future," in *The SAGE Handbook of Organizational Institutionalism*, ed. Royston Greenwood, Christine Oliver, Roy Suddaby, and Kerstin Sahlin (London: SAGE Publications, 2008), 129–48.

29. Amy Binder, "For Love and Money: Organizations' Creative Responses to Multiple Environmental Logics," *Theory and Society* 36, no. 6 (December 2007): 547–71, https://doi.org/10.1007/s11186-007-9045-x; and Donald Tomaskovic-Devey and Dustin Avent-Holt, *Relational Inequalities: An Organizational Approach* (Oxford: Oxford University Press, 2019).

30. Lauren A. Rivera, "Hiring as Cultural Matching: The Case of Elite Professional Service Firms," *American Sociological Review* 77, no. 6 (December 2012): 999–1022, https://doi.org/10.1177/0003122412463213.

31. Stoever, *The Sonic Color Line*.

32. Fred Ferretti, "The White Captivity of Black Radio," *Columbia Journalism Review* 9, no. 2 (Summer 1970): 35–39.

33. Dave Berkman, "Is Educational Broadcasting Segregated?," *National Association of Educational Broadcasters Journal*, January–February 1966.

34. Barlow, *Voice Over*, 247.

35. Elizabeth L. Young Papers (0186-MMC), National Public Radio General File, 1970, box 1, folder 12.0, Special Collections and University Archives, University of Maryland Libraries, https://archives.lib.umd.edu/repositories/2/archival_objects/189663.

36. "March on Washington for Jobs and Freedom: Interview with Al Hulsen," WGBH-FM (Boston) Media Library and Archives, April 29, 2011, http://openvault.wgbh.org/catalog/A_B29FCE218ACD4F0686969643B235B941.

37. Mitchell, *Listener Supported*.

38. Lee C. Frischknecht Papers (1970–1981), National Public Broadcasting Archives, 1. National Public Radio, 1.1. Speeches and Subject Files, box 1.

39. Anderson et al., "A Formula for Change," 69.

40. Anderson et al., "A Formula for Change," xvii.

41. John W. Macy Files, Corporation for Public Broadcasting Records, 1971, National Public Broadcasting Archives.

42. Burt Harrison Collection of Public Radio Oral Histories (0129-MMC-NPBA), Oral History Audiocassettes, Albert Hulsen, October 3, 1978, box 1, folder 5.0, Special Collections and University Archives, University of Maryland Libraries, https://archives.lib.umd.edu/ repositories/2/ archival_objects/165418.

43. Lee C. Frischknecht Papers, National Public Broadcasting Archives, 1. National Public Radio, 1.1. Speeches and Subject Files.

44. Lee C. Frischknecht Papers, National Public Broadcasting Archives, 1. National Public Radio, 1.1. Speeches and Subject Files.

45. The International Executive Service Corps (IESC) is an international economic development not-for-profit organization with headquarters in Washington, DC. The IESC was founded in 1964 by David Rockefeller, States M. Mead III, Frank Pace, Sol Linowitz, and other American business leaders; it has worked in sub-Saharan Africa, Europe and Eurasia, Asia and the Near East, and Latin America and the Caribbean.

46. John W. Macy Files, Corporation for Public Broadcasting Records, 1971.

47. Mitchell, *Listener Supported*.

48. "Al [Hulsen], Liz Young, Bill Kling and secretarial help constituted the Radio Office. Al and Mott worked very well together. They brought in John Witherspoon as a consultant to help design an organization that, unlike PBS, would both produce and acquire and distribute and promote national programming for radio." From "Public Radio Oral History Project, 1977–1982," Burt Harrison Collection of Public Radio Oral Histories (0129-MMC-NPBA), Oral History Audiocassettes.

49. McCauley, *NPR: The Trials and Triumphs*.

50. Elizabeth L. Young Papers, Personal Papers, box 1, July 2017.

51. John W. Macy Files, Corporation for Public Broadcasting Records, 1971.

52. Ray, "A Theory of Racialized Organizations," 42.

53. McCauley, *NPR: The Trials and Triumphs*.

54. John W. Macy Files, Corporation for Public Broadcasting Records, 1971.

55. Savage, *Broadcasting Freedom*.

56. John W. Macy Files, Corporation for Public Broadcasting Records, 1971.

57. There would, however, be more programming for white women than the typical mainstream broadcast. I will discuss that further in the following chapter.

58. Anderson et al., "A Formula for Change," xviii.

59. Cokie Roberts, Susan Stamberg, Noah Adams, John Ydstie, Renée Montagne, Ari Shapiro, and David Folkenflik, *This Is NPR: The First Forty Years* (San Francisco: Chronicle Books, 2010).

60. Loviglio, "Sound Effects."

61. Ralph Engelman, *Public Radio and Television in America: A Political History* (Thousand Oaks, CA: SAGE Publications, 1996).

62. McCauley, *NPR: The Trials and Triumphs*.

63. John W. Macy Files, Corporation for Public Broadcasting Records, 1971.

64. Shepard, "Public Broadcasting Assailed on Race."

65. Savage, *Broadcasting Freedom*; and Jennifer Lynn Stoever, "Fine-Tuning the Sonic Color-Line: Radio and the Acousmatic Du Bois," *Modernist Cultures* 10, no. 1 (March 2015), https://doi .org/10.3366/mod.2015.0100.

66. McCauley, *NPR: The Trials and Triumphs*, 114.

67. Gwyneth Mellinger, *Chasing Newsroom Diversity: From Jim Crow to Affirmative Action* (Urbana: University of Illinois Press, 2013).

68. Anderson et al., "A Formula for Change," xiv.

69. Casillas, *Sounds of Belonging*.

70. Lewis Raven Wallace, *The View from Somewhere: Undoing the Myth of Journalistic Objectivity* (Chicago: University of Chicago Press, 2019), 94.

2. A Trusted Voice

1. Loviglio, "Sound Effects," 71.

2. Chenjerai Kumanyika, "Vocal Color in Public Radio," Transom, January 22, 2015, https://transom.org/2015/chenjerai-kumanyika/. Barnes and Noble is an American bookseller. The company has the largest chain of in-person retail bookstores in the United States, and often has cafés where one can sit and sip warm coffee.

3. Loviglio, "Sound Effects."

4. Alexis Soloski, "When Podcast Hosts Speak, What Do We Hear?," *New York Times*, February 25, 2021, https://www.nytimes.com/interactive/2021/02/25/arts/podcast-voice-sound.html.

5. Susan J. Douglas, *Listening In: Radio and the American Imagination* (Minneapolis: University of Minnesota Press, 2004).

6. Jennifer Gerson, "The Voices of NPR: How Four Women of Color See Their Roles as Hosts," the 19th, April 26, 2023, https://19thnews.org/2023/04/the-voices-of-npr/.

7. Stoever, "Fine-Tuning the Sonic Color-Line," 2.

8. McEnaney, "This American Voice," 113.

9. Napoli, *Susan, Linda, Nina, and Cokie*.

10. Howard S. Becker, *Art Worlds*, 25th Anniversary ed. (Berkeley: University of California Press, 2008), 47–48.

11. Sianne Ngai, *Ugly Feelings* (Cambridge, MA: Harvard University Press, 2005).

12. Summer Kim Lee, "Asian Americanist Critique and Listening Practices of Contemporary Popular Music," in *The Oxford Encyclopedia of Asian American Literature and Culture*, ed. Josephine Lee (Oxford: Oxford University Press, 2020), https://oxfordre.com/literature/view/10.1093/acrefore/9780190201098.001.0001/acrefore-9780190201098-e-819; and A. M. Kanngieser, "Sonic Colonialities: Listening, Dispossession, and the (Re)Making of Anglo-European Nature," *Transactions of the Institute of British Geographers* 48, no. 4 (December 2023): 690–702, https://doi.org/10.1111/tran.12602.

13. Tressie McMillan Cottom, *Thick, and Other Essays* (New York: New Press, 2019), 44.

14. Ellis P. Monk, Michael H. Esposito, and Hedwig Lee, "Beholding Inequality: Race, Gender, and Returns to Physical Attractiveness in the United States," *American Journal of Sociology* 127, no. 1 (July 2021): 194–241, https://doi.org/10.1086/715141; bell hooks, *Killing Rage: Ending Racism* (New York: Henry Holt, 1995); Maxine Leeds Craig, *Ain't I a Beauty Queen? Black Women, Beauty, and the Politics of Race* (Oxford: Oxford University Press, 2002); and Margaret L. Hunter, "'If You're Light You're Alright': Light Skin Color as Social Capital for Women of Color," *Gender and Society* 16, no. 2 (April 2002): 175–93, https://doi.org/10.1177/08912430222104895.

15. John Baugh, "Linguistic Profiling," in *Black Linguistics: Language, Society, and Politics in Africa and the Americas*, ed. Sinfree Makoni, Geneva Smitherman, Arnetha F. Ball, and Arthur K. Spears (London: Routledge, 2003), 155–68.

16. Anne Karpf, *The Human Voice: How This Extraordinary Instrument Reveals Essential Clues about Who We Are* (New York: Bloomsbury, 2006).

17. Jennifer C. Lena, *Entitled: Discriminating Tastes and the Expansion of the Arts* (Princeton, NJ: Princeton University Press, 2019).

18. Loviglio, "Sound Effects."

19. Wallace, *The View from Somewhere*.

20. Napoli, *Susan, Linda, Nina, and Cokie*, 10.

21. Howard N. Fullerton Jr., "Labor Force Participation: 75 Years of Change, 1950–98 and 1998–2025," *Monthly Labor Review* 122, no. 12 (December 1999): 3; and Natalie J. Sokoloff, *Black Women and White Women in the Professions: Occupational Segregation by Race and Gender, 1960–1980* (New York: Routledge, 2014).

22. Betty Friedan, *The Feminine Mystique* (New York: W. W. Norton, 1963).

23. Claudia Goldin, *Career and Family: Women's Century-Long Journey toward Equity* (Princeton, NJ: Princeton University Press, 2021).

24. Angela Garbes, *Essential Labor: Mothering as Social Change* (New York: HarperCollins, 2022).

25. Napoli, *Susan, Linda, Nina, and Cokie*, 78.

26. Napoli, *Susan, Linda, Nina, and Cokie*, 71.

27. National Public Radio, "Susan Stamberg's Cranberry Relish Tradition," November 17, 2023, https://www.npr.org/series/4175681/susan-stamberg-s-cranberry-relish-tradition.

28. Napoli, *Susan, Linda, Nina, and Cokie*, 9.

29. Christine Ehrick, *Radio and the Gendered Soundscape: Women and Broadcasting in Argentina and Uruguay, 1930–1950* (New York: Cambridge University Press, 2015).

30. Karpf, *The Human Voice*, 158.

31. Napoli, *Susan, Linda, Nina, and Cokie*.

32. Napoli, *Susan, Linda, Nina, and Cokie*, 52.

33. Napoli, *Susan, Linda, Nina, and Cokie*.

34. Napoli, *Susan, Linda, Nina, and Cokie*.

35. Douglas, *Listening In*, 286.

36. Loviglio, "Sound Effects."

37. The skit can be found on YouTube at https://www.youtube.com/watch?v=bPpcfH_HHH8.

38. L. Garbes, "Racialized Airwaves," 9.

39. The podcast is created and hosted by Sarah Koenig, who also created *This American Life*; https://serialpodcast.org/.

40. Teddy Wayne, "'NPR Voice' Has Taken Over the Airwaves," *New York Times*, October 24, 2015, https://www.nytimes.com/2015/10/25/fashion/npr-voice-has-taken-over-the-airwaves.html.

41. Laura Sim, "Intimate Publics: Hearing Race in Radio and Podcasts," Academia, 2015, https://www.academia.edu/26841322/intimate_publics_hearing_race_in_radio_and_podcasts.

42. Chávez, *The Sound of Exclusion*, 63.

43. Jillian Hernandez, *Aesthetics of Excess: The Art and Politics of Black and Latina Embodiment* (Durham, NC: Duke University Press, 2020).

44. Chávez, *The Sound of Exclusion*, 68.

45. Doreen St. Félix, "The Twisted Power of White Voice in 'Sorry to Bother You' and 'BlacKkKlansman,'" *New Yorker*, August 13, 2018, https://www.newyorker.com/culture/cultural-comment/the-twisted-power-of-white-voice-in-sorry-to-bother-you-and-blackkklansman.

46. Wallace, *The View from Somewhere*, 100.

47. As noted in the introduction, I explore the case of public radio through the lens of racial inclusion and exclusion, and how these dynamics are inextricably linked with class and gender. For a particularly good exploration of professional workplace experiences that centers class origins in considering limits to professional advancement, see sociologists Sam Friedman and Daniel Laurison's recent book on the topic, *The Class Ceiling: Why It Pays to Be Privileged* (Bristol, England: Policy Press, 2019).

48. Alicia Anstead, cited in McEnaney, "This American Voice," 42.

3. Listeners Like You

1. George Bailey, "Free Riders, Givers, and Heavy Users: Predicting Listener Support for Public Radio," *Journal of Broadcasting and Electronic Media* 48, no. 4 (2004): 607.

2. The quoted segments come from the personal archives of a former employee of an NPR member station. Member identification details have been removed from the list, but these comments were given at the time of donation in response to the prompt: "Tell us why you're donating" on the donation web form during the years 2020 and 2021 during the station's spring and fall member drives.

3. Mitchell, *Listener Supported*.

4. Francie Ostrower, *Why the Wealthy Give: The Culture of Elite Philanthropy* (Princeton, NJ: Princeton University Press, 1997); and Emily Barman, "The Social Bases of Philanthropy," *Annual Review of Sociology* 43 (2017): 271–90, https://doi.org/10.1146/annurev-soc-060116-053524.

5. Pamela Paxton, Kristopher Velasco, and Robert W. Ressler, "Does Use of Emotion Increase Donations and Volunteers for Nonprofits?," *American Sociological Review* 85, no. 6 (December 2020): 1051–83, https://doi.org/10.1177/0003122420960104.

6. Jessica McCrory Calarco, "Avoiding Us versus Them: How Schools' Dependence on Privileged 'Helicopter' Parents Influences Enforcement of Rules," *American Sociological Review* 85, no. 2 (April 2020): 223–46, https://doi.org/10.1177/0003122420905793.

7. Susan Smulyan, *Selling Radio: The Commercialization of American Broadcasting, 1920–1934* (Washington, DC: Smithsonian Institution Press, 1994).

8. Raymond Williams, *Keywords: A Vocabulary of Culture and Society*, rev. ed. (New York: Oxford University Press, 1985).

9. Willard D. Rowland Jr., "Continuing Crisis in Public Broadcasting: A History of Disenfranchisement," *Journal of Broadcasting and Electronic Media* 30, no. 3 (June 1986): 251–74, https://doi.org/10.1080/08838158609386623.

10. Phil McCombs and Jacqueline Trescott, "NPR: Camelot on Crisis," *Washington Post*, August 14, 1983, https://www.washingtonpost.com/archive/lifestyle/1983/08/15/npr-camelot-on-crisis/4594de4b-ec8e-4c7f-bc4a-55db0b2663e5/.

11. *New York Times*, "National Public Radio Opens 'Drive to Survive,'" August 2, 1983, https://www.nytimes.com/1983/08/02/arts/national-public-radio-opens-drive-to-survive.html.

12. Thomas Looker, *The Sound and the Story: NPR and the Art of Radio* (Boston: Houghton Mifflin Harcourt, 1995), 138.

13. Peter P. Nieckarz III, "'All Things Considered': A Comparative Case Study Examining the Commercial Presence within Public Radio" (PhD diss., Western Michigan University, June 1999), https://scholarworks.wmich.edu/dissertations/1523.

14. Loviglio, "Public Radio in Crisis."

15. National Public Radio, "The Friday Podcast: Economists on Federal Funding for NPR," *Planet Money*, March 25, 2011, https://www.npr.org/transcripts/134863998.

16. Arbitron is a radio ratings company. Founded in 1949 under the name American Research Bureau, it was acquired by TV ratings company Nielsen Holdings in 2013 and renamed Nielsen Audio. Ben Sisario, "Nielsen Deal for Arbitron Is Complete," *New York Times*, September 30, 2013, https://www.nytimes.com/2013/10/01/business/media/nielsen-completes-1-26-billion-purchase-of-arbitron.html.

17. Alan G. Stavitsky, "'Guys in Suits with Charts': Audience Research in U.S. Public Radio," *Journal of Broadcasting and Electronic Media* 39, no. 2 (March 1995): 177–89, https://doi.org/10.1080/08838159509364297.

18. Helen Katz, "The Future of Public Broadcasting in the US," *Media, Culture and Society* 11, no. 2 (April 1989): 195–205, https://doi.org/10.1177/016344389011002004; and Rowland, "Continuing Crisis in Public Broadcasting."

19. Tom McCourt, *Conflicting Communication Interests in America: The Case of National Public Radio* (Westport, CT: Praeger, 1999), 15.

20. Samuel G. Freedman, "Television/Radio; Public Radio's Private Guru," *New York Times*, November 11, 2001, https://www.nytimes.com/2001/11/11/arts/television-radio-public-radio-s-private-guru.html.

21. David Barboza, "The 'Enhanced Underwriting' of Public Broadcasting Is Taking a More Commercial Flair," *New York Times*, December 27, 1995, https://www.nytimes.com/1995/12/27/business/media-business-advertising-enhanced-underwriting-public-broadcasting-taking-more.html.

22. National Public Radio, "The Friday Podcast: Economists on Federal Funding for NPR."

23. The images come from an underwriting packet from GCPR, a local station on Florida's Gulf Coast. These packets are given to businesses to convince them to contribute to the station as a sponsor. For another example of such a packet, see https://www.wnmufm.org/sites/wnmu/files/MasterMediaKitWebWNMUFM_0.pdf.

24. Susan Leland, "Public Radio and Sponsors: A Win-Win Relationship," National Public Radio, May 9, 2011, https://www.npr.org/sections/gofigure/2011/05/09/136136378/public-radio-sponsors-a-win-win-relationship.

25. Current, "Study Evaluates Strength of Public Radio's 'Halo' for Sponsors," July 12, 2013, https://current.org/2013/07/study-evaluates-strength-of-public-radios-halo-for-sponsors/.

26. Victor Pickard, *Democracy without Journalism? Confronting the Misinformation Society* (New York: Oxford University Press, 2020); and Chávez, *The Sound of Exclusion*.

27. Chávez, *The Sound of Exclusion*, 14.

28. I have changed the name of the donor group to preserve anonymity.

29. Ellen Berrey, "Diversity Is for White People: The Big Lie behind a Well-Intended Word," *Salon*, October 26, 2015, https://www.salon.com/2015/10/26/diversity_is_for_white_people_the_big_lie_behind_a_well_intended_word/. For research on this insight in a K–12 context, see also Megan R. Underhill, "'Diversity Is Important to Me': White Parents and Exposure-to-Diversity Parenting Practices," *Sociology of Race and Ethnicity* 5, no. 4 (October 2019): 486–99, https://doi.org/10.1177/2332649218790992.

30. prabhdeep singh kehal, "Diversity," in *University Keywords*, ed. Andrew Hines (Baltimore: Johns Hopkins University Press, forthcoming).

31. Megan M. Holland and Karly Serita Ford, "Legitimating Prestige through Diversity: How Higher Education Institutions Represent Ethno-Racial Diversity across Levels of Selectivity," *Journal of Higher Education* 92, no. 1 (2021): 1–30.

32. Usher, *News for the Rich, White, and Blue*.

33. *Get Out* is a 2017 horror-comedy film written and directed by Jordan Peele in which "A young African-American visits his white girlfriend's parents for the weekend, where his simmering uneasiness about their reception of him eventually reaches a boiling point." Internet Movie Database, "*Get Out* (2017)," https://www.imdb.com/title/tt5052448/.

34. Joyce M. Bell and Douglas Hartmann, "Diversity in Everyday Discourse: The Cultural Ambiguities and Consequences of 'Happy Talk,'" *American Sociological Review* 72, no. 6 (December 2007): 895–914, https://doi.org/10.1177/000312240707200603; and Berrey, *The Enigma of Diversity*.

Part II. People of Color in Public Radio Today

1. Roderick Graham and 'Shawn Smith, "The Content of Our #Characters: Black Twitter as Counterpublic," *Sociology of Race and Ethnicity* 2, no. 4 (October 2016): 433–49, https://doi.org/10.1177/2332649216639067.

2. Jeppe Ugelvig, "Portrait: Sandra Mujinga," *Spike*, October 11, 2021, https://spikeartmagazine.com/articles/portrait-sandra-mujinga.

3. Boots Riley, dir., *Sorry to Bother You* (Annapurna Pictures, 2018). The film can be streamed in the United States and some other countries on Tubi at https://tubitv.com/movies/622910/sorry-to-bother-you.

4. Anamik Saha, *Race and the Cultural Industries* (Cambridge: Polity Press, 2018).

5. Saha, *Race and the Cultural Industries.*

6. Collins, "Learning from the Outsider Within," s14–s32.

4. Sounding Like Myself

1. McEnaney, "This American Voice"; and Chávez, *The Sound of Exclusion.*

2. Erving Goffman, *The Presentation of Self in Everyday Life* (New York: Doubleday, 1959).

3. W.E.B. Du Bois, *The Souls of Black Folk: Essays and Sketches* (Chicago: A. C. McClurg and Company, 1903), 190; and José Itzigsohn and Karida L. Brown, "Sociology and the Theory of Double Consciousness: W.E.B. Du Bois's Phenomenology of Racialized Subjectivity," *Du Bois Review: Social Science Research on Race* 12, no. 2 (Fall 2015): 231–48, https://doi.org/10.1017/S1742058X15000107.

4. Stoever, "Fine-Tuning the Sonic Color-Line."

5. Laura Garbes, "When the 'Blank Slate' Is a White One: White Institutional Isomorphism in the Birth of National Public Radio," *Sociology of Race and Ethnicity* 8, no. 1 (January 2022): 79–94, https://doi.org/10.1177/2332649221994619.

6. Alexander Weheliye, "In the Mix: Hearing the Souls of Black Folk," *Amerikastudien / American Studies* 45, no. 4 (2000): 535–54.

7. Du Bois, *Dusk of Dawn*, 27.

8. Du Bois, *The Souls of Black Folk*, 5.

9. Itzigsohn and Brown, "Sociology and the Theory of Double Consciousness."

10. Du Bois, *Dusk of Dawn*, 66.

11. Stoever, *The Sonic Color Line.*

12. Weheliye, "In the Mix."

13. Erving Goffman, *Forms of Talk* (Philadelphia: University of Pennsylvania Press, 1981).

14. Helen Wolfenden, "Just Be Yourself? Talk Radio Performance and Authentic On-Air Selves," in *Radio and Society: New Thinking for an Old Medium*, ed. Matt Mollgaard (Newcastle upon Tyne: Cambridge Scholars Publishing, 2012), 134–48.

15. Nirmal Puwar, *Space Invaders: Race, Gender and Bodies Out of Place* (Oxford: Berg, 2004).

16. Elia Powers, *Performing the News: Identity, Authority, and the Myth of Neutrality* (New Brunswick, NJ: Rutgers University Press, 2024), 119.

17. Kimberle Crenshaw, "Mapping the Margins: Intersectionality, Identity Politics, and Violence against Women of Color," *Stanford Law Review* 43, no. 6 (July 1991): 1241–99, https://doi.org/10.2307/1229039; Collins, "Learning from the Outsider Within"; and Patricia Hill Collins, *Black Feminist Thought: Knowledge, Consciousness, and the Politics of Empowerment* (New York: Routledge, 2000).

18. Anne O'Brien, "Women in Community Radio: A Framework of Gendered Participation," *Feminist Media Studies* 19, no. 6 (August 18, 2019): 787–802, https://doi.org/10.1080/14680777.2018.1508051; and Karpf, *The Human Voice.*

19. Puwar, *Space Invaders.*

20. Ariana Pekary, "How NPR's Ayesha Rascoe Is Changing the Sound of Public Radio," Current, July 19, 2024, https://current.org/2024/07/how-nprs-ayesha-rascoe-is-changing-the-sound-of-public-radio/.

21. Heben Nigatu and Tracy Clayton, "Was That a Microaggression or Just Tuesday?," *Another Round*, episode 19, Buzzfeed News, August 4, 2015, https://www.buzzfeednews.com/article/hnigatu/episode-19-audie-cornish-interview.

22. Nirmal Puwar, "The Racialised Somatic Norm and the Senior Civil Service," *Sociology* 35, no. 3 (August 2001): 659, https://doi.org/10.1177/S0038038501000335.

23. Sekani Robinson, "Black Ballerinas: The Management of Emotional and Aesthetic Labor," *Sociological Forum* 36, no. 2 (June 2021): 491–508, https://doi.org/10.1111/socf.12689; and Marcelo A. Bohrt, "Racial Ideologies, State Bureaucracy, and Decolonization in Bolivia," *Bolivian Studies Journal* 25 (2019): 7–28, https://doi.org/10.5195/bsj.2019.200.

24. Oneya Fennell Okuwobi, *Who Pays for Diversity? Why Programs Fail at Racial Equity and What to Do About It* (Oakland: University of California Press, 2025).

5. Chasing Driveway Moments

1. Melody Joy Kramer and Betsy O'Donovan, "F Is for Future: How to Think about Public Media's Next 50 Years," Knight Foundation, December 2, 2017, https://knightfoundation.org/public-media-white-paper-2017-kramer-o-donovan/.

2. National Public Radio, "Crafting Radio's Driveway Moments," July 20, 2008, https://www.npr.org/2008/07/20/92716706/crafting-radios-driveway-moments.

3. National Public Radio, "Crafting Radio's Driveway Moments."

4. Ari Shapiro, "It Wasn't Just Another Nightclub," *Atlantic*, June 10, 2021, https://www.theatlantic.com/ideas/archive/2021/06/pulse-wasnt-just-another-nightclub/619148/.

5. Loviglio, "Public Radio in Crisis."

6. Sara Ahmed, "Affective Economies," *Social Text* 22, no. 2 (Summer 2004): 117–39, https://doi.org/10.1215/01642472-22-2_79-117.

7. Karin Bijsterveld, "Acoustic Cocooning: How the Car Became a Place to Unwind," *The Senses and Society* 5, no. 2 (July 2010): 189–211, https://doi.org/10.2752/174589210X12668381452809.

8. Loviglio, "Public Radio in Crisis."

9. Sara Ahmed, *The Cultural Politics of Emotion*, 2nd ed. (Edinburgh: Edinburgh University Press, 2014).

10. *Morning Program*, "Pilot Episode 2," SoundCloud, 2015, https://soundcloud.com/stephaniefoo/pilot-episode-2-morning-program.

11. Loviglio, "Public Radio in Crisis."

12. McCauley, *NPR: The Trials and Triumphs*, 112.

13. McCauley, *NPR: The Trials and Triumphs*, 112.

14. National Public Radio, "Hear NPR's First On-Air Original Broadcast from 1971," April 28, 2021, https://www.npr.org/2021/04/28/990230586/hear-nprs-first-on-air-original-broadcast-from-1971.

15. Laura Garbes, "'I Just Don't Hear It': How Whiteness Dilutes Voices of Color at Public Radio Stations," The American Prospect, August 18, 2020, https://prospect.org/api/content/7e7e60c8-e0d5-11ea-b372-1244d5f7c7c6/.

16. Carla Murphy, "Introducing 'Leavers': Results from a Survey of 101 Former Journalists of Color," Source, August 26, 2020, https://source.opennews.org/articles/introducing-leavers-results-survey/.

17. Du Bois, *Dusk of Dawn*, 131.

6. Their Accent Is Too Much

1. Geri Alumit Zeldes, Frederick Fico, and Arvind Diddi, "Differences in the Way Broadcast, Cable and Public TV Reporters Used Women and Non-White Sources to Cover the 2008 Presidential Race," *Mass Communication and Society* 15, no. 6 (November 2012): 831–51, https://doi.org/10.1080/15205436.2011.634084; and Paula M. Poindexter, Laura Smith, and Don Heider, "Race and Ethnicity in Local Television News: Framing, Story Assignments, and Source Selections," *Journal of Broadcasting and Electronic Media* 47, no. 4 (December 2003): 524–36, https://doi.org/10.1207/s15506878jobem4704_3.

2. Elizabeth Jensen, "New On-Air Source Diversity Data for NPR Show Much Work Ahead," National Public Radio, December 17, 2019, https://www.npr.org/sections/publiceditor/2019/12/17/787959805/new-on-air-source-diversity-data-for-npr-shows-much-work-ahead.

3. Andrea D. Wenzel, "Sourcing Diversity, Shifting Culture: Building 'Cultural Competence' in Public Media," *Digital Journalism* 9, no. 4 (2021): 461–80, https://doi.org/10.1080/21670811.2020.1810585.

4. Ian Haney López, "The Social Construction of Race: Some Observations on Illusion, Fabrication, and Choice," *Harvard Civil Rights–Civil Liberties Law Review* 29, no. 1 (Winter 1994): 1–62; José Itzigsohn and Karida Brown, *The Sociology of W.E.B. Du Bois: Racialized Modernity and the Global Color Line* (New York: New York University Press, 2020); Omi and Winant, *Racial Formation in the United States*; and Cedric J. Robinson, *Black Marxism: The Making of the Black Radical Tradition*, 2nd ed. (Chapel Hill: University of North Carolina Press, 2000).

5. David Hesmondhalgh and Sarah Baker, "Creative Work and Emotional Labour in the Television Industry," *Theory, Culture and Society* 25, nos. 7–8 (December 2008): 97–118, https://doi.org/10.1177/0263276408097798.

6. Eduardo Bonilla-Silva, *Racism without Racists: Color-Blind Racism and the Persistence of Racial Inequality in America*, 3rd ed. (Lanham, MD: Rowman and Littlefield, 2009); and Yuen, *Reel Inequality*.

7. Karen E. Fields and Barbara J. Fields, *Racecraft: The Soul of Inequality in American Life* (London: Verso, 2012).

8. Ashlee Bledsoe, "Walk the (Gendered and Racialized) Line: Retrospective Consecration and the Rock and Roll Hall of Fame," *American Behavioral Scientist* 65, no. 1 (January 2021): 59–82, https://doi.org/10.1177/0002764220959686.

9. Damon J. Phillips and David A. Owens, "Incumbents, Innovation, and Competence: The Emergence of Recorded Jazz, 1920 to 1929," *Poetics* 32, nos. 3–4 (June–August 2004): 281–95, https://doi.org/10.1016/j.poetic.2004.06.003.

10. Phillipa Chong, "Reading Difference: How Race and Ethnicity Function as Tools for Critical Appraisal," *Poetics* 39, no. 1 (February 2011): 64–84, https://doi.org/10.1016/j.poetic.2010.11.003.

11. Maryann Erigha, "Racial Valuation: Cultural Gatekeepers, Race, Risk, and Institutional Expectations of Success and Failure," *Social Problems* 68, no. 2 (May 2021): 393–408, https://doi.org/10.1093/socpro/spaa006.

12. Allissa V. Richardson, *Bearing Witness While Black: African Americans, Smartphones, and the New Protest #Journalism* (New York: Oxford University Press, 2020).

13. Trechter and Bucholtz, "White Noise," 5.

14. John Hartigan, *Racial Situations: Class Predicaments of Whiteness in Detroit* (Princeton, NJ: Princeton University Press, 1999).

15. Mo Torres, "Separate from Class? Toward a Theory of Race as Resource Signal," *Social Problems*, August 3, 2024, https://doi.org/10.1093/socpro/spae044.

16. Melissa V. Abad, "Race, Knowledge, and Tasks: Racialized Occupational Trajectories," in *Research in the Sociology of Organizations*, vol. 60, *Race, Organizations, and the Organizing Process*, ed. Melissa E. Wooten (Leeds, England: Emerald Publishing, 2019), 111–30.

17. Jelani Ince, "'Saved' by Interaction, Living by Race: The Diversity Demeanor in an Organizational Space," *Social Psychology Quarterly* 85, no. 3 (September 2022): 259–78, https://doi.org/10.1177/01902725221096373.

18. Stoever, *The Sonic Color Line*, 2.

19. Jonathan Rosa, *Looking Like a Language, Sounding Like a Race: Raciolinguistic Ideologies and the Learning of Latinidad* (New York: Oxford University Press, 2019).

20. Anna North, "How One NPR Host Is Changing the Way We Hear the News," *Vox*, February 19, 2019, https://www.vox.com/2019/2/19/18226436/npr-diversity-race-gender-lulu-garcia-navarro.

Conclusion: Reckoning with Public Radio

1. Chelsea Peterson-Salahuddin, "Opening the Gates: Defining a Model of Intersectional Journalism," *Critical Studies in Media Communication* 38, no. 5 (October 2021): 391–407, https://doi.org/10.1080/15295036.2021.1968014.

2. NextGenRadio, "FAQ," https://nextgenradio.org/faq/.

3. This model, in which there are no prerequisites for an audio journalism program or team, can be useful in allowing people to learn outside the conventions of a genre. Christopher Chávez, in *The Sound of Exclusion*, explains the model in his chapter focusing on Daniel Alarcón's podcast *Radio Ambulante*.

4. Victor Pickard, *America's Battle for Media Democracy: The Triumph of Corporate Libertarianism and the Future of Media Reform* (New York: Cambridge University Press, 2015).

5. Pickard, *Democracy without Journalism?*

6. Pickard, *Democracy without Journalism?*

7. Loviglio, "Public Radio in Crisis."

8. Michael Swerdlow, *The Public's Media: The Case for a Democratically Funded and Locally Rooted News Media in an Era of Newsroom Closures* (Washington, DC: Center for Study of Responsive Law, 2024), https://nader.org/wp-content/uploads/2024/09/the_publics_media.pdf, 13.

9. National Public Radio, "NPR: The Next 50 Years," May 3, 2021, https://www.npr.org/2021/05/03/993132231/npr-the-next-50-years.

10. Patricia A. Banks, "High Culture, Black Culture: Strategic Assimilation and Cultural Steering in Museum Philanthropy," *Journal of Consumer Culture* 21, no. 3 (August 2021): 660–82, https://doi.org/10.1177/1469540519846260.

11. Carla Murphy, "Why We Need a Working-Class Media," *Dissent*, Fall 2019, https://www.dissentmagazine.org/article/why-we-need-a-working-class-media.

12. Victor Pickard, "We Need a Media System That Serves People's Needs, Not Corporations'," *Jacobin*, January 27, 2020, https://jacobinmag.com/2020/01/corporate-media-system-democracy.

13. Christopher Cwynar, "Self-Service Media: Public Radio Personalities, Reality Podcasting, and Entrepreneurial Culture," *Popular Communication* 17, no. 4 (2019): 317–32, https://doi.org/10.1080/15405702.2019.1634811.

14. The most prominent example of this move is Alex Blumberg, an alumnus of *This American Life* and cofounder of the hit NPR show *Planet Money*, who thought there was money to be made in the for-profit sector given podcasting's growing prominence in the 2010s. He partnered with business strategist Matt Lieber to establish Gimlet Media as a startup in 2014. Within its first five years, the company was bought out by Spotify for $200 million. Gimlet Media, based in Brooklyn, has had a self-diagnosed "diversity problem" from its start.

15. Evelynn M. Hammonds, "A Moment or a Movement? The Pandemic, Political Upheaval, and Racial Reckoning," *Signs: Journal of Women in Culture and Society* 47, no. 1 (Autumn 2021): 11–14, https://doi.org/10.1086/715650.

16. Natasha K. Warikoo, *The Diversity Bargain, and Other Dilemmas of Race, Admissions, and Meritocracy at Elite Universities* (Chicago: University of Chicago Press, 2016); Evans and Moore, "Impossible Burdens"; Kriti Budhiraja, "Infrastructures of Sociality: How Disadvantaged Students Navigate Inequity at the University," *Sociological Forum* 38, no. 1 (March 2023): 254–76, https://doi.org/10.1111/socf.12874; Lauren M. Alfrey, "Diversity, Disrupted: A Critique of Neoliberal Difference in Tech Organizations," *Sociological Perspectives* 65, no. 6 (December 2022): 1081–98, https://doi.org/10.1177/07311214221094664; and Bohrt, "Racial Ideologies, State Bureaucracy, and Decolonization in Bolivia."

17. Miranda Fricker, *Epistemic Injustice: Power and the Ethics of Knowing* (Oxford: Oxford University Press, 2007).

18. Fricker, *Epistemic Injustice*, 17.

19. Dreher, "Listening across Difference," 451.

20. Rachel Toor, "Scholars Talk Writing: Tressie McMillan Cottom," *Chronicle of Higher Education*, November 3, 2021, https://www.chronicle.com/article/scholars-talk-writing-tressie-mcmillan-cottom.

21. Carla Murphy, a former journalist and current journalism scholar, did an informal survey of journalists of color who had left the industry. Workplace stress, attributed partly to racism and sexism, was a significant contributing factor to over half of respondents. Carla Murphy, "The 'Leavers' Survey," OpenNews, n.d., https://opennews.org/projects/2020-leavers-survey/.

REFERENCES

Abad, Melissa V. "Race, Knowledge, and Tasks: Racialized Occupational Trajectories." In *Research in the Sociology of Organizations*, vol. 60, *Race, Organizations, and the Organizing Process*, edited by Melissa E. Wooten, 111–30. Leeds, England: Emerald Publishing, 2019.

Acker, Joan. "Hierarchies, Jobs, Bodies: A Theory of Gendered Organizations." *Gender and Society* 4, no. 2 (June 1990): 139–58. https://doi.org/10.1177/089124390004002002.

———. "Inequality Regimes: Gender, Class, and Race in Organizations." *Gender and Society* 20, no. 4 (August 2006): 441–64. https://doi.org/10.1177/0891243206289499.

Ahmed, Sara. "Affective Economies." *Social Text* 22, no. 2 (Summer 2004): 117–39. https://doi.org/10.1215/01642472-22-2_79-117.

———. *Complaint!* Durham, NC: Duke University Press, 2021.

———. *The Cultural Politics of Emotion*. 2nd ed. Edinburgh: Edinburgh University Press, 2014.

Alfrey, Lauren M. "Diversity, Disrupted: A Critique of Neoliberal Difference in Tech Organizations." *Sociological Perspectives* 65, no. 6 (December 2022): 1081–98. https://doi.org/10.1177/07311214221094664.

Anderson, Elijah. "The White Space." *Sociology of Race and Ethnicity* 1, no. 1 (January 2015): 10–21. https://doi.org/10.1177/2332649214561306.

Anderson, Gloria, et al. "A Formula for Change: The Report of the Task Force on Minorities in Public Broadcasting." November 1978. https://eric.ed.gov/?id=ED172269.

Bailey, George. "Free Riders, Givers, and Heavy Users: Predicting Listener Support for Public Radio." *Journal of Broadcasting and Electronic Media* 48, no. 4 (2004): 607–19.

Banks, Patricia A. "High Culture, Black Culture: Strategic Assimilation and Cultural Steering in Museum Philanthropy." *Journal of Consumer Culture* 21, no. 3 (August 2021): 660–82. https://doi.org/10.1177/1469540519846200.

Barlow, William. *Voice Over: The Making of Black Radio*. Philadelphia: Temple University Press, 1999.

Barman, Emily. "The Social Bases of Philanthropy." *Annual Review of Sociology* 43 (2017): 271–90. https://doi.org/10.1146/annurev-soc-060116-053524.

Baugh, John. "Linguistic Profiling." In *Black Linguistics: Language, Society, and Politics in Africa and the Americas*, edited by Sinfree Makoni, Geneva Smitherman, Arnetha F. Ball, and Arthur K. Spears, 155–68. London: Routledge, 2003.

Becker, Howard S. *Art Worlds*. 25th Anniversary ed. Berkeley: University of California Press, 2008.

Bell, Joyce M., and Douglas Hartmann. "Diversity in Everyday Discourse: The Cultural Ambiguities and Consequences of 'Happy Talk.'" *American Sociological Review* 72, no. 6 (December 2007): 895–914. https://doi.org/10.1177/000312240707200603.

Berkman, Dave. "Is Educational Broadcasting Segregated?" *National Association of Educational Broadcasters Journal*, January–February 1966.

Berrey, Ellen. "Diversity Is for White People: The Big Lie behind a Well-Intended Word." *Salon*, October 26, 2015. https://www.salon.com/2015/10/26/diversity_is_for_white_people_the _big_lie_behind_a_well_intended_word/.

———. *The Enigma of Diversity: The Language of Race and the Limits of Racial Justice.* Chicago: University of Chicago Press, 2015.

Binder, Amy. "For Love and Money: Organizations' Creative Responses to Multiple Environmental Logics." *Theory and Society* 36, no. 6 (December 2007): 547–71. https://doi.org/10 .1007/s11186-007-9045-x.

Bledsoe, Ashlee. "Walk the (Gendered and Racialized) Line: Retrospective Consecration and the Rock and Roll Hall of Fame." *American Behavioral Scientist* 65, no. 1 (January 2021): 59–82. https://doi.org/10.1177/0002764220959686.

Bohrt, Marcelo A. "Racial Ideologies, State Bureaucracy, and Decolonization in Bolivia." *Bolivian Studies Journal* 25 (2019): 7–28. https://doi.org/10.5195/bsj.2019.200.

Bonilla-Silva, Eduardo. *Racism without Racists: Color-Blind Racism and the Persistence of Racial Inequality in America.* 3rd ed. Lanham, MD: Rowman and Littlefield, 2009.

———. *Racism without Racists: Color-Blind Racism and the Persistence of Racial Inequality in America.* 4th ed. Lanham, MD: Rowman and Littlefield, 2013.

Bonilla-Silva, Eduardo, Carla Goar, and David G. Embrick. "When Whites Flock Together: The Social Psychology of White Habitus." *Critical Sociology* 32, nos. 2–3 (March 2006): 229–53. https://doi.org/10.1163/156916306777835268.

Bourdieu, Pierre. *Language and Symbolic Power.* Edited by John Thompson. Translated by Gino Raymond and Matthew Adamson. 7th ed. Cambridge, MA: Harvard University Press, 1999.

Brunsma, David L., Nathaniel G. Chapman, Joong Won Kim, J. Slade Lellock, Megan Underhill, Erik T. Withers, and Jennifer Padilla Wyse. "The Culture of White Space: On the Racialized Production of Meaning." *American Behavioral Scientist* 64, no. 14 (December 2020): 2001–15. https://doi.org/10.1177/0002764220975081.

Budhiraja, Kriti. "Infrastructures of Sociality: How Disadvantaged Students Navigate Inequity at the University." *Sociological Forum* 38, no. 1 (March 2023): 254–76. https://doi.org/10.1111 /socf.12874.

Calarco, Jessica McCrory. "Avoiding Us versus Them: How Schools' Dependence on Privileged 'Helicopter' Parents Influences Enforcement of Rules." *American Sociological Review* 85, no. 2 (April 2020): 223–46. https://doi.org/10.1177/0003122420905793.

Casillas, Dolores Inés. *Sounds of Belonging: U.S. Spanish-Language Radio and Public Advocacy.* New York: New York University Press, 2014.

Chávez, Christopher. *The Sound of Exclusion: NPR and the Latinx Public.* Tucson: University of Arizona Press, 2021.

Chong, Phillipa. "Reading Difference: How Race and Ethnicity Function as Tools for Critical Appraisal." *Poetics* 39, no. 1 (February 2011): 64–84. https://doi.org/10.1016/j.poetic.2010 .11.003.

Collins, Patricia Hill. *Black Feminist Thought: Knowledge, Consciousness, and the Politics of Empowerment.* New York: Routledge, 2000.

———. "Learning from the Outsider Within: The Sociological Significance of Black Feminist Thought." *Social Problems* 33, no. 6 (December 1986): s14–s32. https://doi.org/10.2307 /800672.

Corporation for Public Broadcasting. "Diversity." September 25, 2014. https://www.cpb.org/ diverseaudiences.

Couldry, Nick. "Commentary: Rethinking the Politics of Voice." *Continuum* 23, no. 4 (August 2009): 579–82. https://doi.org/10.1080/10304310903026594.

Craig, Maxine Leeds. *Ain't I a Beauty Queen? Black Women, Beauty, and the Politics of Race*. Oxford: Oxford University Press, 2002.

Crenshaw, Kimberle. "Mapping the Margins: Intersectionality, Identity Politics, and Violence against Women of Color." *Stanford Law Review* 43, no. 6 (July 1991): 1241–99. https://doi.org/10.2307/1229039.

Crenshaw, Kimberlé Williams. "Toward a Race-Conscious Pedagogy in Legal Education." *National Black Law Journal* 11, no. 1 (1988): 1–14.

Currid-Halkett, Elizabeth. *The Sum of Small Things: A Theory of the Aspirational Class*. Princeton, NJ: Princeton University Press, 2017.

Cwynar, Christopher. "Self-Service Media: Public Radio Personalities, Reality Podcasting, and Entrepreneurial Culture." *Popular Communication* 17, no. 4 (2019): 317–32. https://doi.org/10.1080/15405702.2019.1634811.

Dane, Alexandra. "Cultural Capital as Performance: Tote Bags and Contemporary Literary Festivals." *Mémoires du livre / Studies in Book Culture* 11, no. 2 (Spring 2020). https://doi.org/10.7202/1070270ar.

Davé, Shilpa. "Racial Accents, Hollywood Casting, and Asian American Studies." *Cinema Journal* 56, no. 3 (Spring 2017): 142–47.

DiMaggio, Paul J., and Walter W. Powell. "The Iron Cage Revisited: Institutional Isomorphism and Collective Rationality in Organizational Fields." In *Advances in Strategic Management*, vol. 17, *Economics Meets Sociology in Strategic Management*, edited by Joel A. C. Baum and Frank Dobbin, 143–66. Leeds, England: Emerald Publishing, 2000.

Doss, Richard C., and Alan M. Gross. "The Effects of Black English and Code-Switching on Intraracial Perceptions." *Journal of Black Psychology* 20, no. 3 (August 1994): 282–93. https://doi.org/10.1177/00957984940203003.

Douglas, Susan J. *Listening In: Radio and the American Imagination*. Minneapolis: University of Minnesota Press, 2004.

Dreher, Tanja. "Listening across Difference: Media and Multiculturalism beyond the Politics of Voice." *Continuum* 23, no. 4 (August 2009): 445–58. https://doi.org/10.1080/10304310903015712.

Du Bois, W.E.B. *Dusk of Dawn: An Essay toward an Autobiography of a Race Concept*. New York: Oxford University Press, 2007.

———. *The Souls of Black Folk: Essays and Sketches*. Chicago: A. C. McClurg and Company, 1903.

Ehrick, Christine. *Radio and the Gendered Soundscape: Women and Broadcasting in Argentina and Uruguay, 1930–1950*. New York: Cambridge University Press, 2015.

Embrick, David G., and Wendy Leo Moore. "White Space(s) and the Reproduction of White Supremacy." *American Behavioral Scientist* 64, no. 14 (December 2020): 1935–45. https://doi.org/10.1177/0002764220975053.

Engelman, Ralph. *Public Radio and Television in America: A Political History*. Thousand Oaks, CA: SAGE Publications, 1996.

Erigha, Maryann. "Racial Valuation: Cultural Gatekeepers, Race, Risk, and Institutional Expectations of Success and Failure." *Social Problems* 68, no. 2 (May 2021): 393–408. https://doi.org/10.1093/socpro/spaa006.

Evans, Louwanda, and Wendy Leo Moore. "Impossible Burdens: White Institutions, Emotional Labor, and Micro-Resistance." *Social Problems* 62, no. 3 (August 2015): 439–54. https://doi.org/10.1093/socpro/spv009.

Ferretti, Fred. "The White Captivity of Black Radio." *Columbia Journalism Review* 9, no. 2 (Summer 1970): 35–39.

Fields, Karen E., and Barbara J. Fields. *Racecraft: The Soul of Inequality in American Life*. London: Verso, 2012.

Fligstein, Neil, and Doug McAdam. *A Theory of Fields*. New York: Oxford University Press, 2012.

Flores, Nelson, and Jonathan Rosa. "Undoing Appropriateness: Raciolinguistic Ideologies and Language Diversity in Education." *Harvard Educational Review* 85, no. 2 (Winter 2015): 149–71. https://doi.org/10.17763/0017-8055.85.2.149.

Fricker, Miranda. *Epistemic Injustice: Power and the Ethics of Knowing*. Oxford: Oxford University Press, 2007.

Friedan, Betty. *The Feminine Mystique*. New York: W. W. Norton, 1963.

Fullerton, Howard N., Jr. "Labor Force Participation: 75 Years of Change, 1950–98 and 1998–2025." *Monthly Labor Review* 122, no. 12 (December 1999): 3–12.

Garbes, Angela. *Essential Labor: Mothering as Social Change*. New York: HarperCollins, 2022.

Garbes, Laura. "'I Just Don't Hear It': How Whiteness Dilutes Voices of Color at Public Radio Stations." The American Prospect, August 18, 2020. https://prospect.org/api/content/7e7e60c8-e0d5-11ea-b372-1244d5f7c7c6/.

———. "Racialized Airwaves: Tracing the Sonic Color Line in the American Public Radio Industry." PhD diss., Brown University, 2022. https://www.proquest.com/docview/2784391272/abstract/6EA38864C974528PQ/1.

———. "When the 'Blank Slate' Is a White One: White Institutional Isomorphism in the Birth of National Public Radio." *Sociology of Race and Ethnicity* 8, no. 1 (January 2022): 79–94. https://doi.org/10.1177/2332649221994619.

Gerson, Jennifer. "The Voices of NPR: How Four Women of Color See Their Roles as Hosts." The 19th, April 26, 2023. https://19thnews.org/2023/04/the-voices-of-npr/.

Goffman, Erving. *Forms of Talk*. Philadelphia: University of Pennsylvania Press, 1981.

———. *The Presentation of Self in Everyday Life*. New York: Doubleday, 1959.

Goldin, Claudia. *Career and Family: Women's Century-Long Journey toward Equity*. Princeton, NJ: Princeton University Press, 2021.

Graham, Roderick, and 'Shawn Smith. "The Content of Our #Characters: Black Twitter as Counterpublic." *Sociology of Race and Ethnicity* 2, no. 4 (October 2016): 433–49. https://doi.org/10.1177/2332649216639067.

Hallett, Tim. "The Myth Incarnate: Recoupling Processes, Turmoil, and Inhabited Institutions in an Urban Elementary School." *American Sociological Review* 75, no. 1 (February 2010): 52–74. https://doi.org/10.1177/0003122409357044.

Hammonds, Evelynn M. "A Moment or a Movement? The Pandemic, Political Upheaval, and Racial Reckoning." *Signs: Journal of Women in Culture and Society* 47, no. 1 (Autumn 2021): 11–14. https://doi.org/10.1086/715650.

Haney López, Ian. "The Social Construction of Race: Some Observations on Illusion, Fabrication, and Choice." *Harvard Civil Rights–Civil Liberties Law Review* 29, no. 1 (Winter 1994): 1–62.

Hartigan, John, Jr. *Racial Situations: Class Predicaments of Whiteness in Detroit*. Princeton, NJ: Princeton University Press, 1999.

Hernandez, Jillian. *Aesthetics of Excess: The Art and Politics of Black and Latina Embodiment*. Durham, NC: Duke University Press, 2020.

Hesmondhalgh, David, and Sarah Baker. "Creative Work and Emotional Labour in the Television Industry." *Theory, Culture and Society* 25, nos. 7–8 (December 2008): 97–118. https://doi.org/10.1177/0263276408097798.

Hill, Jane H. "Language, Race, and White Public Space." *American Anthropologist* 100, no. 3 (September 1998): 680–89.

Holland, Megan M., and Karly Serita Ford. "Legitimating Prestige through Diversity: How Higher Education Institutions Represent Ethno-Racial Diversity across Levels of Selectivity." *Journal of Higher Education* 92, no. 1 (2021): 1–30.

hooks, bell. *Killing Rage: Ending Racism*. New York: Henry Holt, 1995.

Hunter, Margaret L. "'If You're Light You're Alright': Light Skin Color as Social Capital for Women of Color." *Gender and Society* 16, no. 2 (April 2002): 175–93. https://doi.org/10.1177/08912430222104895.

Ince, Jelani. "'Saved' by Interaction, Living by Race: The Diversity Demeanor in an Organizational Space." *Social Psychology Quarterly* 85, no. 3 (September 2022): 259–78. https://doi.org/10.1177/01902725221096373.

Internet Movie Database. "*Get Out* (2017)." https://www.imdb.com/title/tt5052448/.

Itzigsohn, José, and Karida L. Brown. "Sociology and the Theory of Double Consciousness: W.E.B. Du Bois's Phenomenology of Racialized Subjectivity." *Du Bois Review: Social Science Research on Race* 12, no. 2 (Fall 2015): 231–48. https://doi.org/10.1017/S1742058X15000107.

Itzigsohn, José, and Karida L. Brown. *The Sociology of W.E.B. Du Bois: Racialized Modernity and the Global Color Line*. New York: New York University Press, 2020.

Jensen, Elizabeth. "New On-Air Source Diversity Data for NPR Show Much Work Ahead." National Public Radio, December 17, 2019. https://www.npr.org/sections/publiceditor/2019/12/17/787959805/new-on-air-source-diversity-data-for-npr-shows-much-work-ahead.

Kanngieser, A. M. "Sonic Colonialities: Listening, Dispossession, and the (Re)Making of Anglo-European Nature." *Transactions of the Institute of British Geographers* 48, no. 4 (December 2023): 690–702. https://doi.org/10.1111/tran.12602.

Karpf, Anne. *The Human Voice: How This Extraordinary Instrument Reveals Essential Clues about Who We Are*. New York: Bloomsbury, 2006.

Katz, Helen. "The Future of Public Broadcasting in the US." *Media, Culture and Society* 11, no. 2 (April 1989): 195–205. https://doi.org/10.1177/016344389011002004.

kehal, prabhdeep singh. "Diversity." In *University Keywords*, edited by Andrew Hines. Baltimore: Johns Hopkins University Press, forthcoming.

Kim, Claire Jean. *Asian Americans in an Anti-Black World*. Cambridge: Cambridge University Press, 2023.

Kondabolu, Hari. *The Problem with Apu*. Apple TV, 2017. https://tv.apple.com/us/show/the-problem-with-apu/umc.cmc.79ccp9drj3lwqvctz77ct5eie.

Kramer, Melody Joy, and Betsy O'Donovan. "F Is for Future: How to Think about Public Media's Next 50 Years." Knight Foundation, December 2, 2017. https://knightfoundation.org/public-media-white-paper-2017-kramer-o-donovan/.

LaFrance, Adrienne. "How NPR Tote Bags Became a Thing." *Atlantic*, April 16, 2015. https://www.theatlantic.com/business/archive/2015/04/how-npr-tote-bags-became-a-thing/390657/.

Lagos, Danya. "Hearing Gender: Voice-Based Gender Classification Processes and Transgender Health Inequality." *American Sociological Review* 84, no. 5 (October 2019): 801–27. https://doi.org/10.1177/0003122419872504.

Laws, Mike. "Why We Capitalize 'Black' (and Not 'White')." *Columbia Journalism Review*, June 16, 2020. https://www.cjr.org/analysis/capital-b-black-styleguide.php.

Lee, Summer Kim. "Asian Americanist Critique and Listening Practices of Contemporary Popular Music." In *The Oxford Encyclopedia of Asian American Literature and Culture*, edited by Josephine Lee. Oxford: Oxford University Press, 2020. https://oxfordre.com/literature/view/10.1093/acrefore/9780190201098.001.0001/acrefore-9780190201098-e-819.

Leland, Susan. "Public Radio and Sponsors: A Win-Win Relationship." National Public Radio, May 9, 2011. https://www.npr.org/sections/gofigure/2011/05/09/136136378/public-radio-sponsors-a-win-win-relationship.

Lena, Jennifer C. *Entitled: Discriminating Tastes and the Expansion of the Arts*. Princeton, NJ: Princeton University Press, 2019.

Lewis, Amanda E., and John B. Diamond. *Despite the Best Intentions: How Racial Inequality Thrives in Good Schools*. New York: Oxford University Press, 2015.

Lippi-Green, Rosina. *English with an Accent: Language, Ideology, and Discrimination in the United States*. 2nd ed. London: Routledge, 2011.

Lipsitz, George. *How Racism Takes Place*. Philadelphia: Temple University Press, 2011.

Looker, Thomas. *The Sound and the Story: NPR and the Art of Radio*. Boston: Houghton Mifflin Harcourt, 1995.

Loviglio, Jason. "Public Radio in Crisis." In *Radio's New Wave: Global Sound in the Digital Era*, edited by Jason Loviglio and Michele Hilmes, 34–52. New York: Routledge, 2013.

———. "Sound Effects: Gender, Voice and the Cultural Work of NPR." *Radio Journal: International Studies in Broadcast and Audio Media* 5, nos. 2–3 (July 2008): 67–81. https://doi.org/10.1386/rajo.5.2-3.67_1.

Mallapragada, Madhavi. "*The Problem with Apu*, Whiteness, and Racial Hierarchies in US Media Industries." *JCMS: Journal of Cinema and Media Studies* 60, no. 1 (Fall 2020): 148–52.

Martin, Alison. "Plainly Audible: Listening Intersectionally to the Amplified Noise Act in Washington, DC." *Journal of Popular Music Studies* 33, no. 4 (December 2021): 104–25. https://doi.org/10.1525/jpms.2021.33.4.104.

Massey, Douglas S., and Garvey Lundy. "Use of Black English and Racial Discrimination in Urban Housing Markets: New Methods and Findings." *Urban Affairs Review* 36, no. 4 (March 2001): 452–69. https://doi.org/10.1177/10780870122184957.

May, Stephen. "Linguistic Racism: Origins and Implications." *Ethnicities* 23, no. 5 (October 2023): 651–61. https://doi.org/10.1177/14687968231193072.

McCauley, Michael P. *NPR: The Trials and Triumphs of National Public Radio*. New York: Columbia University Press, 2005.

McCombs, Phil, and Jacqueline Trescott. "NPR: Camelot on Crisis." *Washington Post*, August 14, 1983. https://www.washingtonpost.com/archive/lifestyle/1983/08/15/npr-camelot-on-crisis/4594de4b-ec8e-4c7f-bc4a-55db0b2663e5/.

McCourt, Tom. *Conflicting Communication Interests in America: The Case of National Public Radio*. Westport, CT: Praeger, 1999.

McEnaney, Tom. "This American Voice: The Odd Timbre of a New Standard in Public Radio." In *The Oxford Handbook of Voice Studies*, edited by Nina Sun Eidsheim and Katherine Meizel, 96–123. New York: Oxford University Press, 2019.

McMillan Cottom, Tressie. *Thick, and Other Essays*. New York: New Press, 2019.

Melaku, Tsedale M. "Black Women in White Institutional Spaces: The Invisible Labor Clause and the Inclusion Tax." *American Behavioral Scientist* 66, no. 11 (October 2022): 1512–25. https://doi.org/10.1177/00027642211066037.

Mellinger, Gwyneth. *Chasing Newsroom Diversity: From Jim Crow to Affirmative Action*. Urbana: University of Illinois Press, 2013.

Mitchell, Jack W. *Listener Supported: The Culture and History of Public Radio*. Westport, CT: Praeger, 2005.

Monk, Ellis P., Michael H. Esposito, and Hedwig Lee. "Beholding Inequality: Race, Gender, and Returns to Physical Attractiveness in the United States." *American Journal of Sociology* 127, no. 1 (July 2021): 194–241. https://doi.org/10.1086/715141.

Moore, Wendy Leo. "The Mechanisms of White Space(s)." *American Behavioral Scientist* 64, no. 14 (December 2020): 1946–60. https://doi.org/10.1177/0002764220975080.

———. *Reproducing Racism: White Space, Elite Law Schools, and Racial Inequality*. Lanham, MD: Rowman and Littlefield, 2008.

Mora, G. Cristina, Reubén Pérez, and Nicholas Vargas. "Who Identifies as 'Latinx'? The Generational Politics of Ethnoracial Labels." *Social Forces* 100, no. 3 (March 2022): 1170–94. https://doi.org/10.1093/sf/soab011.

Moreton-Robinson, Aileen, Maryrose Casey, and Fiona Nicoll. *Transnational Whiteness Matters.* Lanham, MD: Lexington Books, 2008.

Morning Program. "Pilot Episode 2." SoundCloud, 2015. https://soundcloud.com/stephaniefoo/pilot-episode-2-morning-program.

Murphy, Carla. "Introducing 'Leavers': Results from a Survey of 101 Former Journalists of Color." Source, August 26, 2020. https://source.opennews.org/articles/introducing-leavers-results-survey/.

———. "The 'Leavers' Survey." OpenNews, n.d. https://opennews.org/projects/2020-leavers-survey/.

———. "Why We Need a Working-Class Media." *Dissent*, Fall 2019. https://www.dissentmagazine.org/article/why-we-need-a-working-class-media.

Nader, Ralph, Consumer Advocate. "New Report Reveals Corporate Capture in NPR and Local Stations Report Calls for New Approach to Public Media to Ensure Stable Public Funding and Community Representation." PR Newswire, September 19, 2024. https://www.prnewswire.com/news-releases/new-report-reveals-corporate-capture-in-npr-and-local-stations-report-calls-for-new-approach-to-public-media-to-ensure-stable-public-funding-and-community-representation-302253371.html.

Napoli, Lisa. *Susan, Linda, Nina, and Cokie: The Extraordinary Story of the Founding Mothers of NPR.* New York: Harry N. Abrams, 2021.

National Public Radio. "Crafting Radio's Driveway Moments." July 20, 2008. https://www.npr.org/2008/07/20/92716706/crafting-radios-driveway-moments.

———. "Diversity in Action at NPR." https://www.npr.org/diversity.

———. "The Friday Podcast: Economists on Federal Funding for NPR." *Planet Money*, March 25, 2011. https://www.npr.org/transcripts/134863998.

———. "Hear NPR's First On-Air Original Broadcast from 1971." April 28, 2021. https://www.npr.org/2021/04/28/990230586/hear-nprs-first-on-air-original-broadcast-from-1971.

———. "NPR: The Next 50 Years." May 3, 2021. https://www.npr.org/2021/05/03/993132231/npr-the-next-50-years.

———. "Susan Stamberg's Cranberry Relish Tradition." November 17, 2023. https://www.npr.org/series/4175681/susan-stamberg-s-cranberry-relish-tradition.

New York Times. "National Public Radio Opens 'Drive to Survive.'" August 2, 1983. https://www.nytimes.com/1983/08/02/arts/national-public-radio-opens-drive-to-survive.html.

NextGenRadio. "FAQ." https://nextgenradio.org/faq/.

Ngai, Sianne. *Ugly Feelings.* Cambridge, MA: Harvard University Press, 2005.

Nieckarz, Peter P., III. "'All Things Considered': A Comparative Case Study Examining the Commercial Presence within Public Radio." PhD diss., Western Michigan University, June 1999. https://scholarworks.wmich.edu/dissertations/1523.

Nigatu, Heben, and Tracy Clayton. "Was That a Microaggression or Just Tuesday?" *Another Round*, episode 19. Buzzfeed News, August 4, 2015. https://www.buzzfeednews.com/article/hnigatu/episode-19-audie-cornish-interview.

Nkomo, Stella M. "The Emperor Has No Clothes: Rewriting 'Race in Organizations.'" *Academy of Management Review* 17, no. 3 (July 1992): 487–513. https://doi.org/10.5465/AMR.1992.4281987.

O'Brien, Anne. "Women in Community Radio: A Framework of Gendered Participation." *Feminist Media Studies* 19, no. 6 (2019): 787–802. https://doi.org/10.1080/14680777.2018.1508051.

Okuwobi, Oneya Fennell. *Who Pays for Diversity? Why Programs Fail at Racial Equity and What to Do About It.* Oakland: University of California Press, 2025.

Omi, Michael, and Howard Winant. *Racial Formation in the United States: From the 1960s to the 1990s.* 2nd ed. New York: Routledge, 1994.

Ostrower, Francie. *Why the Wealthy Give: The Culture of Elite Philanthropy*. Princeton, NJ: Princeton University Press, 1997.

Paxton, Pamela, Kristopher Velasco, and Robert W. Ressler. "Does Use of Emotion Increase Donations and Volunteers for Nonprofits?" *American Sociological Review* 85, no. 6 (December 2020): 1051–83. https://doi.org/10.1177/0003122420960104.

Pekary, Ariana. "How NPR's Ayesha Rascoe Is Changing the Sound of Public Radio." Current, July 19, 2024. https://current.org/2024/07/how-nprs-ayesha-rascoe-is-changing-the-sound -of-public-radio/.

Perry, Imani. *More Beautiful and More Terrible: The Embrace and Transcendence of Racial Inequality in the United States*. New York: New York University Press, 2011.

Peterson-Salahuddin, Chelsea. "Opening the Gates: Defining a Model of Intersectional Journalism." *Critical Studies in Media Communication* 38, no. 5 (October 2021): 391–407. https://doi .org/10.1080/15295036.2021.1968014.

Phillips, Damon J., and David A. Owens. "Incumbents, Innovation, and Competence: The Emergence of Recorded Jazz, 1920 to 1929." *Poetics* 32, nos. 3–4 (June–August 2004): 281–95. https://doi.org/10.1016/j.poetic.2004.06.003.

Pickard, Victor. *America's Battle for Media Democracy: The Triumph of Corporate Libertarianism and the Future of Media Reform*. New York: Cambridge University Press, 2015.

———. *Democracy without Journalism? Confronting the Misinformation Society*. New York: Oxford University Press, 2020.

———. "We Need a Media System That Serves People's Needs, Not Corporations'." *Jacobin*, January 27, 2020. https://jacobinmag.com/2020/01/corporate-media-system-democracy.

Poindexter, Paula M., Laura Smith, and Don Heider. "Race and Ethnicity in Local Television News: Framing, Story Assignments, and Source Selections." *Journal of Broadcasting and Electronic Media* 47, no. 4 (December 2003): 524–36. https://doi.org/10.1207/s15506878jobem4704_3.

Purnell, Thomas, William Idsardi, and John Baugh. "Perceptual and Phonetic Experiments on American English Dialect Identification." *Journal of Language and Social Psychology* 18, no. 1 (March 1999): 10–30. https://doi.org/10.1177/0261927X99018001002.

Puwar, Nirmal. "The Racialised Somatic Norm and the Senior Civil Service." *Sociology* 35, no. 3 (August 2001): 651–70. https://doi.org/10.1177/S0038038501000335.

———. *Space Invaders: Race, Gender and Bodies Out of Place*. Oxford: Berg, 2004.

Ray, Victor. "A Theory of Racialized Organizations." *American Sociological Review* 84, no. 1 (February 2019): 26–53. https://doi.org/10.1177/0003122418822335.

Richardson, Allissa V. *Bearing Witness While Black: African Americans, Smartphones, and the New Protest #Journalism*. New York: Oxford University Press, 2020.

Riley, Boots, dir. *Sorry to Bother You*. Annapurna Pictures, 2018.

Rivera, Lauren A. "Hiring as Cultural Matching: The Case of Elite Professional Service Firms." *American Sociological Review* 77, no. 6 (December 2012): 999–1022. https://doi.org/10.1177 /0003122412463213.

Roberts, Cokie, Susan Stamberg, Noah Adams, John Ydstie, Renée Montagne, Ari Shapiro, and David Folkenflik. *This Is NPR: The First Forty Years*. San Francisco: Chronicle Books, 2010.

Robinson, Cedric J. *Black Marxism: The Making of the Black Radical Tradition*. 2nd ed. Chapel Hill: University of North Carolina Press, 2000.

Robinson, Russell K. "Perceptual Segregation." *Columbia Law Review* 108, no. 5 (June 2008): 1093–180.

Robinson, Sekani. "Black Ballerinas: The Management of Emotional and Aesthetic Labor." *Sociological Forum* 36, no. 2 (June 2021): 491–508. https://doi.org/10.1111/socf.12689.

Rosa, Jonathan. *Looking Like a Language, Sounding Like a Race: Raciolinguistic Ideologies and the Learning of Latinidad*. New York: Oxford University Press, 2019.

Rowland, Willard D., Jr. "Continuing Crisis in Public Broadcasting: A History of Disenfranchise-ment." *Journal of Broadcasting and Electronic Media* 30, no. 3 (June 1986): 251–74. https://doi.org/10.1080/08838158609386623.

Royster, Deirdre. *Race and the Invisible Hand: How White Networks Exclude Black Men from Blue-Collar Jobs*. Berkeley: University of California Press, 2003.

Saha, Anamik. *Race and the Cultural Industries*. Cambridge: Polity Press, 2018.

Savage, Barbara Dianne. *Broadcasting Freedom: Radio, War, and the Politics of Race, 1938–1948*. Chapel Hill: University of North Carolina Press, 1999.

Schmidt, Thomas R. "Challenging Journalistic Objectivity: How Journalists of Color Call for a Reckoning." *Journalism* 25, no. 3 (March 2024): 547–64. https://doi.org/10.1177/14648849231160997.

Scott, W. Richard. *Institutions and Organizations: Ideas, Interests and Identities*. Thousand Oaks, CA: SAGE Publications, 1995.

Shepard, Richard F. "Public Broadcasting Assailed on Race." *New York Times*, November 26, 1978. https://www.nytimes.com/1978/11/26/archives/public-broadcasting-assailed-on-race-recommendations-sought.html.

Shepperd, Josh. *Shadow of the New Deal: The Victory of Public Broadcasting*. Urbana: University of Illinois Press, 2023.

Shiffman, Dan. "A Standard for the Wise and Honest: The 'Americans All . . . Immigrants All' Radio Broadcasts." *Studies in Popular Culture* 19, no. 1 (October 1996): 99–107.

Siemering, Bill. "Radio with a Purpose: Bill Siemering on NPR's Original Mission Statement." National Public Radio, May 7, 2021. https://www.npr.org/2021/05/07/993569986/radio-with-a-purpose-bill-siemering-on-nprs-original-mission-statement.

Sim, Laura. "Intimate Publics: Hearing Race in Radio and Podcasts." Academia, 2015. https://www.academia.edu/26841322/intimate_publics_hearing_race_in_radio_and_podcasts.

Slotten, Hugh Richard. *Radio's Hidden Voice: The Origins of Public Broadcasting in the United States*. Urbana: University of Illinois Press, 2009.

Smulyan, Susan. *Selling Radio: The Commercialization of American Broadcasting, 1920–1934*. Washington, DC: Smithsonian Institution Press, 1994.

Sokoloff, Natalie J. *Black Women and White Women in the Professions: Occupational Segregation by Race and Gender, 1960–1980*. New York: Routledge, 2014.

Soloski, Alexis. "When Podcast Hosts Speak, What Do We Hear?" *New York Times*, February 25, 2021. https://www.nytimes.com/interactive/2021/02/25/arts/podcast-voice-sound.html.

Stavitsky, Alan G. "'Guys in Suits with Charts': Audience Research in U.S. Public Radio." *Journal of Broadcasting and Electronic Media* 39, no. 2 (March 1995): 177–89. https://doi.org/10.1080/08838159509364297.

St. Félix, Doreen. "The Twisted Power of White Voice in 'Sorry to Bother You' and 'BlacKkKlans-man.'" *New Yorker*, August 13, 2018. https://www.newyorker.com/culture/cultural-comment/the-twisted-power-of-white-voice-in-sorry-to-bother-you-and-blackkklansman.

Stoever, Jennifer Lynn. "'Doing Fifty-Five in a Fifty-Four': Hip Hop, Cop Voice and the Cadence of White Supremacy in the United States." *Journal of Interdisciplinary Voice Studies* 3, no. 2 (November 2018): 115–31. https://doi.org/10.1386/jivs.3.2.115_1.

———. "Fine-Tuning the Sonic Color-Line: Radio and the Acousmatic Du Bois." *Modernist Cultures* 10, no. 1 (March 2015): 99–118. https://doi.org/10.3366/mod.2015.0100.

———. *The Sonic Color Line: Race and the Cultural Politics of Listening*. New York: New York University Press, 2016.

Sullivan, Margaret. *Ghosting the News: Local Journalism and the Crisis of American Democracy*. New York: Columbia Global Reports, 2020.

Swerdlow, Michael. *The Public's Media: The Case for a Democratically Funded and Locally Rooted News Media in an Era of Newsroom Closures.* Washington, DC: Center for Study of Responsive Law, 2024. https://nader.org/wp-content/uploads/2024/09/the_publics_media.pdf.

The Takeaway. "Reckoning with Race in Public Media." July 9, 2020. https://www.wnycstudios.org/podcasts/takeaway/segments/reckoning-systemic-racism-public-media.

Tomaskovic-Devey, Donald, and Dustin Avent-Holt. *Relational Inequalities: An Organizational Approach.* Oxford: Oxford University Press, 2019.

Toor, Rachel. "Scholars Talk Writing: Tressie McMillan Cottom." *Chronicle of Higher Education*, November 3, 2021. https://www.chronicle.com/article/scholars-talk-writing-tressie-mcmillan-cottom.

Torres, Mo. "Separate from Class? Toward a Theory of Race as Resource Signal." *Social Problems*, August 3, 2024. https://doi.org/10.1093/socpro/spae044.

Trechter, Sara, and Mary Bucholtz. "White Noise: Bringing Language into Whiteness Studies." *Journal of Linguistic Anthropology* 11, no. 1 (January 2001): 3–21. http://escholarship.org/uc/item/78b5t2xq.

Underhill, Megan R. "'Diversity Is Important to Me': White Parents and Exposure-to-Diversity Parenting Practices." *Sociology of Race and Ethnicity* 5, no. 4 (October 2019): 486–99. https://doi.org/10.1177/2332649218790992.

Usher, Nikki. *News for the Rich, White, and Blue: How Place and Power Distort American Journalism.* New York: Columbia University Press, 2021.

Vidal-Ortiz, Salvador, and Juliana Martínez. "Latinx Thoughts: Latinidad with an X." *Latino Studies* 16, no. 3 (October 2018): 384–95. https://doi.org/10.1057/s41276-018-0137-8.

Wallace, Lewis Raven. *The View from Somewhere: Undoing the Myth of Journalistic Objectivity.* Chicago: University of Chicago Press, 2019.

Ward, Jane. "White Normativity: The Cultural Dimensions of Whiteness in a Racially Diverse LGBT Organization." *Sociological Perspectives* 51, no. 3 (September 2008): 563–86. https://doi.org/10.1525/sop.2008.51.3.563.

Warikoo, Natasha K. *The Diversity Bargain, and Other Dilemmas of Race, Admissions, and Meritocracy at Elite Universities.* Chicago: University of Chicago Press, 2016.

Wayne, Teddy. "'NPR Voice' Has Taken Over the Airwaves." *New York Times*, October 24, 2015. https://www.nytimes.com/2015/10/25/fashion/npr-voice-has-taken-over-the-airwaves.html.

Weheliye, Alexander. "In the Mix: Hearing the Souls of Black Folk." *Amerikastudien / American Studies* 45, no. 4 (2000): 535–54.

Wenzel, Andrea D. "Sourcing Diversity, Shifting Culture: Building 'Cultural Competence' in Public Media." *Digital Journalism* 9, no. 4 (2021): 461–80. https://doi.org/10.1080/21670811.2020.1810585.

Williams, Raymond. *Keywords: A Vocabulary of Culture and Society.* Rev. ed. New York: Oxford University Press, 1985.

Wingfield, Adia Harvey. "Are Some Emotions Marked 'Whites Only'? Racialized Feeling Rules in Professional Workplaces." *Social Problems* 57, no. 2 (May 2010): 251–68. https://doi.org/10.1525/sp.2010.57.2.251.

Wingfield, Adia Harvey, and Renée Skeete Alston. "Maintaining Hierarchies in Predominantly White Organizations: A Theory of Racial Tasks." *American Behavioral Scientist* 58, no. 2 (February 2014): 274–87. https://doi.org/10.1177/0002764213503329.

Wolfenden, Helen. "Just Be Yourself? Talk Radio Performance and Authentic On-Air Selves." In *Radio and Society: New Thinking for an Old Medium*, edited by Matt Mollgaard, 134–48. Newcastle upon Tyne: Cambridge Scholars Publishing, 2012.

Wooten, Melissa, and Andrew J. Hoffman. "Organizational Fields: Past, Present and Future." In *The SAGE Handbook of Organizational Institutionalism*, edited by Royston Greenwood, Christine Oliver, Roy Suddaby, and Kerstin Sahlin, 129–48. London: SAGE Publications, 2008.

Yuen, Nancy Wang. *Reel Inequality: Hollywood Actors and Racism*. New Brunswick, NJ: Rutgers University Press, 2017.

Zeldes, Geri Alumit, Frederick Fico, and Arvind Diddi. "Differences in the Way Broadcast, Cable and Public TV Reporters Used Women and Non-White Sources to Cover the 2008 Presidential Race." *Mass Communication and Society* 15, no. 6 (November 2012): 831–51. https://doi.org/10.1080/15205436.2011.634084.

Page numbers followed by *f* indicate a figure

A NOTE ON THE TYPE

This book has been composed in Adobe Text and Gotham. Adobe Text, designed by Robert Slimbach for Adobe, bridges the gap between fifteenth- and sixteenth-century calligraphic and eighteenth-century Modern styles. Gotham, inspired by New York street signs, was designed by Tobias Frere-Jones for Hoefler & Co.

GPSR Authorized Representative: Easy Access System Europe - Mustamäe tee
50, 10621 Tallinn, Estonia, gpsr.requests@easproject.com

www.ingramcontent.com/pod-product-compliance
Lightning Source LLC
Jackson TN
JSHW022149050725
87054JS00001B/3